The Southern Front

By the Editors of Time-Life Books

Alexandria, Virginia

TIME LIFE®

The Third Reich

Other Publications:

THE NEW FACE OF WAR
HOW THINGS WORK
WINGS OF WAR
CREATIVE EVERYDAY COOKING
COLLECTOR'S LIBRARY OF THE UNKNOWN
CLASSICS OF WORLD WAR II
TIME-LIFE LIBRARY OF CURIOUS AND UNUSUAL FACTS
AMERICAN COUNTRY
VOYAGE THROUGH THE UNIVERSE
THE TIME-LIFE GARDENER'S GUIDE
MYSTERIES OF THE UNKNOWN
TIME FRAME
FIX IT YOURSELF
FITNESS, HEALTH & NUTRITION
SUCCESSFUL PARENTING
HEALTHY HOME COOKING
UNDERSTANDING COMPUTERS
LIBRARY OF NATIONS
THE ENCHANTED WORLD
THE KODAK LIBRARY OF CREATIVE PHOTOGRAPHY
GREAT MEALS IN MINUTES
THE CIVIL WAR
PLANET EARTH
COLLECTOR'S LIBRARY OF THE CIVIL WAR
THE EPIC OF FLIGHT
THE GOOD COOK
WORLD WAR II
HOME REPAIR AND IMPROVEMENT
THE OLD WEST

The Cover: German guards parade American and British troops captured at Anzio past Rome's Coliseum in March 1944. The bitter fighting that began with the Allied invasion of North Africa in November 1942 and ended in northern Italy in May 1945 drained some of the best Axis and Allied troops from other fronts. Germany's war effort was especially hampered by the loss of twenty divisions tied down in the Mediterranean.

This volume is one of a series that chronicles the rise and eventual fall of Nazi Germany. Other books in the series include:
The SS
Fists of Steel
Storming to Power
The New Order
The Reach for Empire
Lightning War
Wolf Packs
Conquest of the Balkans
Afrikakorps
The Center of the Web
Barbarossa
War on the High Seas
The Twisted Dream
The Road to Stalingrad
The Shadow War
The Heel of the Conqueror

First printing. Printed in U.S.A.

Published simultaneously in Canada.
School and library distribution by Silver Burdett Company, Morristown, New Jersey 07960.

Library of Congress Cataloging in Publication Data
The Southern front / by the editors of Time-Life Books.
p. cm. — (The Third Reich)
Includes bibliographical references and index.
ISBN 0-8094-7016-0
ISBN 0-8094-7017-9 (lib. bdg.)
1. World War, 1939-1945—Campaigns—Africa, North. 2. World War, 1939-1945—Campaigns—Italy.
I. Time-Life Books. II. Series.
D766.82.S56 1991 940.54'23—dc20 90-20032

General Consultants

Col. John R. Elting, USA (Ret.), former associate professor at West Point, has written or edited some twenty books, including *Swords around a Throne, The Superstrategists,* and *American Army Life,* as well as *Battles for Scandinavia* in the Time-Life Books World War II series. He was chief consultant to the Time-Life series The Civil War.

Charles V. P. von Luttichau is an associate at the U.S. Army Center for Military History in Washington, D.C., and coauthor of *Command Decision and Great Battles.* From 1937 to 1945, he served in the German air force and taught at the Air Force Academy in Berlin. After the war, he emigrated to the United States and was a historian in the office of the Chief of Military History, Department of the Army, from 1951 to 1986, when he retired.

Contents

1 **Finale in the Desert** 4

2 **A Slugging Match for Sicily** 50

3 **Knocking on the Door of Axis Europe** 98

4 **The Eternal City and Beyond** 142

ESSAYS

Through the Eyes of a Soldier 39

Rescuing the Duce 86

The Destruction of Monte Cassino 130

Bitter Fruits of Alliance with Hitler 176

Acknowledgments 186

Picture Credits 186

Bibliography 187

Index 188

ONE

Finale in the Desert

Field Marshal Erwin Rommel, retreating from Egypt on November 8, 1942, after the defeat at El Alamein, received the worst possible news: To Rommel's west, British and American troops were pouring ashore by the tens of thousands at nine different landing sites around Casablanca, Oran, and Algiers. The Desert Fox had instantly sized up the situation. The days of his famed Afrikakorps were numbered. As he wrote in his diary: "This spelled the end of the army in Africa."

Rommel had been withdrawing westward along the coast of North Africa, the British Eighth Army at his heels, since November 4, always hoping that he could rally, strike back, and resume his drive to Alexandria. Now, with Allied troops landing to the rear of the Afrikakorps, that hope was dashed. Rommel realized immediately that he had no course but further retreat.

Clarion calls to stand and hold poured in from Mussolini, Hitler, and Comando Supremo, the Rome-based Italian high command. But Rommel concluded that the first reasonable place to regroup was at the Mersa Brega Line, 600 miles west of El Alamein. So the retreat continued with amazing speed, and as they went, the Germans relinquished all their previous gains: Sidi Barrani was lost on November 9, the Sollum-Halfaya Line on the 11th; hard-won Tobruk fell without a fight on the 13th, Martuba two days later; Benghazi was yielded on the 20th, the fifth time that that battered town had changed hands in two years.

It was a hellish, unceasing ordeal. Withdrawing at night meant navigating through minefields with only a hand-held compass for a guide. In the darkness, the Royal Air Force dropped flares that illuminated the German troops for the fighter planes and bombers that followed.

One survivor remembered such a scene, the parachutes slowly dropping with their incandescent flares: "They struck me as emerging from the darkness with an almost idiotic exultancy. In a few minutes the heavens were filled with 'Christmas trees.' We raced madly amid the thunder and the flashes. If we halted and went to ground, the aircraft attacked even solitary soldiers whom they caught erect: Their grotesque shadows danced revealingly across the ground."

Field Marshal Albert Kesselring flashes his habitual grin as he confers with Field Marshal Erwin Rommel in Egypt shortly before the Desert Fox returned to Germany on sick leave in September 1942. Later that autumn, Rommel's weakened force was sent reeling in retreat by the British at El Alamein.

How had Rommel, the intrepid and fearsome Desert Fox, come to this grievous pass? Even before the British Eighth Army had turned the tide in North Africa with its searing victory at El Alamein, Rommel's main problem had become, and would remain, one of supply. Hitler had never grasped the strategic importance of the North African campaign; he considered it Mussolini's war, far less important than Germany's life-and-death struggle against the Soviet Union. Therefore, the supplies that were forever promised to the Afrikakorps were only grudgingly assigned and rarely delivered intact—provided they could be sent through at all. Alerted to departure times and planned routes by Ultra, London's secret code-cracking operation, British naval and air forces were able to anticipate and sink Axis convoys in the Mediterranean that were bound for Rommel's army.

A major impediment to Axis shipping was the British crown colony of Malta, which lies between Sicily and the Libyan and Tunisian ports—directly athwart the Axis supply routes to Africa. Planes belonging to the RAF, along with British ships and submarines, were launched from Malta to devastate Axis resupply efforts. Soon three-quarters of the equipment and reinforcements sent to Rommel were being lost en route; it has been estimated that twice as many German tanks lie at the bottom of the Mediterranean as ever reached the battlefront.

Thus, while Rommel's pursuit of the British in the summer of 1942 had put him almost within sight of the pyramids, he lacked enough manpower and armor to push farther and was desperately short of gasoline to supply the vehicles he did have. Conversely, the opposing Eighth Army was growing stronger by the day and had acquired a demanding and determined new commander, Lieut. General Bernard Law Montgomery.

The German assault on British lines at the end of August had run out of fuel. When Montgomery failed to counterattack, a month-long stalemate fell over the desert—the first chance in four months that weary Axis soldiers had had to rest, shore up their defenses, and redeploy. Rommel himself had been in the desert for twenty months, far longer than junior officers and troops half his age. The strain was beginning to tell.

Rommel finally heeded his doctor's demands that he return home for rest and treatment of dangerously low blood pressure, chronic gastritis, and desert sores. On the way there, he stopped in Rome to plead with Mussolini for reinforcements and resupply. The duce recalled that Rommel seemed "physically and morally shaken." Faced with Rommel's urgent requests for matériel, Hitler presented him with a field marshal's baton. The Führer was little moved by Rommel's gloomy assessments. "Don't worry," Hitler told him. "I mean to give Africa all the support needed."

In fact, by October 1942, the British Eighth Army held a two-to-one

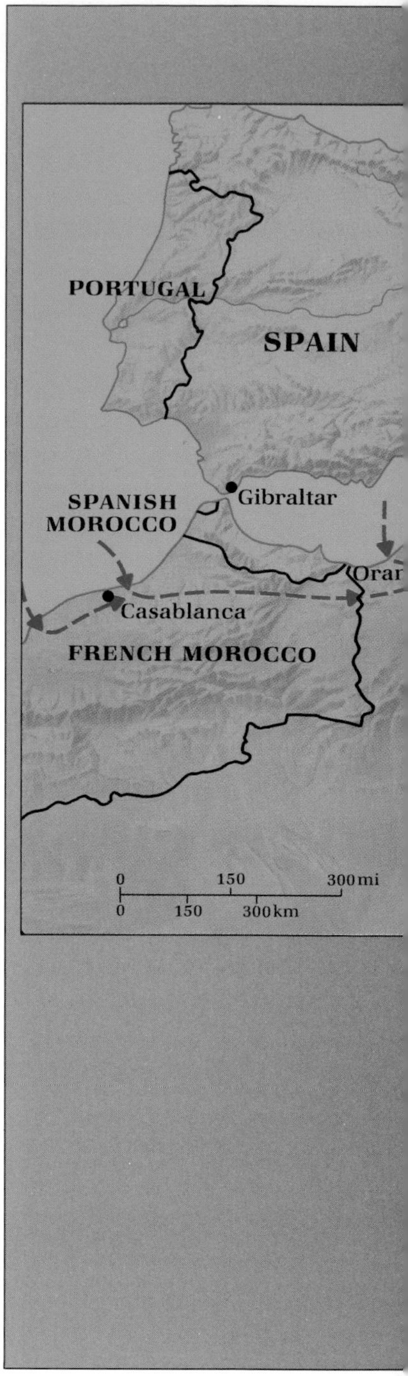

Action on Mediterranean Shores

On November 8, 1942, four days after the Axis troops of Field Marshal Erwin Rommel began withdrawing from Egypt in the wake of their defeat at El Alamein *(far right)*, three Allied task forces carrying 107,000 men—three-quarters of them American, the rest British—began landing on the shores of French North Africa at Casablanca, Oran, and Algiers. Their goal was to quickly neutralize the French Vichy forces, push east into Tunisia, and close the back door on Rommel's German-Italian Panzer Army. Both sides now began a race for Tunisia. While Rommel fell back through Libya with the British Eighth Army at his heels, the Germans moved troops into Bizerte, Sfax, and Gabès to check the advance of the Allied forces, grouped together as the British First Army, who were descending on Tunisia from the west. By February 1943, with the survivors of Rommel's army dug in behind the Mareth Line, the newly formed Fifth Panzer Army had pulled back into commanding positions in Tunisia's Eastern Dorsal mountains, setting the stage for the final months of fighting in North Africa.

advantage in men and tanks, and triple the amount of field artillery. The RAF, with twice as many planes as the Luftwaffe, controlled the skies. Montgomery was finally ready. The battle of El Alamein opened with the greatest artillery barrage since World War I. Rommel arrived back at his post at sundown the following evening, and his first reaction was: "It is obvious that from now on the British will destroy us bit by bit."

Soon enough, events would prove him right. "Alamein was lost before it was fought," said General Johann Cramer, of Rommel's staff. "We had not enough petrol." Another key officer, General Fritz Bayerlein, recalled, "Rommel could do nothing. He took over a battle in which all his reserves were already committed. No major decisions that could alter the course of events were possible." Within a week, the battered Axis forces were driven from their positions, and one of the epic military retreats in history was under way. For some members of the Afrikakorps, it was the fourth march across the hostile, parched Sahara.

Rommel never received enough supplies to allow him to make a stand, let alone to counterattack. There was not even enough fuel to permit his remaining armor to move to the rear in an orderly fashion. The retreat bogged down in massive traffic jams along the one paved coastal road, while RAF planes attacked at will. And always there was the threat of a British flanking movement that might envelop and destroy the entire army.

As if all this were not enough, Rommel's command was a hodgepodge of German and Italian units whose order of battle was constantly being reorganized. More than half of the troops were Italian, but they counted for little in the Germans' eyes. German scorn for their ally was summed up by Rommel's chief of staff, Colonel Siegfried Westphal, who admitted that "sometimes" the Italian soldiers were brave, but "their tendency to give way to emotion made them lack the steadiness that is the sine qua non of a soldier, particularly in a tight corner." Westphal added sarcastically that they were "dashing in an attack, so long as there were no serious obstacles."

And Rommel, while generally in command of the battlefield, had to clear his major decisions with nominally superior Italian generals, who in turn reported to the high command in Rome. Their decisions often reflected Mussolini's and Hitler's political priorities rather than combat realities. Furthermore, to Rommel's distress, he had to depend on them for supply.

This tangled command structure and overlapping authority would undermine the defense of North Africa to the very end. Even as the retreat began, a bombastic order from Hitler arrived: "The position requires that El Alamein be held to the last man. There is to be no retreat, not so much as one millimeter. Victory or death!"

Field Marshal Albert Kesselring, Rommel's superior, authorized him to ignore Hitler's order, but that helped little. The weakened panzer units were in no position to cover the disorganized infantry along the already clogged coastal road. So Rommel had no choice but to let his foot soldiers fend for themselves across the unforgiving desert.

While Rommel estimated that 70,000 Axis troops remained, the scattered units were greatly reduced: The two panzer divisions were down to 2,200 men and eleven tanks; the other divisions counted 1,800 men between them; Ramcke's Paratroop Brigade had just 600 survivors, who had become separated from the main force and were struggling back through open desert to the south. In the whole German force, twenty-five antitank guns remained—hardly equal to the task of stopping hundreds of British tanks.

Still, the Afrikakorps survived the first crucial days of its retreat, thanks in part to the speed with which Rommel ordered the withdrawal to begin.

Two Afrikakorps veterans slump exhaustedly in their combat vehicle during the hurried retreat out of Egypt and across Libya. The enormous battle losses at El Alamein, along with attrition, had virtually destroyed Rommel's fighting power; his two panzer divisions retained only 11 tanks of an original 370.

Montgomery, with no plan prepared and his soldiers exhausted after El Alamein, delayed the start of his pursuit to, in his words, "tidy up" the battlefield. The RAF failed to take full advantage of its air superiority, and even Nature took a hand, blessing Rommel with a two-day downpour that mired his pursuers, who had left the road to flank him, in a sandy morass.

But now the greatest naval armada ever seen up to that time was landing more than 100,000 British and American troops in French Morocco and Algeria, almost 2,000 miles to Rommel's rear. The Afrikakorps was caught in an enormous vise, and the sides were squeezing shut.

And so the Germans retreated westward, pursued across Libya and into Tunisia by the relentless but often disorganized British. Day after day, undermanned German units, sometimes as small as squads, were able to slow and blunt the Eighth Army reconnaissance patrols, maintaining control of the highway and frustrating the advance of British supply trucks.

Perhaps the most effective defense of all was that of the panzer engineers, who developed the lowly art of minelaying into one of diabolic effectiveness. Roads, houses, ditches, embankments—anything was fair game. Sometimes they planted lattices of dummy mines, lulling the Allied sappers into enough overconfidence that they would wave the convoys onward into the real mines that lay beyond. The German sappers also learned to booby-trap everything—doorways, burned-out vehicles, discarded rifles, officers' fine leather map cases—until the British soldiers became afraid to

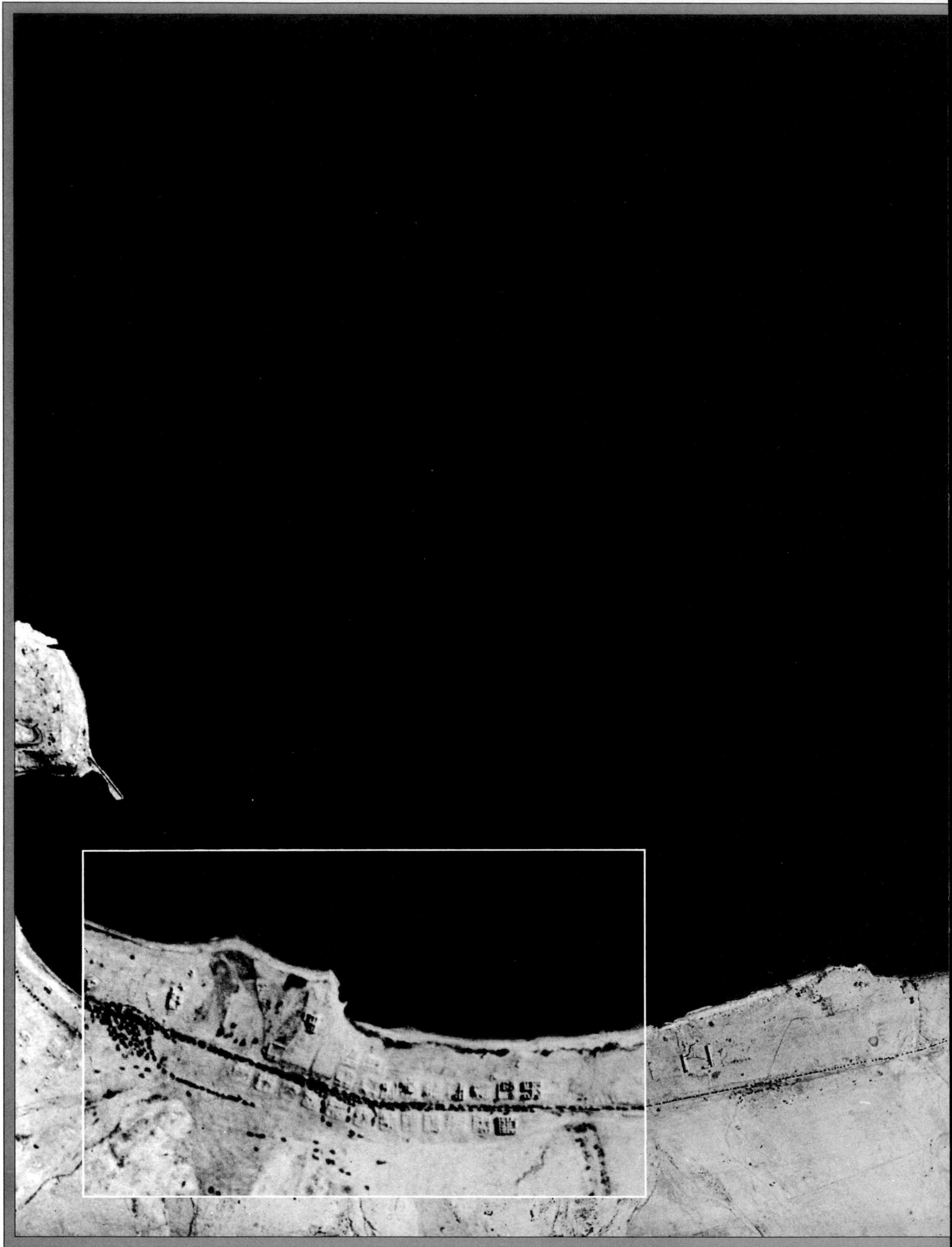

An aerial reconnaissance photograph, part of which is enlarged in the inset, shows Afrikakorps vehicles jamming a forty-mile

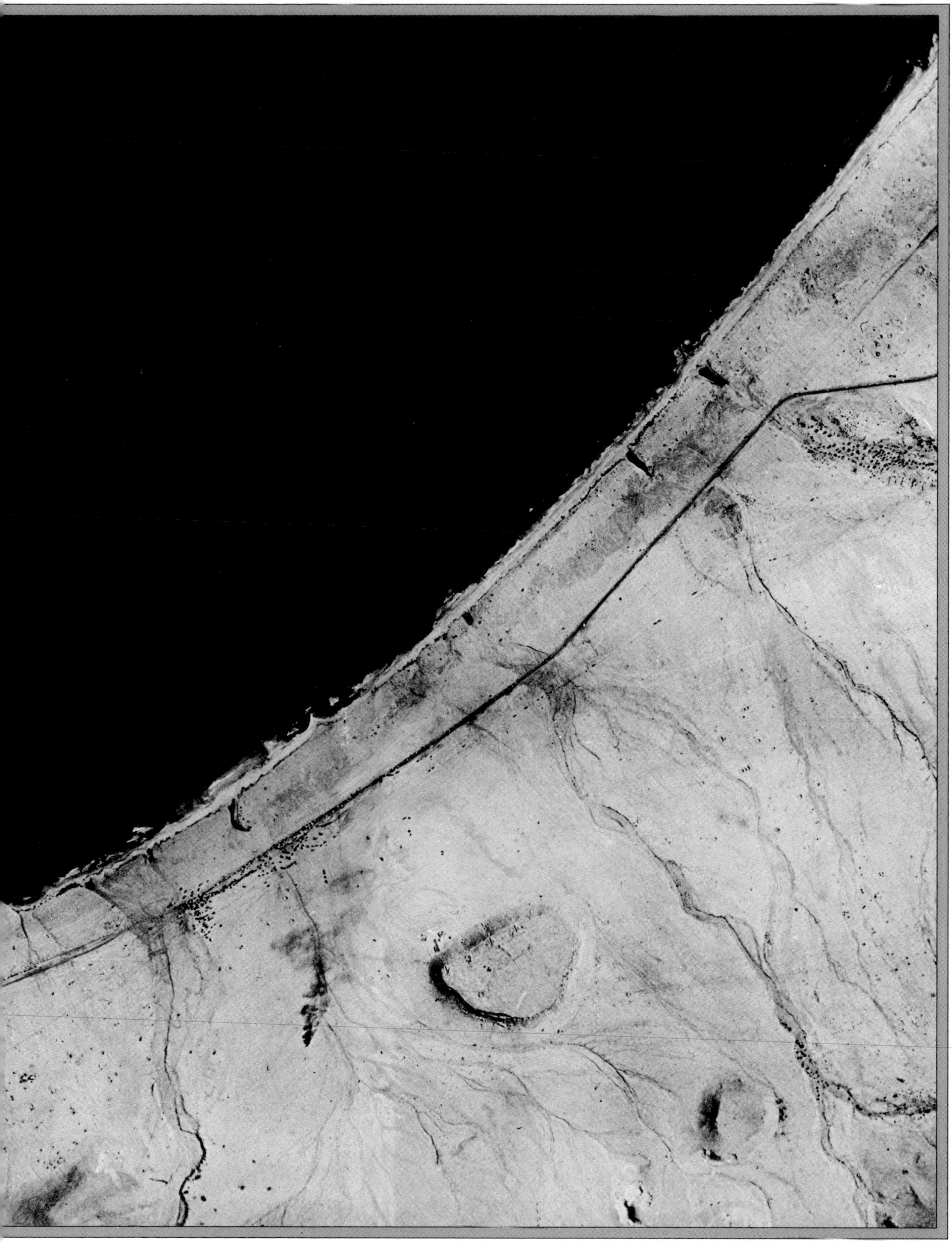

length of the Egyptian coastal road as Rommel's army struggled to reach Sollum *(far left)* and the Libyan border on November 11.

touch anything. The new "S" mine, called the Bouncing Betty, which sprayed shrapnel waist-high for forty yards around, proved especially lethal. With guile and grit and not much else, the minelaying squads slowed their tormentors just long enough for the retreat to re-form and continue. From Tobruk to Mersa Brega, a stretch of 400 miles, Rommel could boast that he lost hardly a man, but his situation was no less desperate.

Among the infantry who had been left to fend for themselves in the desert to the south, matters were even worse. Twenty thousand Italian troops surrendered en masse. But even here, heroic episodes took place. General Ramcke's Paratroop Brigade, with half a pint of water per man and a sixty-mile march to Fuka on the coastal road, stumbled on a British transport column. They captured it outright: trucks, gasoline, water, corned beef, canned pineapples, and cigarettes. The 600 men then fought their way across 200 miles of desert and reported back to a surprised Rommel.

On November 23, Rommel's troops reached the relative security of the Mersa Brega Line, halfway between Egypt and Tunisia. Here, finally, was a position that could be defended. Rommel was fully aware that his troops were too weak to attempt a protracted defense, let alone a counterattack, but he also knew that Montgomery would need time to stabilize his extended supply lines before he could mount a credible attack.

And he knew that German and Italian reinforcements had begun flowing into Tunisia, behind his forces, to block the Allied advance from the west. Tired of always getting the lowest priority and of "the mismanagement, operational blunders, prejudices, the everlasting search for scapegoats" that emanated from the German armed forces high command (OKW) and Comando Supremo, Rommel resolved to fly once again to Hitler's Wolf's Lair in East Prussia. He hoped to win Hitler's agreement to a plan that might forestall disaster. The forces at his command had only a third of their pre-Alamein fighting strength—little more than one division. Now, when Italian Marshal Ettore Bastico, Comando Supremo representative in Libya, relayed an order to "resist to the end in Mersa Brega," Rommel responded briskly: "We either lose the position four days earlier and save the army, or lose both position and army four days later." It was clear that the moment had come to try to force the high command to face reality.

His interview with the Führer took place on November 28, with Reich Marshal Hermann Göring also in attendance. The timing of the visit was less than propitious. On the Russian front, the German Sixth Army had just been encircled and trapped at Stalingrad, and Hitler and Göring were preoccupied by the disaster. Rommel detected a "noticeable chill in the atmosphere." He had intended to set out a logical long-term strategy to salvage matters in North Africa. First, he would abandon the rest of Libya immediately in favor of the defensive position at Gabès, a third of the way up the Tunisian coast. It would take Montgomery a long time to bring an assault-size force so far forward, and Gabès was shielded from flank attack by a vast salt marsh, Chott Djerid. Thus protected, Rommel could link up with the newly formed Axis army in Tunis, turn on the inexperienced Allied troops who were working their way east through Tunisia, and perhaps hurl them all the way back to Algeria. Once that was accomplished, his reinforced panzers could turn their attention to the Eighth Army once again.

Instead of presenting his case in this manner, however, Rommel short-circuited his own argument and came too quickly to his final point: In the long run, North Africa would have to be abandoned, and the best course available was a Dunkirk-style evacuation before the enemy forces gained more strength. "The mere mention of the strategic question worked like a spark in a powder keg," he wrote in his memoirs. "The Führer flew into a fury and directed a stream of completely unfounded attacks upon us." Hitler and Göring took turns accusing Rommel of fleeing when there was no need, of abandoning his armor, of throwing away rifles. "I no longer want to hear such rubbish from your lips!" Hitler screamed. "North Africa will be defended as Stalingrad will. That is an order, Herr Field Marshal. Go! I have other things to do than talk to you." Rommel saluted and turned on his heel. In another account of the episode, Hitler ran after him and put his arm around his shoulder. "You must excuse me," he said. "I'm in a very nervous state. Come and see me tomorrow and we will talk about it calmly."

Instead, he turned Rommel over to Göring with the instruction, "See that the Afrikakorps is supplied with all that Rommel needs." The Luftwaffe chief, and the Führer's second in command, invited Rommel and his wife to join him on a trip to Rome aboard his private railroad car. But all Göring wanted to talk about was his jewelry and his plans for loading up the train with paintings and sculpture for the return journey. To Rommel's frustration, he was unable to involve Göring in his military problems.

The Allied landings—code-named Operation Torch—were a logistical masterpiece. More than 500 British and American ships had gathered off Gibraltar. Undetected by German U-boats or aircraft, they delivered some 83,000 American and 26,000 British troops to landing sites around Casablanca, Oran, and Algiers. The Germans were oblivious to the situation until the last minute. Reports of an unusual assemblage of naval traffic were assumed to refer to yet another convoy headed for Malta. Hitler discounted the idea of Allied landings in French Africa, reasoning that if a seaborne assault occurred, Sardinia or southern France would be the logical target.

The invasion created a complex and dangerous diplomatic imbroglio.

Heinkel 111 bombers wing over the domed harbor buildings of Benghazi in Libya. Rommel abandoned the town to the advancing British on November 20, hastily falling back to the old, defensible Mersa Brega Line to the south near El Agheila. There, he held off Montgomery's Eighth Army for almost three weeks.

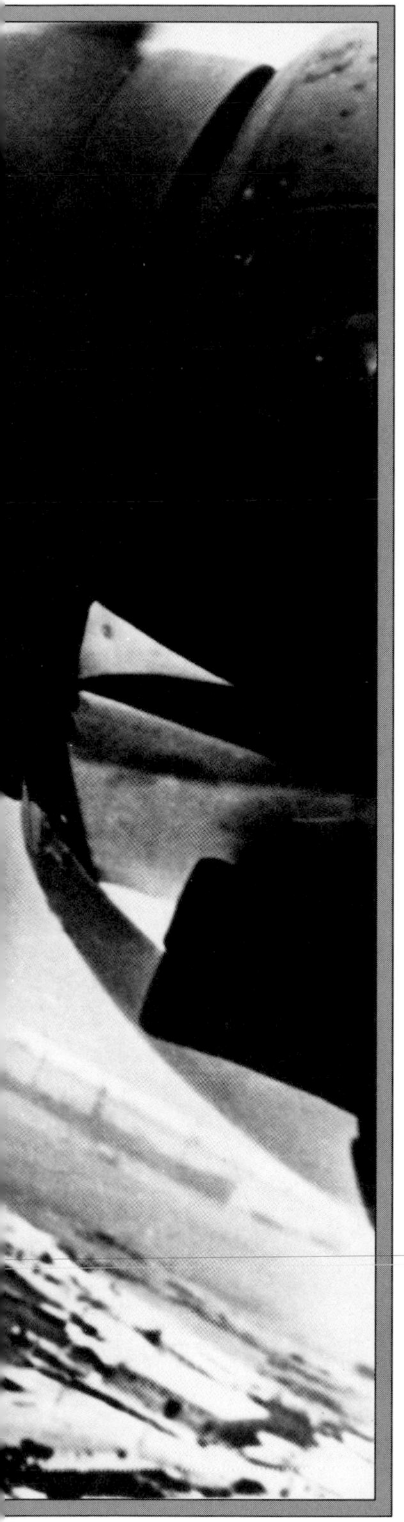

The terms of the 1940 French surrender specified that the colonies of France remain nominally independent, albeit subject to the government in Vichy. This meant that there was not a single German or Italian soldier in Morocco or Algeria to resist the Allied landings. Some of the American troops, expecting to be welcomed as liberators, waded ashore with loud-speakers blaring, "*Ne tirez pas. Nous sommes vos amis. Nous sommes Americains.*" (Don't shoot. We are your friends. We are Americans.)

It was not to be that simple. The French colonies were under military administration, and while few of the officers were pro-Nazi, many were anti-British. If they threw in with the Allies, Vichy France would be occupied and the colonies' theoretical independence would end quickly. Foreseeing this dilemma, Winston Churchill had proclaimed that the first North African conflict would be the "battle to have no battle with the French."

Accordingly, in the hope of gaining French support, the American general Mark Clark had boated ashore from a British submarine for a secret meeting with Robert Murphy, United States counselor to the Vichy government, and a pro-American French general. They met at an isolated villa on the Algerian coast. Clark could not be specific about his plans; consequently, when the assault troops began their encircling movements around the three invasion sites, the French response was whatever the local commanders decreed. In some places, they ordered troops to surrender without a fight, but in Algiers, two British destroyers attempting to deliver American infantry came under withering fire from shore batteries; one ship was sunk, the other had to withdraw. In Oran, two more ships loaded with troops were surprised by French patrol boats and sunk, resulting in heavy loss of life. A planned linkup with British paratroopers at the airports around Oran went awry; a total of 39,000 troops of the U.S. II Corps came ashore, but it took forty-eight hours for the soldiers to wrest control of the city. In Casablanca, where the landings were commanded by Major General George S. Patton, resistance was even stronger. The 35,000-ton French battleship *Jean Bart* opened up with four fifteen-inch guns while a task force of seven destroyers, eight submarines, and a cruiser attacked the troopships as the men tried to board their landing craft.

Despite the resistance, all three cities were occupied by November 11. But that did not solve the crisis of alliances. Local French commanders did not know whose orders to follow, or where they would come from. Normally, the military commander in Algiers was General Alphonse-Pierre Juin, whose sympathies were pro-Allied. But by a twist of fate, the Vichy regime's number-two man, the pro-Pétain, anti-British admiral Jean François Darlan, had just arrived in North Africa to visit his ailing son.

Murphy sent a French officer to fetch Darlan to Juin's headquarters on an urgent matter of state. It was a trap: As soon as he arrived, he was gently arrested and pressured to switch his allegiance. Within hours, Darlan ordered all French resistance to cease. In instant revenge, ten German and six Italian divisions took control of previously unoccupied southern France, and a German advance guard flew into Tunis to protect the port from capture. Nevertheless, within three days a provisional government that would collaborate with the Allies had been established in North Africa with Darlan at its head, and within a week most of the French forces in the region who had not surrendered to the Germans were joining the Allies.

The swiftness with which the landings had been secured and the relative ease with which the French had been turned around gave the Allies a false sense of confidence. Within a few weeks, they thought, the drive to capture Tunis and Bizerte could be completed, laying the groundwork for an invasion of Europe. But they underestimated the speed and intensity of the Axis reaction, and perhaps just as serious, they miscalculated how difficult it would be to fight in Tunisia. The terrain is mostly steep and mountainous. The flat valleys vary from marshy to barren and are vulnerable to enfilading artillery. The passes are narrow, with dense brush that facilitates ambushes. Paved roads were few, so whoever controlled the junctions could dictate the course of battle. The broken terrain allowed defenders to pull back from ridge to ridge while covering the valleys below.

The weather in November 1942 was windy and cold, with low-hanging clouds that hindered air support. Driving, seemingly endless rains turned the earth to a clay paste that sucked the boots from infantrymen's feet and mired the tanks to the tops of their treads. It was not much like the glamorous, freewheeling desert war the troops had heard about, with fifty-mile daily advances and wide-sweeping encounters waged like naval battles over sand. The combat-hardened Germans, some of whom had been transferred to Tunisia from the Russian front, would quickly adapt to these harsh conditions. But the unseasoned Americans and British, barely off their ships, were in for some ugly surprises.

Even before the landing sites were under Allied control, the German high command had awakened to the magnitude and significance of the threat. While the French were still dithering over which side they were fighting on, the Luftwaffe secured Tunis airport and began landing fighter planes, Stuka dive bombers, and Junkers troop carriers. By November 15, a regiment was on the ground; by the end of the month, 15,000 men had arrived. The OKW ordered Lieut. General Walther Nehring, who was recovering from an arm wound suffered while fighting with the Afrikakorps the previous summer, to organize them immediately into a defensive force.

The race for Tunis had begun. On paper it was an absurdly unequal

Italian troops newly arrived in Tunis line up to receive desert gear. From November 1942 through January 1943, approximately 112,000 Axis troops, including 31,000 Italians, were shipped to northwest Africa to reinforce the crumbling front.

struggle: Nehring estimated the enemy's total strength at between nine and thirteen divisions, although only a fraction were available for immediate attack. Against them, even with local air superiority, the Germans' two patched-together paratroop battalions were not enough to maintain a front, but only a series of defensive strongpoints. The Allied offensive was assigned to the Eastern Task Force that had captured Algiers. It was rechristened British First Army, although it also included the U.S. 1st Armored Division. This force had re-formed within three days of coming ashore and was already moving eastward by land, by air, even by sea. A small amphibious group had been assigned to capture harbors along the north coast as a first step toward isolating Bizerte and Tunis.

At first the Allies advanced swiftly, for Nehring had no choice but to make his stand at defensive strongpoints close to his coastal starting point and supply base. That meant his best option was to try to block the Allies at the gates of Bizerte and Tunis. He assigned the paratroop-engineer battalion commanded by Major Rudolf Witzig to dig in along the road from Mateur to Djebel Abiod, southwest of Bizerte. They did so, stopped the advance units of the British 78th Infantry Division, and in a brilliant rearguard action, brought them to a halt at the mouth of a road and rail tunnel. The British were pinned down there until January.

General Nehring faced another threat that demanded immediate attention. The coastal town of Gabès, some 200 miles south of Tunis, was defended by only a few ill-equipped French troops under the command of General Joseph Welvert. If the British and Americans reached the coast here, Nehring's opportunity to join forces with Rommel's army was gone, and with it any chance of a real counteroffensive. The only hope was an airborne assault by Lieut. Colonel Koch's 5th Paratroop Regiment, one of the first to arrive at Tunis. Their first attempt, on November 17, was waved off after it encountered heavy machine-gun fire. They landed successfully the next day. The French fled, and the Germans secured the airport.

Three days later, the first American tank patrols arrived at the edge of Gabès. A handful of Koch's paratroopers held them at bay long enough for two battalions of the Italian Superga Division to reinforce them. The Americans fell back. Gabès and a coastal perimeter were safe for the moment.

While these skirmishes were taking place, more Axis troops were arriving in Tunis and Bizerte by plane and ship, and the Luftwaffe was providing invaluable air cover. For the defense of Tunis itself, Nehring was able to call upon a new regiment under the command of Colonel Walther Barenthin. It arrived November 20 and immediately set out to reinforce the thinly held front—stretching from Mateur, twenty miles south, to the crossroads town of Tébourba, nineteen miles west of Tunis.

In the first assault, on November 26, the entire British 36th Brigade of Guards, enough men to cut a swath all the way to Bizerte, slammed into one of Barenthin's battalions. But suddenly the British withdrew and began digging defensive breastworks of their own. An Arab sheik had falsely warned the British that they were facing a regiment of crack paratroopers from Crete. It was not the first time, or the last, that Arabs would help the Germans confound the Allies. They would barter and sell food to either side, and strip the dead of their weapons and uniforms impartially, but on the whole they preferred Germans to the friends of their colonial masters.

The British tried again three days later, but by this time Barenthin had been reinforced and was able to throw them back. On Barenthin's flank, however, Koch's paratroopers had put the entire defensive perimeter at risk by probing miles beyond Tébourba to the town of Medjez-el-Bab. Then they ran directly into elements of the British 36th Brigade and the U.S. 1st Armored Division. A fierce seesaw firefight raged back and forth through the town, and the Germans found themselves overpowered.

Once they were beaten back, the road to Tébourba and beyond was open. The Americans quickly exploited the break: A battalion of M-3 light tanks commanded by Lieut. Colonel John K. Waters sped right past the town and, to their own amazement, overran an undefended airport containing thirty-eight Messerschmitt and Junkers aircraft. The Americans destroyed all but two of the planes, along with their hangars and machine shops.

It looked as though the Allies might be in Tunis by the end of November—

A clash between American forces and German armor is captured in these frames from a newsreel taken by U.S. Signal Corps photographers during the struggle for Tébourba in early December 1942. In the first frame *(reading left to right)*, a German 88-mm gun, hidden in a haystack, opens fire on American tanks advancing from the upper left. Allied artillery then gets the range of the gun, igniting the haystack, and repelling several Panzer IV tanks, which wheel around to evade the incoming shells. The retreat was temporary; German armor soon hurled back the early British-American push toward Tunis. The team of photographers was led by Hollywood mogul Darryl F. Zanuck, who was promoted to colonel during the war.

but then they learned about the Germans' 88-mm guns. Probably the best artillery piece used in the war, the 88 had been designed as an antiaircraft gun, but with its barrel lowered, it was devastating against tanks. "It could go through all our tanks like butter," said one British soldier.

For the next few days there was heavy fighting all up and down the line. Nehring had to detach an infantry unit to surround an assault force of 500 amphibious troops that had landed near Cape Serrat, west of Bizerte; another German company supported by Italian infantry captured some 500 British paratroopers who had jumped in south of Medjez-el-Bab, looking for a weak spot in the Tunis defenses. The heaviest fighting continued around Tébourba itself, but here, the beleaguered Nehring was finally getting some real help. Strong elements of General Wolfgang Fischer's 10th Panzer Division were landing at Bizerte and Tunis, ready to move in any direction. Their weaponry included the first contingent of sixty-three ton Tiger tanks, impenetrably armored and carrying 88-mm guns of their own.

Everything that could move was thrown into the battle, which raged for four days. The outnumbered Germans won decisively. Entire Allied units —the British 11th Brigade and the U.S. Combat Force B—lost all their equipment; the U.S. 18th Infantry suffered heavy losses, and one British battalion was wiped out; 1,100 prisoners were taken; 134 Allied tanks, 40 guns, and 47 planes were lost. It was a serious setback for the Allied timetable and morale. On Christmas Eve, the Allies tried for the second time to capture Djebel Ahmera, known to them as Longstop Hill, which overlooked Tunis and controlled two important roads leading into the city. In a hideous, rain-soaked night battle, this assault too was thrown back. The race for Tunis had been won by the Axis.

It was clear to everybody but Hitler, Mussolini, and Kesselring, however, that the Afrikakorps could not hold off the invaders forever. The Allies already held a huge advantage in manpower and equipment, with more arriving steadily, and they would not remain inexperienced for long. While the fighting along the Tébourba Line was still in progress, Hitler established the Tunisian second front by summoning a Prussian general named Jürgen von Arnim from Russia and christening his new unit Fifth Panzer Army. Arnim's command relationship to Rommel was left unclear, adding yet another layer of friction to the already muddled Axis command structure.

By the time Arnim relieved General Nehring on December 9, German and Italian transport commands were taking full advantage of the major port facilities and all-weather airports at Tunis and Bizerte. By the end of the year, seven infantry battalions, two armored reconnaissance companies, batteries of field guns, and scores of tanks—including a few of the giant Panzer VI Tigers—had been landed. By the time the climactic battles of the

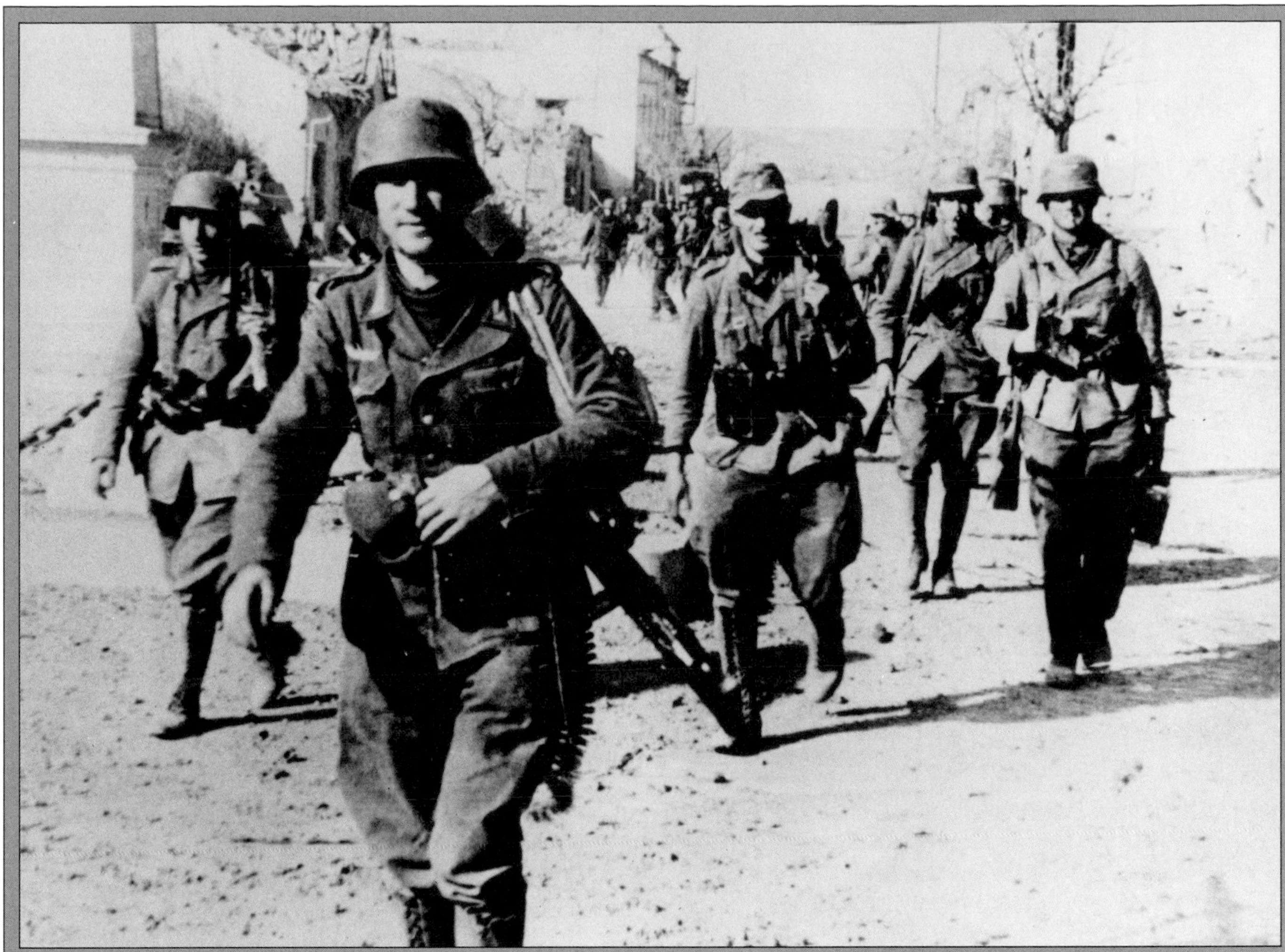

A detachment of German troops hustles into Tébourba after the 10th Panzer had expelled inexperienced British and American forces from the strategically valuable road and rail junction. The counterattack mounted by the Germans virtually destroyed the Allied force at Tébourba, knocking out more than 100 tanks and capturing 1,100 soldiers.

coming campaign were joined, the Axis had a force of 100,000 men on the ground, including the newly arrived and formidable 10th Panzer Division.

If half of these reinforcements had been directed to Rommel two months earlier, he might have been eating Christmas dinner at Shepheard's Hotel in Cairo. Instead, almost out of gasoline, he was virtually immobilized. One of his staff officers estimated his November troop strength at 25,000 Italians of questionable reliability and 10,000 Germans, and his armored resources at only 100 tanks. The long Mersa Brega Line was impossible to defend with such meager forces, but Rommel doubted his ability to mount a successful retreat to Buerat, the next defensible position. Even to withdraw, he would need 400 tons of fuel a day, 50 tons of ammunition, another 50 tons of food and supplies. It was a lucky day when he received a fourth of that amount, and there was little hope of improvement. During December alone, 5,883 tons of fuel, 262 tons of ammunition, and 447 tons of other supplies were sunk en route to Libya. Again, although Rommel did not know it, an unseen adversary was Ultra, which allowed the British to decode Axis radio messages about the routes the convoys were planning to take.

Rommel was still being bombarded with unrealistic orders from the OKW and Comando Supremo: "Resist to the end in Mersa Brega." "There will be no retreat from Tripoli." Rommel had foreseen this impasse on the day he flew back to Africa from his disastrous interview with Hitler. "I realized that we were now completely thrown back on our resources," he

The Roar of a Brand-New Tiger

The sixty-three-ton Panzer VI Tiger I tank, which the Germans unleashed against the western Allies in North Africa, was one of the first of Hitler's superweapons. German armor experts had been long demanding a heavy tank. The Führer was so impressed by the Henschel Company model unveiled on his birthday, April 20, 1942, that he ordered production to begin as soon as testing could be completed.

Plated with frontal armor up to 100 millimeters thick and armed with a modified version of the Luftwaffe's dread 88-mm flak gun, the Tiger was a formidable weapon. But its virtues made it costly to produce and hampered its performance in the field. The massive turret traversed with agonizing slowness. And with a top cross-country speed of only twelve miles per hour and a fuel consumption of 2.75 gallons per mile, the tank's mobility was limited. But its killing power and thick skin overshadowed these flaws, and caused Allied soldiers to recoil when the behemoth lumbered onto the battlefields.

1. 88-mm gun
2. Hull machine gun
3. Periscope
4. Radio operator's hatch
5. Gear selector
6. Hydraulic steering wheel
7. Accelerator
8. Forward/reverse lever
9. Brake
10. Clutch
11. Hand brake
12. Smoke dischargers
13. Vision port
14. Turret machine gun
15. Binocular telescope
16. Traverse handwheel

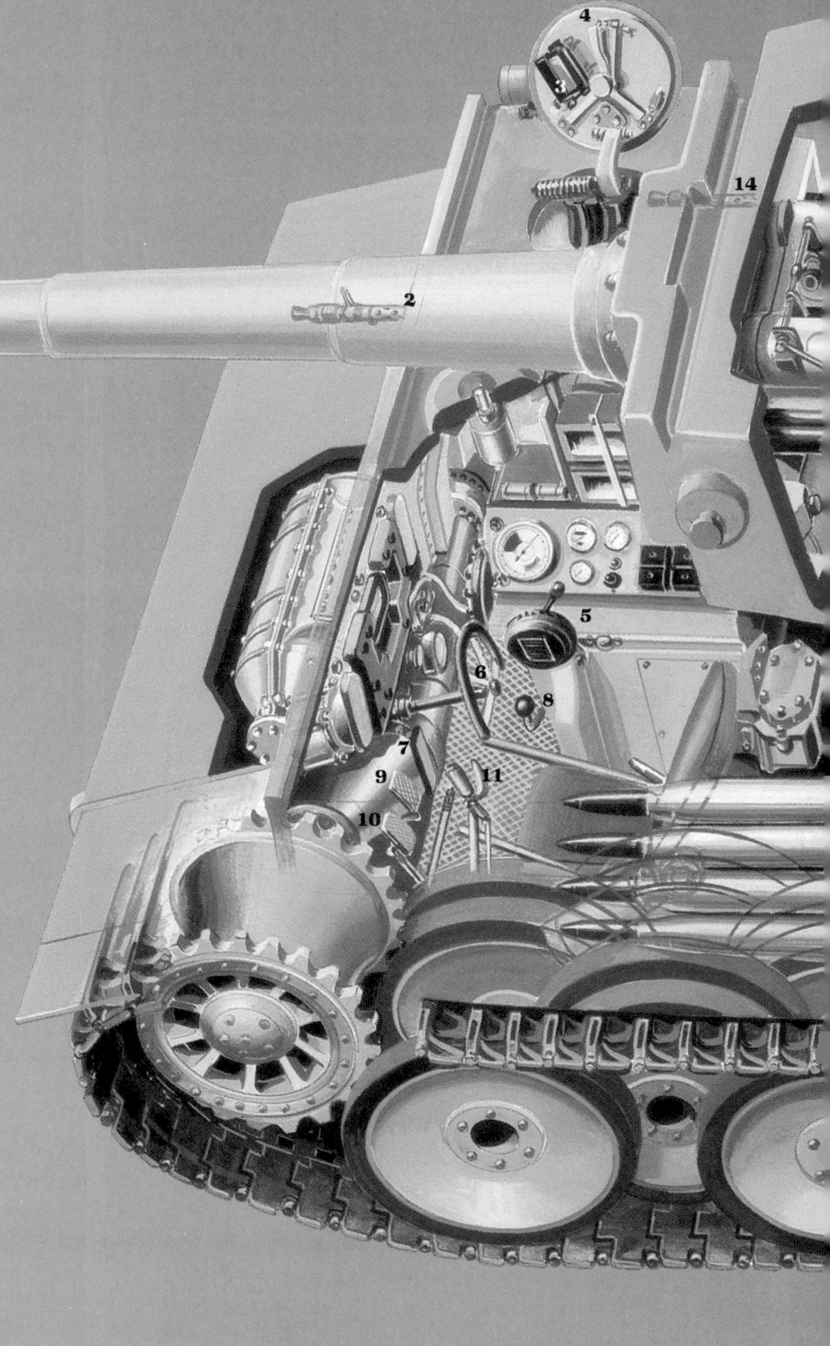

Panzer VI Tiger I

The Tiger employed the same five-man crew arrangement used in the Panzer III and IV—driver and radio operator forward in the hull, the gunner, loader, and commander in the turret. In combat, the radio operator manned the hull machine gun, while the three turret crewmen teamed up to select, sight, and kill targets with the deadly 88-mm gun. Using foot pedals, the turret gunner also fired a second machine gun.

17. Turret machine gun firing pedal
18. Hydraulic traverse foot control
19. Machine gun ammunition pouches
20. Water flask
21. Loader's seat
22. 88-mm ammunition
23. Commander's independent traverse wheel
24. Gunner's seat
25. Turret traverse mechanism
26. Ventilator fan
27. Escape hatch
28. Turret fuse box
29. Commander's cupola
30. Empty shell case container
31. Commander's seat
32. Pistol port
33. Drive shaft
34. Battery
35. Torsion bar suspension
36. Gas tank
37. Desert air intakes
38. Maybach V-12 engine
39. Air filters
40. Exhausts

wrote later, "and that to keep the army from being destroyed as the result of some crazy order or other would need all our skill."

Time and again, the great master of the counterattack had impotently watched British thrusts and flanking maneuvers that he could have demolished if only he had been mobile. He saw his troops fight off encirclement again and again while waiting for enough fuel to allow them to retreat through the final gap. His half-starved forces continued the retreat by filtering the Italian infantry back from the Mersa Brega Line in late November, with the last defenders abandoning it by December 13. By Christmas, even the rear guard was at Sirte, a few miles east of Buerat.

"We vamped up a Christmas tree out of a wooden pole in which we had bored holes to carry camel-thorn branches," a survivor recalled. "We decorated the tree with silver paper, and we improvised candles of a sort. As Christmas fare, each of my men received three cigarettes—we had been hoarding them for some time. The contents of a light mailbag of letters from home were handed out. The letters were the best of Christmas presents." A few miles away, the New Zealand patrol that was shadowing the retreat settled down for their own Christmas dinner featuring turkey and roast pork, fresh vegetables, plum pudding, and two bottles of beer for each man.

Rommel had a slight respite at Buerat: A violent winter storm at Benghazi

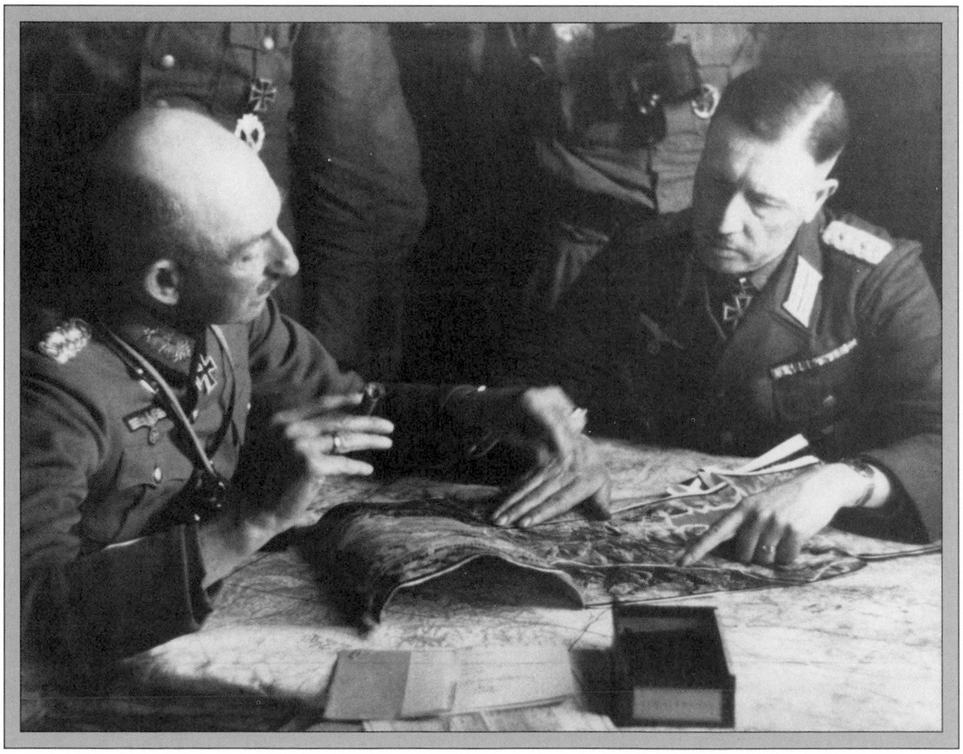

General Jürgen von Arnim *(left)*, dispatched to Tunisia to command the new Fifth Panzer Army, confers with one of his division commanders, Colonel Friedrich Weber, at a command post at Pont-du-Fahs, a key point in the defense of Tunis.

A group of German and Italian officers study Allied troop dispositions from an observation post. The plumed helmet identifies one of the Italians as belonging to an elite Bersaglieri infantry unit. Both the 5th Bersaglieri and tanks from the Italian Centauro Division took part in Rommel's March offensive at Kasserine Pass.

had broken up docks and smashed or sunk many British resupply vessels, slowing Montgomery's pursuit. But by mid-January, Rommel's depleted units were on the move again. He had been ordered to transfer his favored 21st Panzer Division northward to Arnim's command; the remaining troops, hounded by the New Zealanders' repeated flanking movements, reached the Tarhuna-Homs Line on January 19 and Tripoli on the 23rd.

Pushed along by cold winds, they finally crossed into Tunisia on February 4. Only 100 miles remained before they reached the Mareth Line, an easily defended natural corridor between the sea and a range of barren hills. There, the 1,500-mile retreat would end, and the Afrikakorps would turn to face the British. Rommel found time to write to his wife: "I simply can't tell you how hard it is for me to undergo this retreat and all that goes with it. Day and night I'm tormented by the thought that things might really go wrong here in Africa. I'm so depressed that I can hardly do my work."

The next day, Comando Supremo informed him that due to his poor state of health, he was to be relieved of command once his troops reached Mareth. An Italian, General Giovanni Messe, was being transferred from the Russian front to replace him. The orders incongruously left up to Rommel the actual date of the transfer of command.

Even after the Afrikakorps reached the Mareth Line, there could be little rest for the weary troops. The prewar complex of hills and marshes linked by crumbling French fortifications needed extensive preparation prior to the inevitable Eighth Army attack. But there was an even more urgent crisis.

To Rommel's rear, Allied forces had reached the town of Gafsa, less than 100 miles from the coast. Before them loomed the Eastern Dorsal, a 200-mile-long mountain range running north to south, parallel to and about 60 miles inland from Tunisia's east coast. Once the Allies poured through the Eastern Dorsal passes, Arnim's forces to the north could easily be severed from Rommel's, and the hard-won Tunisian bridgehead lost for good. Comando Supremo finally approved Rommel's proposal to mount a major, two-pronged Axis offensive. Under Operation *Frühlingswind* (Spring Wind), Arnim's Fifth Army was to drive westward to secure and seal off the Allied approach at Faïd and Sidi-Bou-Zid. Operation *Morgenluft* (Morning Air), with German and Italian components blocking the American advance at Gafsa itself, was supposed to push the Allies back to the Western Dorsal, another mountain range separated from the Eastern Dorsal by a wide plain.

Arnim at least would be starting his drive from near the point of attack, with the relatively well-supplied 10th and 21st Panzer divisions. But for Rommel, the offensive meant a 100-mile march from the Mareth Line, and almost as far again to secure his goals. He was woefully underequipped. The 90th Light Infantry Division was without field guns, defenseless against armored attack; fighting had severely reduced the strength of its regiments. The entire 164th Infantry had only one battery of field guns. Somehow, Rommel summoned the will to mount the offensive. Perhaps he took courage from his belief that the "Americans had as yet no practical battle experience, and it was now up to us to instill in them from the outset an inferiority complex of no mean order." Or perhaps Kesselring had hinted to him that if all went well, Rommel might yet be given overall command of the North African theater.

The Allied forces that he and Arnim would engage were not only untested in combat but also hampered by a command structure even more cumbersome than Comando Supremo's. General Dwight D. Eisenhower was commander in chief, but he was too tied down with political and logistical problems to take charge of operations. His field commander was General Sir Harold Alexander, a brilliant, quick-thinking British tactician. The northern end of the line was under the control of Kenneth Anderson, a Scottish general who had hardly distinguished himself in the November race for Tunis. The center was held by the French, with antiquated equipment and leaders who refused to serve under any English general, insisting on their own chain of command. The southern sector, where the coming action was to take place, was primarily the preserve of the U.S. II Corps. It had its own problems, notably in the person of its commander, Major General Lloyd Fredendall, an erratic, overbearing officer who preferred to direct battles from a bombproofed headquarters fifty miles behind the

German paratroopers in their distinctive bowl-shape helmets prepare for an assault beyond their own defensive concertina wire. Two airborne regiments, fighting as regular infantry, were among General Arnim's forces in northern Tunisia that counterattacked the Allied columns advancing on Bizerte.

front, and who was barely on speaking terms with his senior subordinate, Major General Orlando Ward of the 1st Armored Division. So on both sides of the line, animosities, backbiting, and failures to communicate would play major parts in the bloody encounter that lay ahead.

The Kasserine Pass in the Western Dorsal is an imposing defensive position, with rocky heights rising 5,000 feet on either side of a valley that narrows to a 1,500-yard-wide funnel at the eastern end. A week of bitter fighting climaxed there, but in fact the battle of Kasserine Pass was a series of bloody engagements that covered a 100-square-mile area. The first assault, on February 14, began at dawn in the Eastern Dorsal in the Faïd Pass area, under the direction of Arnim's deputy, General Heinz Ziegler. The German plan called for coordinated attacks by the 10th and 21st Panzer divisions. Two battle groups of the 10th would attack through the pass and then diverge, one moving toward Sidi-Bou-Zid, the second northward toward Lessouda. Meanwhile, armored elements of the 21st Panzer would breach a second pass to the south and then head north to help form a pincers movement around Sidi-Bou-Zid.

The panzers surged through the mountains at Faïd and, under the cover of a sandstorm, rumbled toward their destination. Visibility improved as the morning progressed, and the advancing armor began to encounter effective American artillery, followed by attacking tank units. But this time the panzers were numerically superior, and their cannon had greater range. By afternoon the Germans held the village, and the relatively inexperienced Americans had been driven from the field, leaving sixty-eight destroyed vehicles behind. Something far more serious had been left behind as well: Two infantry battalions, which had been sited on djebels, or hills, by Fredendall, now found themselves surrounded. The next day, American armored units counterattacked to relieve them but again were outmaneuvered and cut to pieces. The American command airdropped a message to the infantry: They were on their own and would have to fight their way out as best they could. They tried to escape that night, but most of them were captured. By the end of the second day, II Corps had lost two entire battalions of armor, two of artillery, and two of infantry. The remaining units were ordered to pull back across the plain to new defensive positions along the Western Dorsal, where they were reinforced with hastily assembled French and British elements from the north.

Advancing to Gafsa on the 15th, Rommel found the town already abandoned and deployed Colonel Menton's Special Unit 288—the illustrious Panzergrenadier Regiment Afrika—to occupy it. Then, he immediately ordered other Afrikakorps reconnaissance units to advance to Fériana,

A Bold Bid at Kasserine Pass

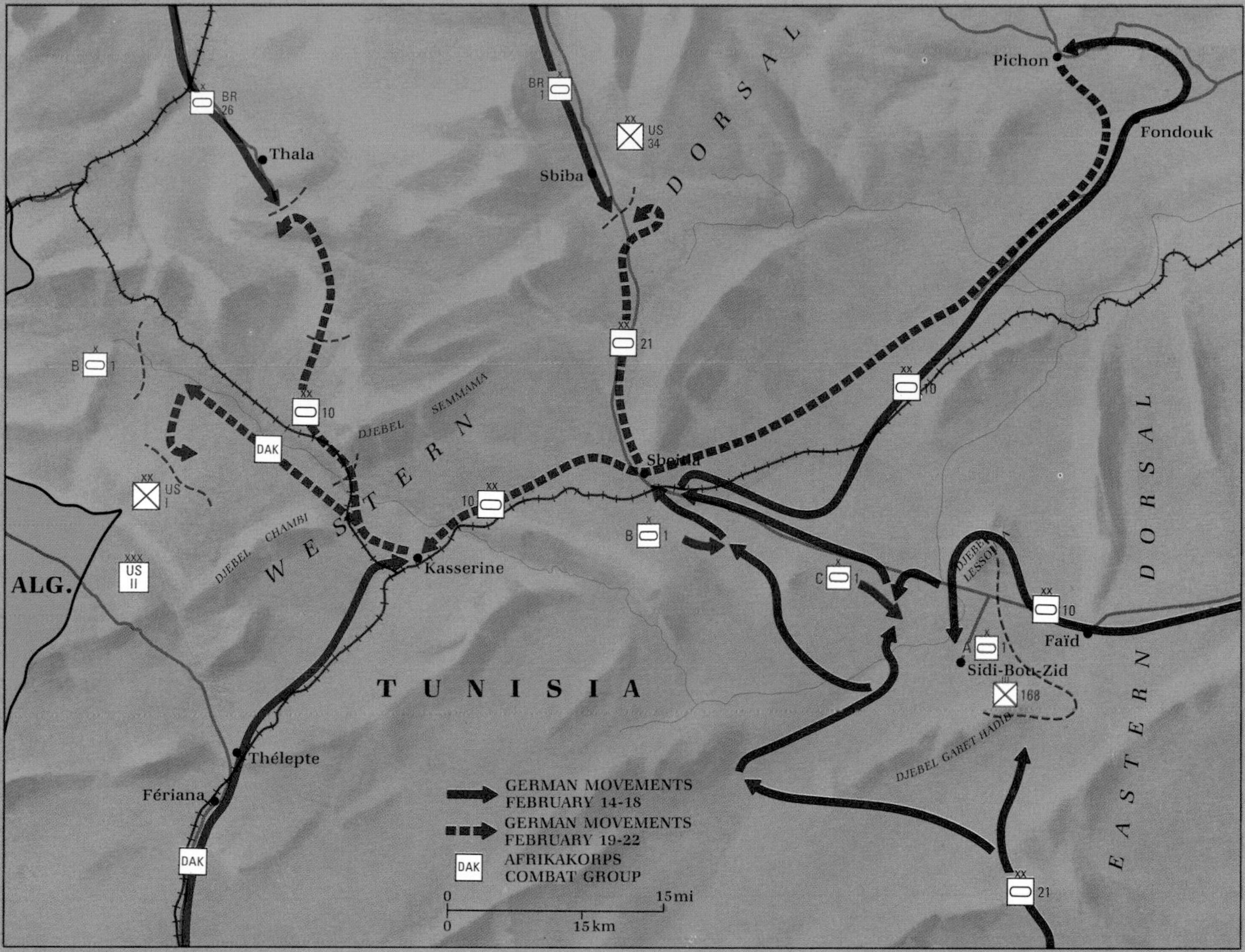

On February 14, 1943, the Germans struck suddenly against the Allied center held by inexperienced American forces in a daring attempt to cut them off from their bases in Algeria. While an Afrikakorps combat group under Rommel moved northward toward Kasserine Pass, along the flank of the Western Dorsal range, Arnim's 10th and 21st Panzer divisions attacked through two passes in the Eastern Dorsal. Arnim's pincer movement trapped units of the U.S. II Corps around Sidi-Bou-Zid and drove the Americans back on Sbeitla. On February 19, having been given control of Arnim's units by Kesselring, Rommel ordered the 21st Panzer toward Sbiba and sent the 10th Panzer to Kasserine Pass. On February 22, Rommel's forces broke through, only to be turned back by stiffening Allied resistance.

forty miles up the road. From the time the joint offensive had first been ordered, Rommel had argued for an all-out assault that would push the Allies back through the passes and across the Algerian border to their big supply base at Tebessa. With the equipment and supplies that could be captured, there was no end to what Rommel might accomplish.

Command authority remained divided, however. Rommel and Arnim, who had little use for each other, operated as coequals and failed to coordinate their campaigns. Rommel wanted flat-out pursuit; Arnim preferred to husband his limited manpower and resources. He declined to release troops he was supposed to shift to Rommel, intending to use them farther north in an offensive that would enhance his own ambitions.

For the moment, Rommel got his way: After a time-consuming debate that gave the Allies time to regroup, General Ziegler, who had led the Sidi-Bou-Zid assault, was directed by Kesselring and Comando Supremo to transfer the 10th and 21st Panzer divisions to Rommel. He in turn used some of them on a thrust northwest toward Sbeitla and began organizing separate assault groups to attack Kasserine Pass. Meanwhile, the Afrikakorps captured the American airfield at Thélepte just north of Fériana.

Orders from above stopped short of granting Rommel permission for a headlong westward dash to take Tebessa. He was told instead to direct his main effort northward through the pass toward Thala and on to Le Kef, halfway to Tunisia's northern coast. Thala was far more powerfully defended than Tebessa, so Rommel considered this plan an "appalling and unbelievable piece of shortsightedness" that ultimately caused his overall operation to fail. But the directive was stated so ambiguously that he adapted it to his own ends. Accordingly, an Afrikakorps combat group started directly toward Kasserine; 21st Panzer proceeded northward up an adjoining valley; and units from 10th Panzer moved up in its wake to Sbeitla, from whence they could reinforce either thrust, depending on the need.

On February 19, Afrikakorps panzers under General Karl Buelowius attempted to blast through the bottleneck on the eastern end of Kasserine Pass, only to be repulsed. That night, Buelowius sent infantry patrols on a flanking maneuver through the mountains overlooking the pass. They worked their way into the heights north of the pass and descended to the rear of the Allies defending the roads to Tebessa and Thala. The unexpected and silent arrival of the Germans in the pitch-black night panicked many of the Allied soldiers, and the defense of Kasserine seemed on the verge of disintegration. Only the arrival of reinforcements during the night kept the German armor from breaking through the entrance to Kasserine.

Rommel, driven by a sense of urgency, now committed 10th Panzer to the assault of Kasserine Pass. He knew that he had to secure a victory quickly, for far to the east, the British forces of General Montgomery were approaching the Mareth Line. Soon the Desert Fox would have to reverse his steps to reinforce the rear guard he left to defend Mareth.

Rommel exhorted Buelowius to make an extra effort to breach the narrow entrance to Kasserine. On the 20th, in the wake of a massive artillery barrage, elements of the 10th Panzer and the Afrikakorps, including the Italian Centauro Division, broke the Allied hold on the pass and swept into the valley beyond. A night attack by veteran tankmen of the 8th Panzer Regiment pinned a II Corps armored formation against the mountains and demolished it. By dawn, panzers were probing down the roads leading to both Thala and Tebessa and encountering little resistance. The way seemed clear for Rommel to drive on deep into Allied territory.

A German armored personnel carrier leads a parade of vehicles, many of them captured American trucks, after Rommel's defeat of the U.S. II Corps in the battle of Kasserine Pass. Rommel's bold plan, frustrated ultimately by command indecision, was to drive into Algeria, threatening the rear of Allied troops in Tunisia and forcing them to withdraw.

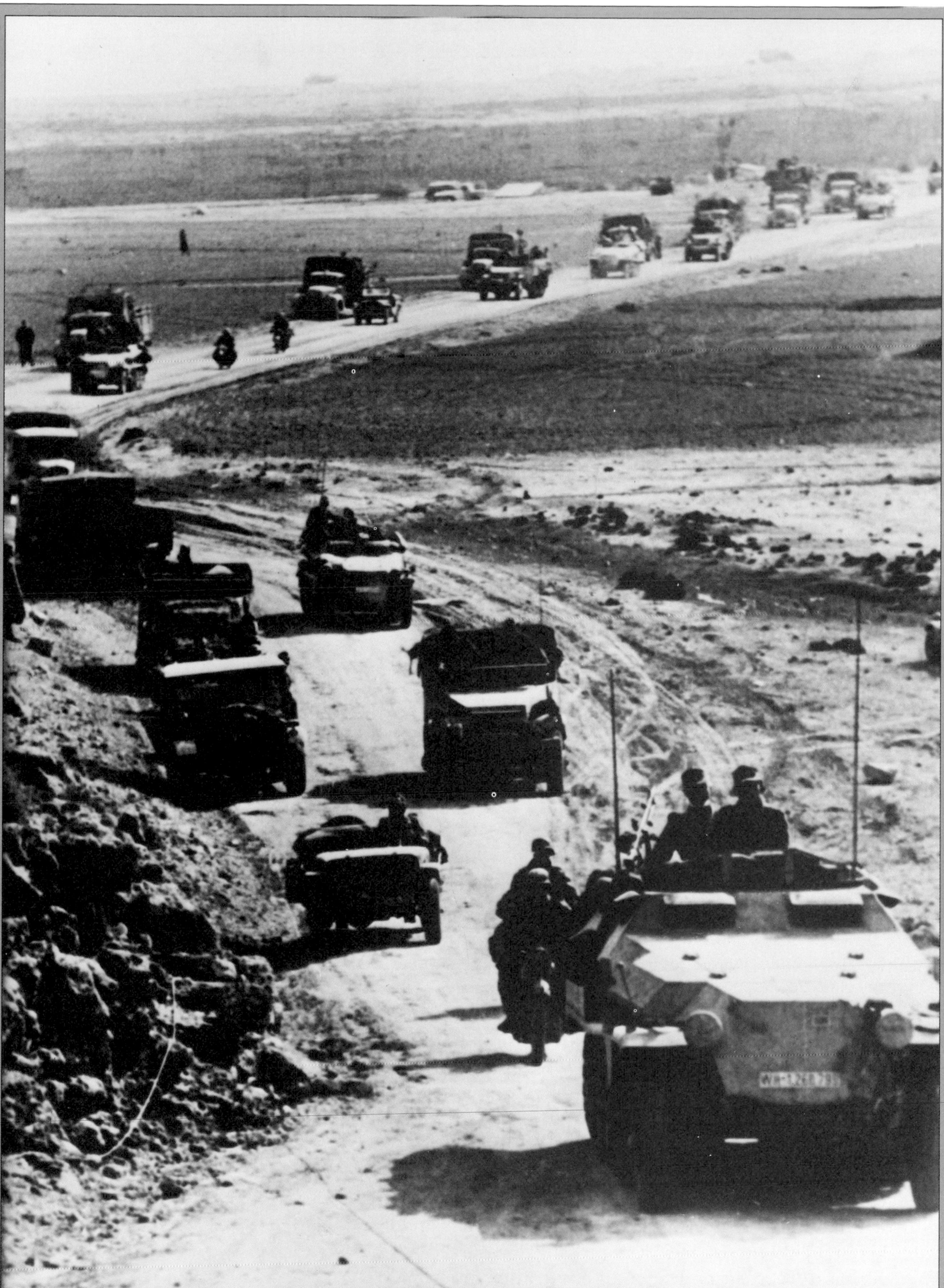

Now, however, Rommel hesitated and halted the advance. He expected a counterattack on the 21st and wanted to make sure that his troops were consolidated and well prepared to meet the Allied thrust. It was a costly mistake. The attack never came that day, but while the Axis forces remained stationary, Allied reinforcements arrived to bolster the faltering defense.

Then suddenly, a dramatic turnaround occurred. After a four-day, 800-mile forced march from western Algeria, the artillery battalions of the U.S. 9th Infantry Division appeared on the Thala road in the afternoon and spent the night digging in. At dawn, as the panzers resumed their advance toward Thala, the bone-tired Allied artillerymen began pumping shells into the approaching German columns. The presence of the gunners and their forty-eight howitzers stiffened the resolve of the British infantrymen, who had been falling slowly back along the road. More important, the artillery barrage convinced Rommel and General Fritz von Broich, commanding the Thala assault group, that major Allied reinforcements had arrived and the counteroffensive was imminent.

Grave doubts now beset Rommel. After his panzers had swept through the pass, he had inspected the captured American equipment and had envied and admired its quality and abundance. He was also impressed by the swift flow of Allied reinforcements to the Kasserine area. In contrast, the Axis forces that had breached the Kasserine defenses were down to one day's ammunition, six days' food, and 120 miles' fuel per vehicle. Rommel now concluded that continuing his offensive would only drown his soldiers in a sea of superior enemy numbers and matériel.

The great gamble had failed: On February 22, Rommel and Kesselring agreed to call off the offensive and withdraw by stages. Twenty-four hours elapsed before the Allies realized they were gone. The Afrikakorps left 6,300 II Corps Americans dead, wounded, or missing and captured another 4,026; they had destroyed 183 Allied tanks, 194 half-tracks, 512 trucks and jeeps and, by one estimate, demolished more matériel and supplies than all the reserve stores in Algeria and Morocco combined. A relatively few Germans—201—were killed; 536 were wounded, and 252 were missing.

The high command's confidence in Rommel plummeted. The Italians, aghast at the loss of Libya, their most important colony, had been urging his removal. Kesselring thought that ever since El Alamein, Rommel had not been "fighting back with the uncompromising vigor I have been accustomed to expect," and now, after Kasserine Pass, Kesselring referred to the "pigheadedness" of both Rommel and Arnim. Astonishingly, he then recommended Rommel as temporary commander of a newly designated Army Group Africa, with authority over both Arnim and Giovanni Messe, the Italian general who had already been designated to succeed him.

End Game in Africa

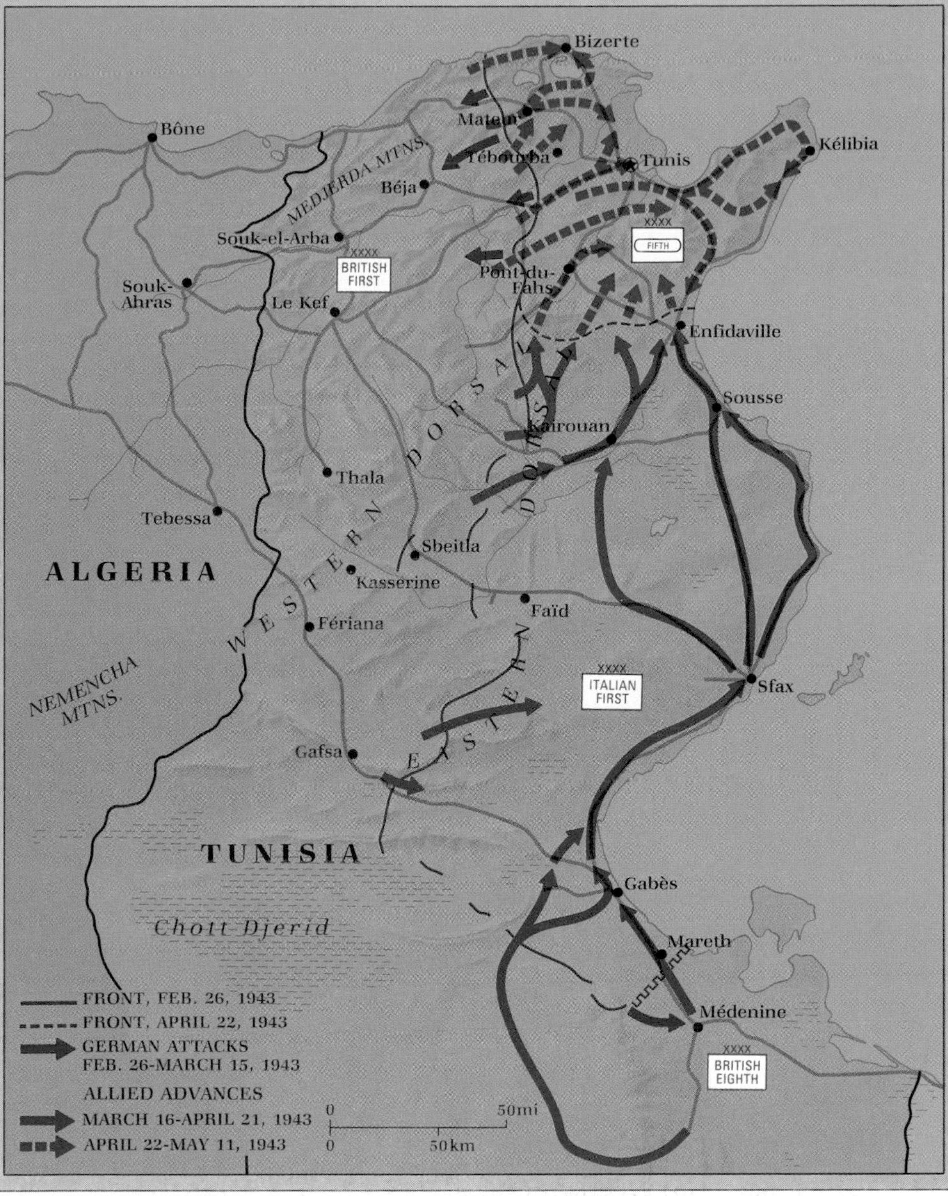

Buying time after the setback at Kasserine, Rommel, now the overall commander in Tunisia, launched two attacks in late February and early March, first with Arnim's Fifth Panzer Army against the Allied front in the north, and finally against the British Eighth Army at Médenine. Both attacks failed with heavy losses. On March 9, Rommel—a sick man—was ordered home and replaced by Arnim. On March 20, Montgomery outflanked the Mareth Line and pushed up the coast while other Allied units advanced through the Eastern Dorsal. The retreating Axis forces managed to avoid encirclement, but not for long. Beginning on April 22, the Allies launched their final drive against the Axis bridgehead. After Allied forces cut the Bizerte-Tunis road on May 9, Axis troops, with no hope of evacuation and short of ammunition, began surrendering in droves. By May 13, it was all over.

Perhaps Kesselring believed that only Rommel could accomplish the task that immediately confronted the Germans in North Africa—beating back the British Eighth Army, now arrayed in force below the Mareth Line. Typically, Hitler's orders were to hold the position to the last man; but no reinforcements or adequate matériel were forthcoming. Knowing that he had only skeletal forces to work with, Rommel wanted to withdraw to more logical defensive positions at the narrow Gabès Line. Instead, he mounted one more desperate assault in an attempt to break Montgomery's line at the village of Médenine, south-southeast of Mareth.

The battle lasted only one day, March 6, 1943. Montgomery, who was renowned for fighting defensively before launching his own assaults, was well prepared. Air reconnaissance and Ultra interceptions had pinpointed the approach of the Germans precisely. Three British divisions and two additional brigades were dug in, with 460 antitank guns, 350 field guns, and 300 tanks in position. They had laid 70,000 mines. When the three attacking

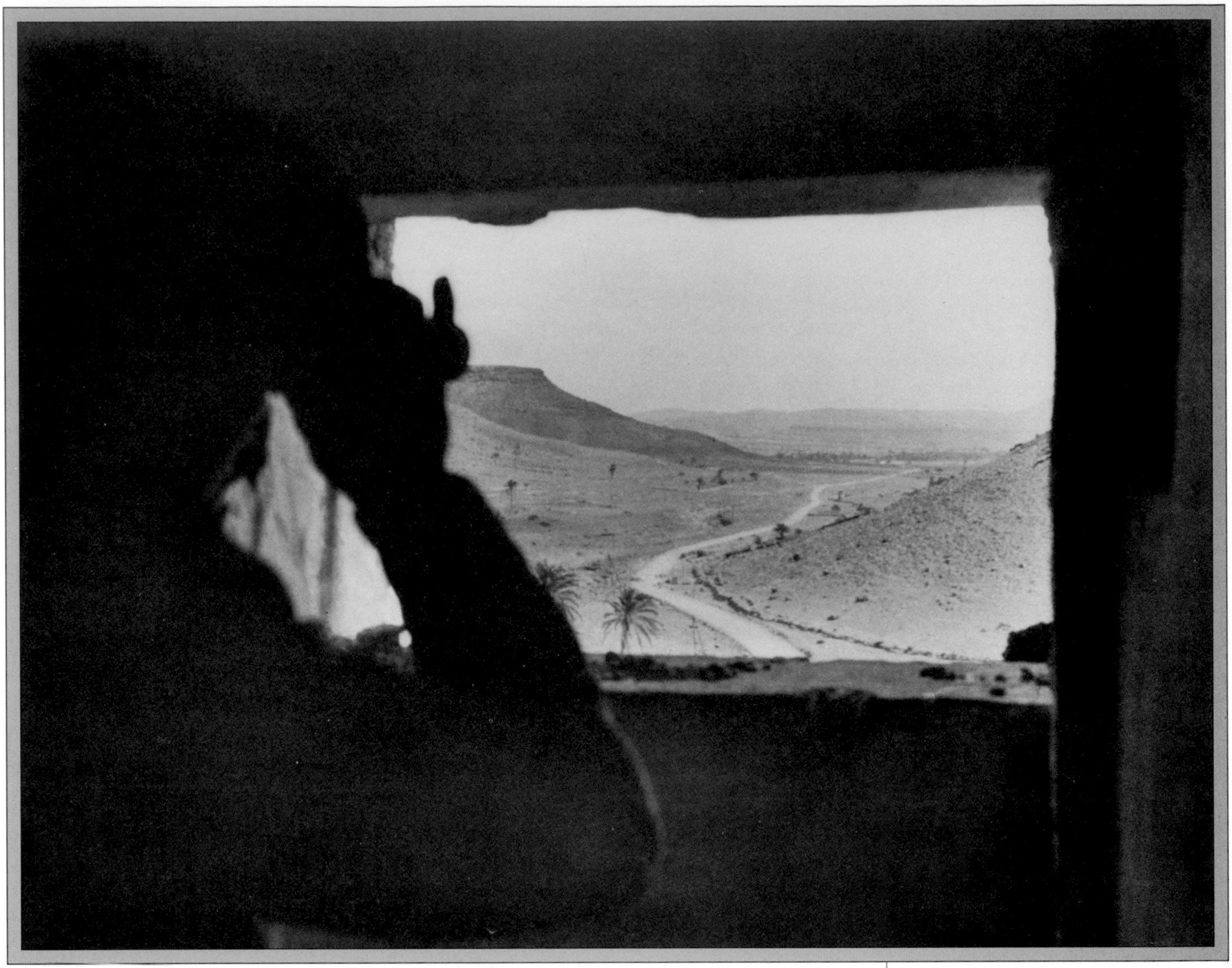

An Axis soldier with field glasses peers from a concrete strongpoint in the Mareth Line, the French-built, twenty-five-mile-long belt of fortified positions blocking the direct route from Libya into Tunisia. German and Italian engineers added extra machine-gun and artillery emplacements, wire, and minefields to the line, making it a formidable obstacle for the British Eighth Army.

panzer divisions poured out of the passes, with the 90th Light and Italian Spezia divisions on their flanks, they were cut to pieces under a hurricane of British shelling. By nightfall it was all over, the defeat so devastating that suspicions lingered in the German ranks that their plans had been betrayed by someone in the Italian command.

Rommel had fought his last battle in Africa. He left secretly three days later, never to return. Back in Germany, he pleaded once more with Hitler for an evacuation, arguing that it was suicidal for the German forces to remain in Africa. Instead, he was awarded the highest order of the Iron Cross and told to go on sick leave. Africa must be held, Hitler maintained.

So the slaughter continued. Montgomery launched a frontal assault on the main Mareth Line, but was stopped dead for two days. An alternate Allied scheme, however, was already in progress: Eighth Army's New Zealand Corps, whose flanking "left hooks" had dogged the Germans all through their long retreat, had been dispatched on a week-long, 200-mile march behind the mountain passes to attack the Germans from the rear. On March 26, supported by the U.S. 1st Armored Division, they struck. Their brilliant maneuver broke the Mareth defense, but they could not trap the defending armies. Germans and Italians streamed north, to dig in just north of Gabès, in the narrow gap between the Chott Djerid salt marshes and the coast—the line Rommel had wanted to defend from the very first.

Brilliant muzzle flashes signal the start of the furious 300-gun British bombardment of the Mareth Line on March 20, 1943. Despite the pounding, the German and Italian defenders threw back the attacking British infantry and armor with heavy losses, abandoning the position only when they were outflanked by a circling attack from desert areas to the southwest.

By now the Axis fortunes in North Africa were in precipitous decline. The Luftwaffe had virtually been driven from the sky, and resupply from Europe had all but dried up. Perhaps 80 percent of the Junkers transports were being shot down en route to Africa by Allied warplanes. The Royal Navy controlled the Mediterranean routes to Tunis. The Axis still had 150,000 combat troops in Africa, but that was not enough to defend a 500-mile front

In a huge, wire-enclosed tent city outside Bizerte, captured German troops line up for a water ration at an American army tank.

Most of the 275,000 Axis troops taken prisoner in Tunisia were shipped across the Atlantic to the United States and Canada.

against the far stronger Allied forces. Axis troops were also short of all essential supplies—gasoline, ammunition, and food.

The British Eighth Army continued to press from the south; the U.S. II Corps—now under the aggressive command of General George Patton—was pushing in from the west; while in the northern sector, the British First Army and the French corps renewed their campaign against the perimeter defending Tunis and Bizerte.

In mid-April, the Axis troops retreating northward along the east coast reached the village of Enfidaville and linked up with the forces defending the northern tip of Tunisia. A ragged front had been established that meandered north and west from Enfidaville to the coast not far from Cape Serrat. On one side stood Eisenhower, Alexander, and Montgomery, with fifteen fully equipped British divisions, five American divisions, and the French corps, and with total control of the sea and sky as well. On the other side stood Arnim, whose nine exhausted German divisions had been reduced to two-fifths of normal strength, and Messe, whose six Italian divisions had been rendered virtually useless for combat. With only the pride of the old Afrikakorps to sustain them, the Germans stubbornly defended the hills and yielded ground grudgingly, at a high cost to their foes.

It could not go on forever. The surrender took place during the second week of May, unit by unit. A British officer recalled watching the "white flags go up: first in small clusters, turning into larger groups as platoons merged with companies. White everywhere, as if butterflies were dancing over the hills. It had been a long haul from El Alamein. But there was a sense of compassion. This had been a good enemy. The last phase in the life of the Afrikakorps had been entirely worthy of its astonishing debut."

Axis casualties in Tunisia alone amounted to some 315,000—275,000 captured and 40,000 killed, wounded, or missing. Rommel's great terrain-chewing war machine, respected by every adversary, ceased to exist.

For Hitler, the defeat in North Africa meant far more than loss of territory. His hopes of knocking Britain out of the war by seizing the Suez Canal and cutting Britain's lifeline to oil supplies and to Asia were permanently shattered. Hundreds of thousands of German troops who might have escaped to defend their homeland would fight no more. Italy's losses of men, colonies, and pride had broken her will, and Fortress Europe would soon be defended by Germans alone.

The battered Axis survivors who escaped the Allied net in North Africa withdrew across 100 miles of water to Sicily, where they dug in to wait for their enemy. The Mediterranean was now an Allied sea, and the Anglo-American forces were massing a mighty, battle-hardened armada to spearhead a new campaign against the Axis in its home territory—Italy.

Standing by a breached wall at Carthage, Sergeant Wolfgang Horn plays the tourist as waves break at his feet. He and four fellow soldiers visited the ancient city, nine miles northeast of Tunis, soon after their arrival in North Africa.

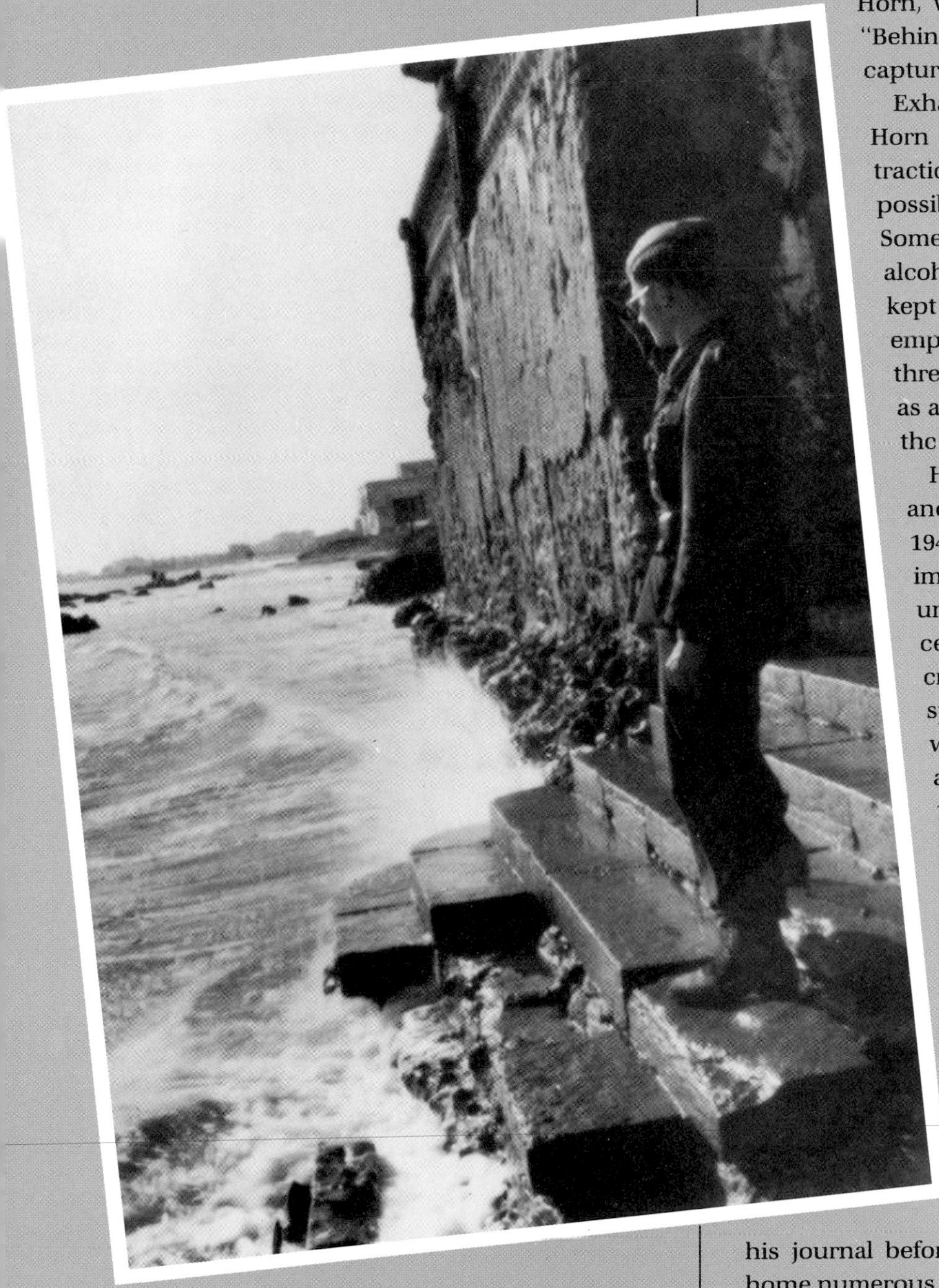

Through the Eyes of a Soldier

"I express only a weak hope that we can hold out until the end of the war," a young German soldier, Wolfgang Horn, wrote from Tunisia in March 1943. "Behind us is the sea, so we face certain capture or death in the battlefield."

Exhausted by the war and ill-supplied, Horn and his comrades sought "any distraction from the misery, the dirt, and the possibility of being ripped apart by a shell." Some of the men in his unit turned to alcohol and card games to escape, another kept pet newts and desert scorpions in an empty ammunition box. But the twenty-three-year-old Horn turned to his camera as a diversion and chronicled his part of the war with photographs.

Having survived the Russian enemy and the brutal Soviet winter of 1941-1942, Horn and parts of his artillery regiment were transferred to Tunisia with units of the 10th Panzer Division in December 1942 to help reinforce the crumbling North African front. They spent three weeks sightseeing in Tunis while waiting for their equipment to arrive. Although other elements of the 10th Panzer traveled south to join Rommel's forces at Kasserine Pass, Horn's unit remained under Arnim's Fifth Army command in the Medjerda Valley. In addition to acting as the regiment's unofficial photographer, Horn also served as a surveyor and artillery forward observer.

The war ended for him on May 9, 1943, when he surrendered to American troops and was shipped to Texas for internment. Although he gave up his camera and buried his journal before going into captivity, he had sent home numerous rolls of film and letters to his parents. Published here for the first time, they provide a remarkable record of the Axis's last stand in the desert.

Disembarking at Ancient Tunis

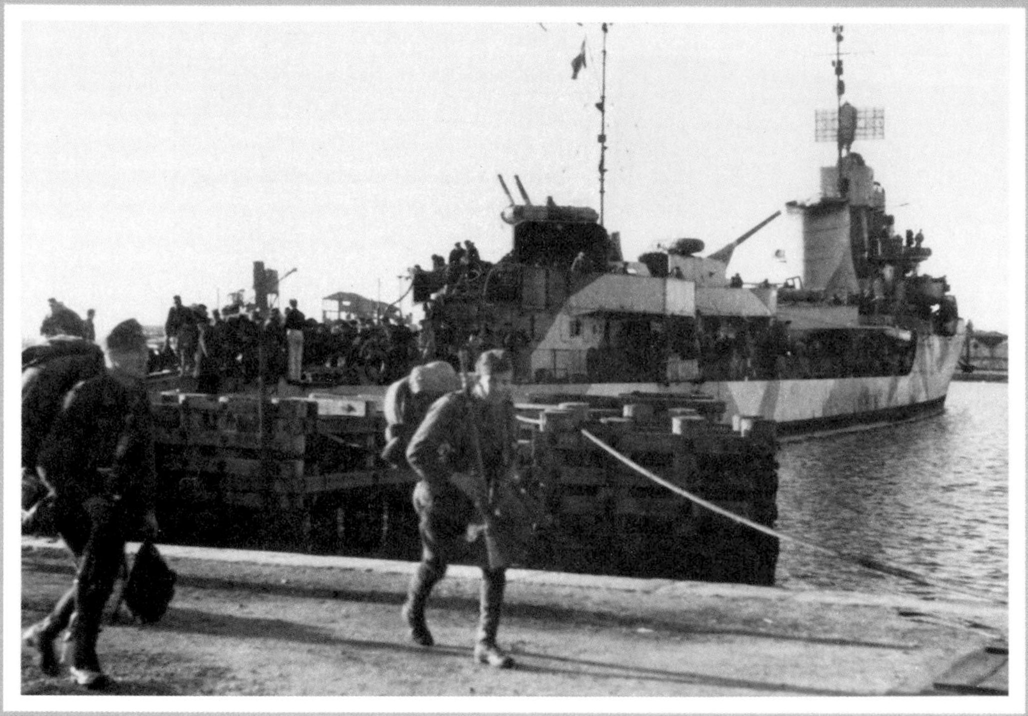

After a choppy overnight crossing from Sicily, members of Horn's division disembark from an Italian destroyer on the morning of December 29, 1942. "We land at the small, damaged harbor of La Goulette," Horn wrote, "outside the city of Tunis."

The newly arrived artillerymen follow a wagon laden with their packs. "We are lucky to be able to hire a donkey cart to transport our luggage to the former French army barracks where we are to stay," Horn commented. "We hesitate to put so much on the cart, but the owner insists that his donkey will be able to pull the full load."

Tunis's two prominent gates lead into the old city, a densely populated district of whitewashed buildings, inner courtyards, and narrow streets. Horn was struck by the alien architecture, so different from his native Germany, and described the "imposing walls," "decorative stucco," and "large arches that had to be passed to enter narrower streets."

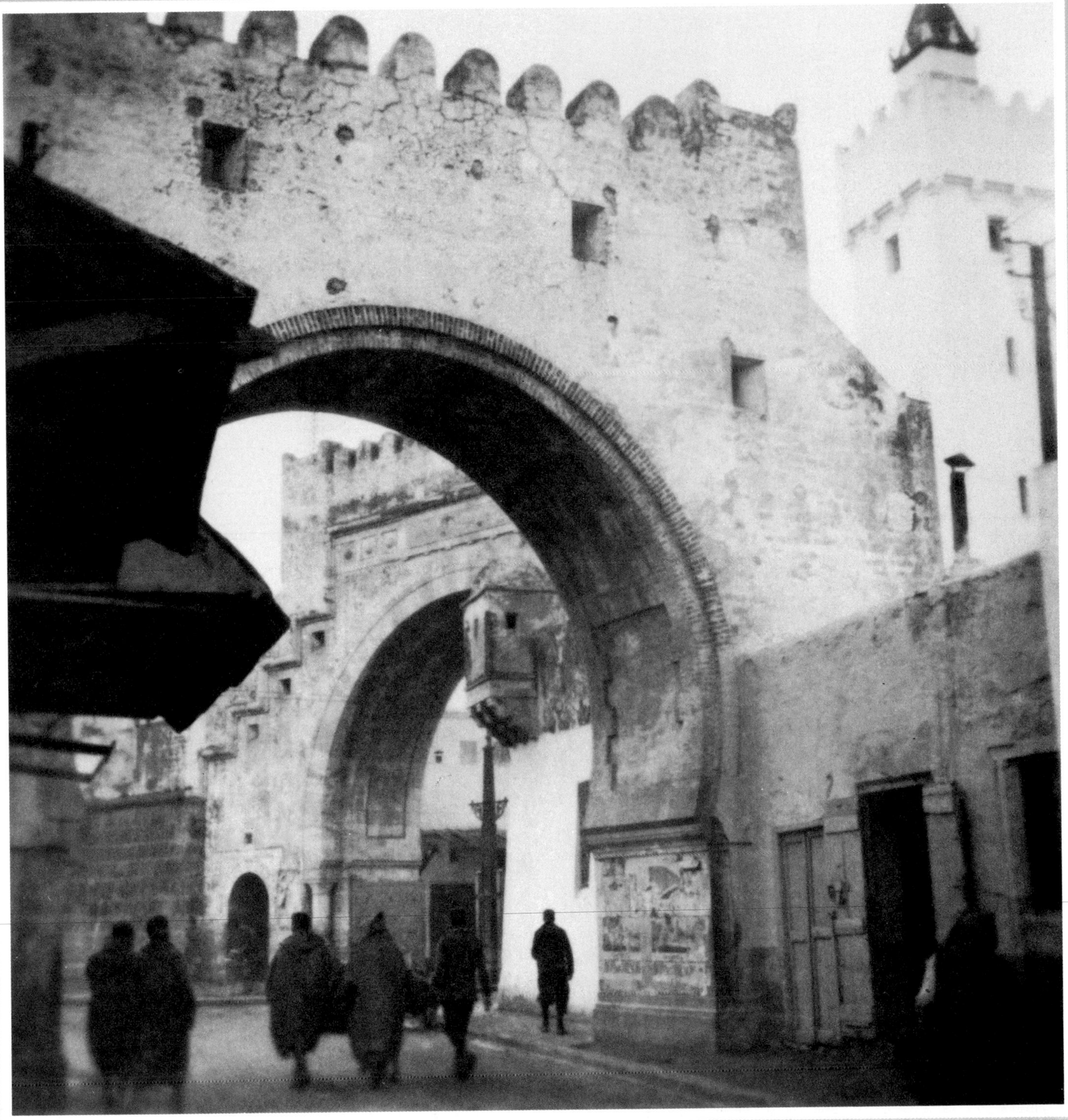

Enchantments of an Exotic Land

A classical Venus at the Museum of Bardo is one of many sights Horn photographed. He noted the "beautiful Greek statues, saved out of a depth of forty meters from a sunken vessel."

After a visit to the Jewish cemetery in Tunis *(below)*, Horn observed, "A special quarter was inhabited nearly exclusively by Jews, and there we were not looked at very kindly."

Beams of sunlight angle through a covered bazaar or souk *(far left)*. Horn was enchanted by the "romantic aspect of the souks" as well as their practical design. "The streets are covered by arches as protection against the sun, but small round holes in the ceiling let light through."

Intent on his work, this wizened Arab cobbler *(left)* is unaware of Horn's watchful eye. "I walked for hours through the crowded streets," Horn explained. "Men of all shades were loitering, trading, and working all around."

Members of Horn's unit tour the Roman arena at Carthage, sacked by the Arabs in 698. "Huge parts of the ruins reach down to the sea. In the arena is a chapel to the memory of the martyrs Felicitas and Perpetua, torn apart by wild beasts." The two soldiers in the foreground are looking skyward at a swarm of Ju 52 transport planes bringing supplies from Sicily.

Preparing to Face the Enemy

Horn's comrades build a new bunker. In a note to his parents, Horn describes the process: "We start by digging a large hole for a bunker (two by three by one meter). Most of the work has to be done with our pickaxes, since the clay soil is so hard that a shovel just doesn't do. On top we place trees, after their branches have been chopped off. Then we cover it with lots of stones and earth, to protect us against smaller caliber shells."

Outside of Tunis, a soldier smiles gamely for the camera as his comrades dig a trench in early January 1943. "We rise at 5 a.m., and march fifteen kilometers to flat hills to dig trenches for a defensive line outside of the city," Horn recorded dutifully. "To get more done, we hire Arabs at relatively low fees, which are here normal."

Short of weapons and ammunition, Horn's battery constructed this dummy gun emplacement near Medjez-el-Bab. "To fool the enemy about our strength, we put up a position with wooden beams, which we partly hide under branches of olives, so they might look like artillery to a reconnaissance plane," Horn wrote. "We make lots of tracks, which suggest that it is supplied with ammunition."

Artillerymen gingerly attach an explosive to a destroyed enemy tank during the course of a demolition exercise *(above)*. "I was sent with a few other selected men to be trained in the destruction of tanks with mines and hollow charges, which had to be pressed to the side of tanks, where they adhered magnetically," Horn reported.

In the distance, a tank explodes in flame and black smoke during a training session. Horn related the procedure: After a soldier attached a hollow charge to the destroyed tank, a "cord had to be pulled, and one had to get away as quickly as possible."

Gun crew members load a camouflaged 105-mm howitzer with fifteen-kilogram shells. Both the Axis and Allied forces made use of the abundant olive groves in the Medjerda Valley sector to disguise their weapons.

Camp Life among the Locals

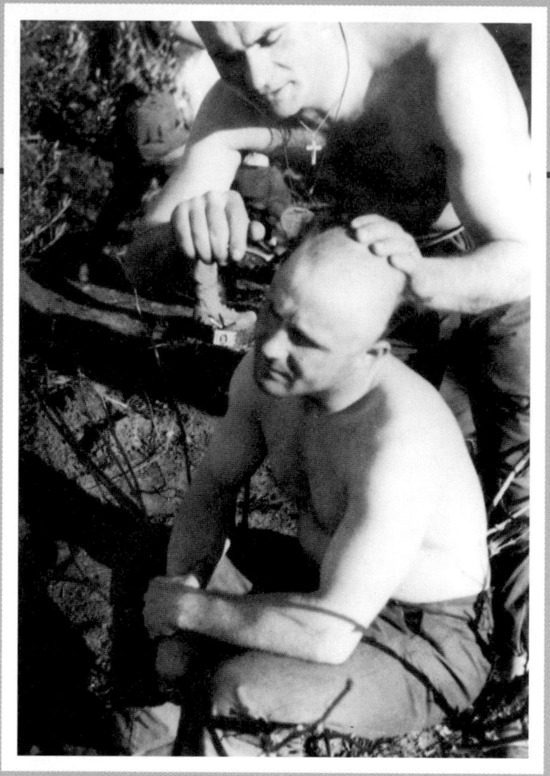

A corporal submits to a drastic haircut, having heard the "rumor that shaving your head might promote the growth of healthier hair and avoid infestation with lice." Horn explained that the men had given up any hope of furloughs by this point, February, and that there would be ample time for hair to grow back before returning home.

Arabs, who generally preferred the Germans to the allies of the French, their colonial masters, barter with artillerymen *(right)*. "Every day we buy oranges from an Arab who passes close to our position," Horn recalled. "He could be a spy, but we are less often harassed by enemy artillery than in the beginning, so he is probably harmless."

In the tent they share with Horn, two corporals relax under an unusual wartime pinup. The photograph hanging at left is of a sculpture of the Virgin Mary by the sixteenth-century German artist Tilman Riemenschneider.

Horn and a friend squat before a fire as they fry eggs in olive oil. The fresh fruit and eggs that they purchased from native Arabs provided welcome relief from a diet of army rations.

German soldiers and native Berber women draw water from a well in northern Tunisia. "There is a well two kilometers from our position. I took some free time to wash myself from top to foot with two buckets of water, an unusual luxury these days," Horn recollected, adding that the "water is salty, and full of algae and frogs."

Artillery Duels with a Distant Foe

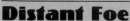

A German corporal examines a British Spitfire that was downed by antiaircraft fire near Horn's regiment. Horn noted that the British fighter's "two 20-mm cannon and four machine guns" were "pretty good armament."

A howitzer crew *(right)* fires at the highest possible elevation in order to duel with distant Allied artillery. "Even when we can see an enemy battery, we are allowed to shell them only with our daily ration of twenty-four shells," Horn complained.

From a bunker covered with earth and corrugated iron, Horn looks through a scissors scope, the "best instrument to observe the enemy positions." He photographed an enemy emplacement at Medjez-el-Bab *(below, right)* through one lens of the scope.

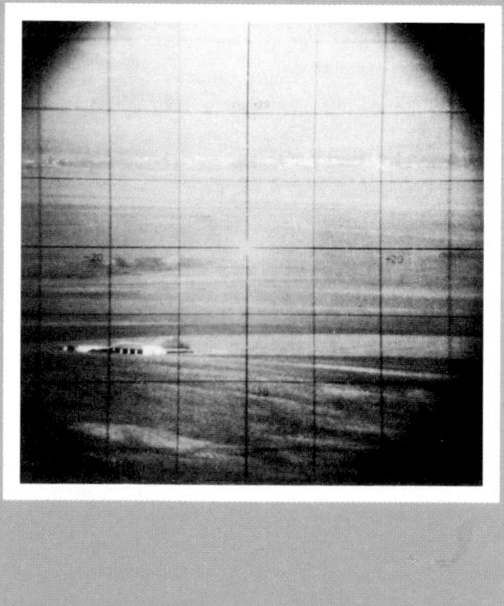

In the distance, a salvo of four fear-inducing British shells rains down on a German position. Horn vividly remembered the "ominous sound of approaching shells," which "emit a peculiar odor and kind of fog."

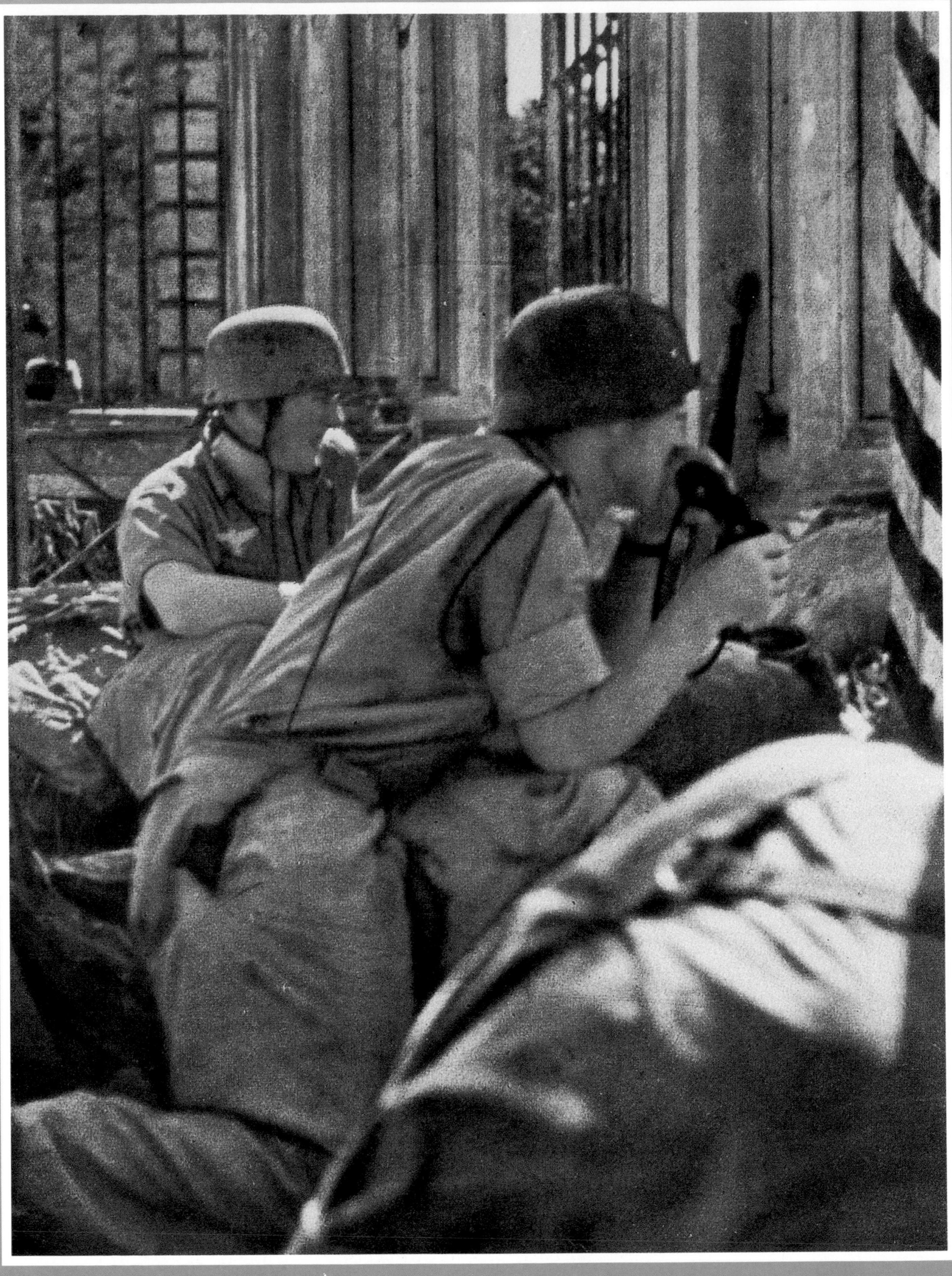

TWO

A Slugging Match for Sicily

German army intelligence officers could scarcely believe their good fortune. On April 30, 1943, two weeks before the end of the fighting in North Africa, a fisherman found a man's body drifting off the shore of southern Spain. The corpse was evidently the victim of an air crash at sea, and the local Abwehr agent was alerted. The agent copied and forwarded to Berlin the documents found in the courier case manacled to the man's wrist. The papers identified him as Major William Martin, an amphibious-landings expert in the British Royal Marines.

The documents also revealed information of vital strategic importance to the Germans. All spring, even as battles raged in Tunisia, the German high command had debated where the Allies would strike next. Speculation centered on the northern Mediterranean and ranged from southern France to Italy to the region Hitler was certain the enemy would target—the economically significant Balkan States, with their oil and other raw materials. A letter found in the dead man's case, addressed to General Sir Harold Alexander, the British commander in North Africa, confirmed at least part of Hitler's theory. The letter, which was signed by the vice chief of the British Imperial General Staff, indicated that the Allies would attack both Greece and the island of Sardinia—but only after feigning an assault on another large Italian island, Sicily.

Sheltered in ruins, two soldiers from Germany's 1st Paratroop Division monitor Allied troop movements with binoculars after the Anglo-American invasion of Sicily in July 1943.

Although the rightly skeptical Italian high command never doubted that the invasion would hit Sicily, the Führer was fooled utterly. Convinced that the documents were authentic, Hitler responded quickly to this tantalizing new intelligence. He ordered the swift reinforcement of German garrisons in Sardinia and Greece. Indeed, an entire panzer division was dispatched from France to southern Greece. This hasty journey of more than 1,000 miles turned out to be a wild-goose chase, for the Allies had no plans to invade either Greece or Sardinia. With counterfeit documents and a corpse that had been given the identity of a man who never existed, then set adrift, British counterintelligence had staged the entire affair to divert attention from the true objective—Sicily.

Sicily had been targeted by the British and American leaders nearly four months earlier. Meeting in January at Casablanca, they had selected this largest of the Italian islands for their first major thrust at the "soft underbelly of the Axis," in Churchill's pungent phrase. They wanted to divert German pressure from the Russian front while preparing for the invasion of northern France that was scheduled for a year hence. A battleground since earliest-recorded history, Sicily has great strategic importance. Only ninety miles from the tip of Tunisia, it not only commands the western Mediterranean but also, by virtue of its position within rowing distance of the toe of Italy across the Strait of Messina, offers a convenient steppingstone to the mainland.

The Axis forces were vulnerable to invasion in Sicily—and virtually anywhere in the western Mediterranean for that matter. German power was sapped in large measure by the depletion of Italy's military strength. The Italian navy, with its large surface fleet anchored at Spezia and Taranto for nearly a year, lacked the fuel and aggressive leadership to intercept an Allied armada. British and American warships, meanwhile, had effectively choked off the passage of German U-boats through the Strait of Gibraltar. The Italian air force had always depended on substantial German support, and since the beginning of the year, Allied bombers and fighters had slashed the combined Axis air strength in the region by half, to about 1,000 serviceable planes. Since 147,000 men had marched into captivity in Tunisia, the Italian army had been spread dangerously thin. After the commitment of 1.2 million Italian soldiers in Russia and the Balkans, fewer than a million remained for the defense of the homeland.

Most of all, Hitler doubted the determination of his southern partner. Referring to Sicily, he told a staff conference on May 20: "What worries me is that these people have no will to defend it; you can see they've no will. The duce may have the best intentions, but he will be sabotaged."

Hitler was beginning to doubt even his old friend and fellow dictator. Their personal relationship and ideologies, rather than any common values or objectives, had welded together Germany and Italy in the so-called Pact of Steel since May 1939. But Hitler saw Mussolini failing in health and resolve, even advocating measures such as a truce with the Soviet Union.

Now, in May 1943, under pressure from his own high command, the duce was averse to Hitler's offer of German troops to bolster the defense of the Italian homeland. In all, Hitler offered five Wehrmacht divisions that month; Mussolini agreed to take only the three that were already in Italy being re-formed from the remnants of units that had been largely destroyed in North Africa. This reluctance made Hitler so suspicious that he ordered his high command to prepare a secret plan, code-named *Alarich,* for the

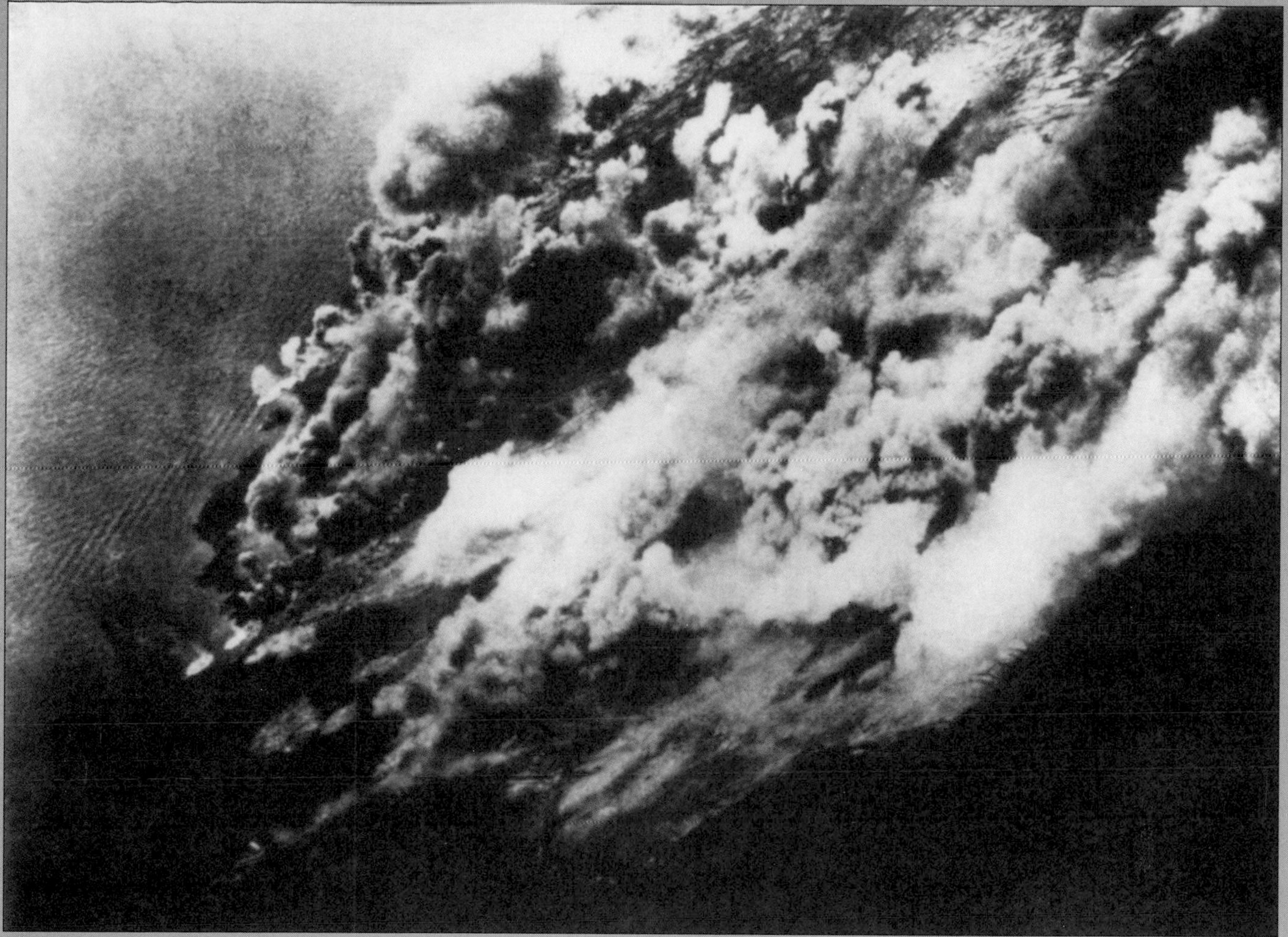

In early June 1943, near the end of a month-long bombardment by Allied planes, thick smoke enshrouds Pantelleria, an island midway between Sicily and Tunisia. After Mussolini's forces surrendered the tiny island on June 11, Allied troops began using its airport as a forward base for the assault on Sicily.

German occupation of Italy in the event the Italians defected to the Allies.

Hitler soon saw dramatic new confirmation of his suspicions in yet another dismal performance by Italian troops. The British and Americans, seeking a nearby airfield to support their planned invasion of Sicily, decided to seize Pantelleria, some sixty-five miles southwest of Sicily. The tiny volcanic island bristled with coastal batteries, underground aircraft hangars hewn from solid rock, and a garrison of nearly 12,000 Italian defenders.

Allied bombers battered the fortress for nearly a month. The bombardment, joined by naval guns, reached a round-the-clock crescendo in early June when more than 5,000 tons of bombs poured down in just five days. It was such an awesome demonstration that some Allied air-power advocates were convinced that the Axis could be bombed into submission. Astonishingly, the bombs killed and wounded fewer than 400 troops, but they smashed the Italians' water supply and morale. On June 11, a brigade of British infantry put ashore, and to Hitler's great chagrin, the Italian garrison surrendered after firing scarcely a shot. Apparently the only British casualty was a soldier bitten by a shell-shocked mule.

The surrender of Pantelleria on June 11, together with that of the smaller island of Lampedusa on the following day, jolted Mussolini as well. The Allied attacks pointed toward the next target as Sicily or perhaps Sardinia, both uncomfortably close to home. Mussolini agreed to accept not only the two additional German divisions he had rejected previously, but another as well. These reinforcements enabled the Axis forces to stiffen their precarious defenses on Sicily. By the end of June, two German mechanized divisions had arrived there. Both had been rebuilt from the wreckage of divisions shattered in North Africa: the 15th Panzergrenadier Division and the Hermann Göring Panzer Division, a Luftwaffe ground unit.

The German troops—some 30,000, counting support and antiaircraft units—joined a motley force of about 200,000 Italians on Sicily. The Italians had four partly mobile divisions. In addition, there were five static coastal divisions and three smaller units made up mostly of Sicilian recruits and overage reservists who hated the Germans. In an army notorious for poor leadership, training, and equipment, the coastal units ranked at the bottom. Responsible for the defense of nearly 500 miles of coastline, they were so deficient in artillery that each antitank gun had to cover five miles of shore. Island fortifications were so shoddy that Kesselring later termed them "mere eyewash" and "so much gingerbread." When an Italian general came by to inspect some concrete defense works, a soldier was heard to mutter about the need for "fewer generals and more engineers."

The defense of Sicily was also afflicted by a Byzantine command structure. Under a recent agreement, all Axis troops on the island came under the overall direction of General Alfredo Guzzoni, commander of the Italian Sixth Army. Though recently called back from retirement at age sixty-six and unfamiliar with the island, Guzzoni was a competent strategist and leader. But from his headquarters at Enna in the center of the island, he had to cope with parallel chains of command. In addition to the formal channels that led from Italian and German units through Guzzoni to Rome, the Wehrmacht maintained its own chain of command. German unit leaders frequently turned to their liaison officer at Enna, who in turn reported to Kesselring, the Reich's theater commander in Rome. And Reich Marshal Hermann Göring, commander in chief of the Luftwaffe, further complicated matters by sometimes bypassing both chains of command to communicate directly with the commander of his namesake division.

Unlike many Germans, who treated Italian troops and their generals with disdain, Kesselring got along well with Guzzoni. Both men had long felt certain that Sicily was the Allies' next objective. Kesselring, the only senior German commander to appreciate the threat, was experienced as both a soldier and an airman. He realized that Sicily was the only major target within range of land-based Allied fighter planes. He and Guzzoni also agreed that the main invasion most likely would strike the southeastern corner of the island.

The two commanders could not agree, however, on the deployment of the two German divisions. Guzzoni wanted to keep them as a strong reserve

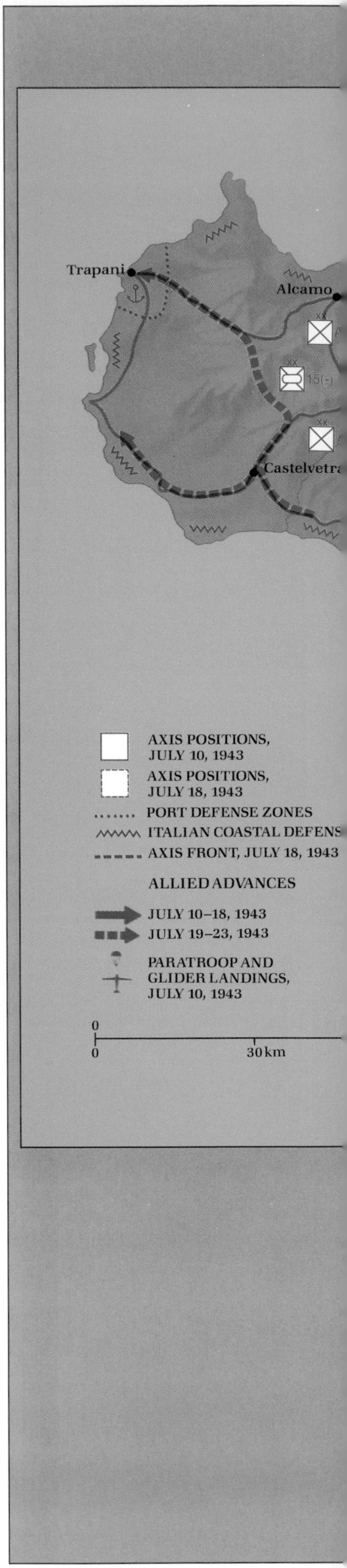

Stubborn Defenses in Rugged Terrain

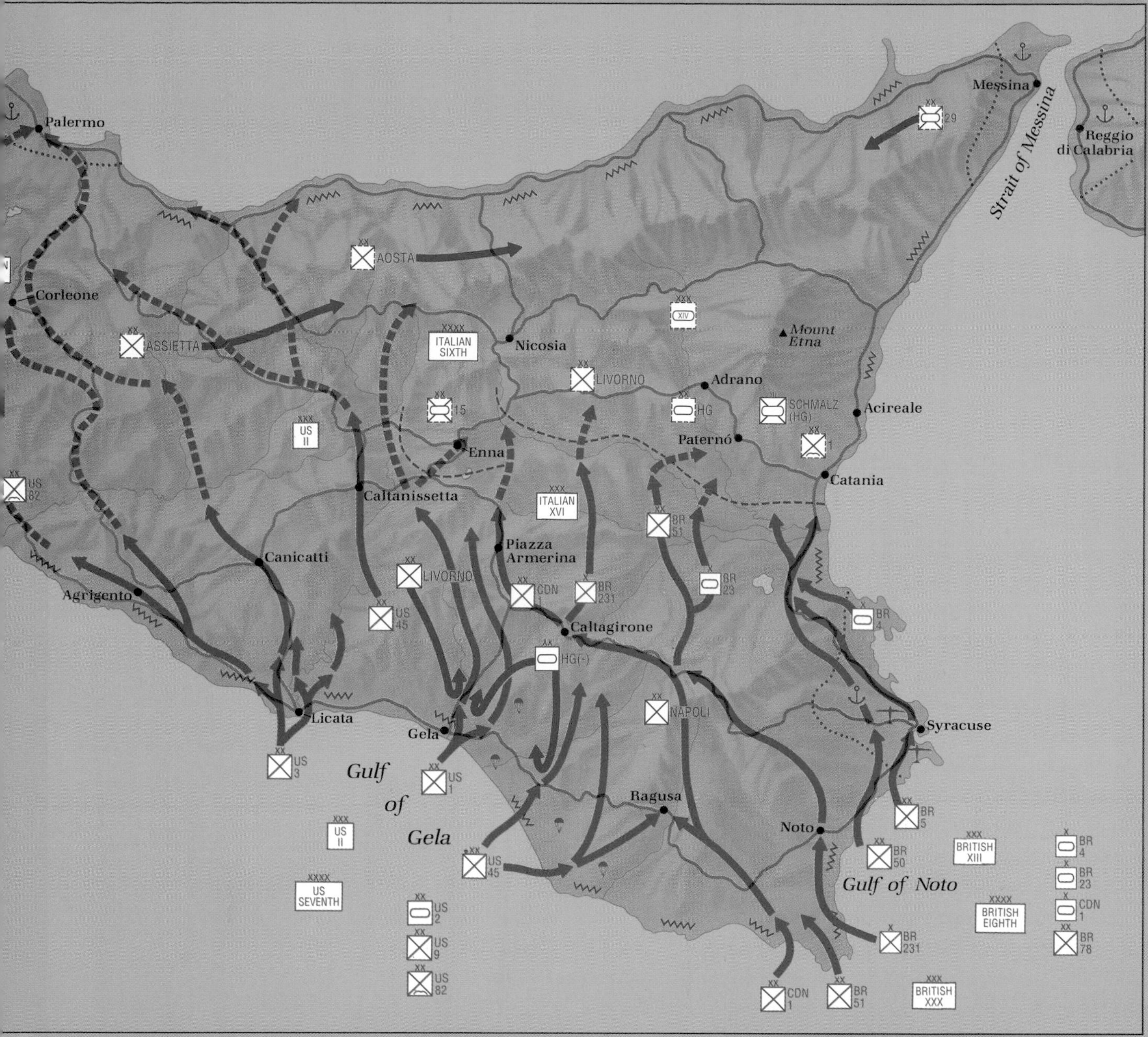

At dawn on July 10, 1943, amphibious forces from two Allied armies, Patton's Seventh and Montgomery's Eighth, stormed ashore along the southern coast of Sicily, brushing aside the Italian coastal defenses. The Italian Sixth Army commander, Guzzoni, with Kesselring's approval, ordered an immediate counterattack against the American beachhead. The assault by the Livorno Division failed miserably, but the Hermann Göring Panzer Division managed to get within a mile of the shoreline before being driven off. The Axis high command quickly realized that the Allies were far too powerful to be driven back into the sea and instead decided to stage a fighting withdrawal back to the northeastern corner of the island where they could establish a defensive line anchored at Mount Etna. Within a week of the Allied landing, the Italians were on the verge of collapse, and Sicily's defense now fell largely under the control of Hube's newly arrived XIV Panzer Corps staff. Abandoning the western end of the island to the Americans, the Germans threw four divisions (Hermann Göring Panzer, 15th Panzergrenadier, and two reinforcing divisions, the 1st Paratroop and the 29th Panzergrenadier) into the path of the main Allied push toward Messina. Outnumbered three to one and continuously harassed by Allied aircraft, the defenders capitalized on their skillful use of the Italian terrain and held the two Allied armies at bay for nearly two weeks.

Allied ships crowd a North African harbor just before the start of Operation Husky. "There were tankers and cargo vessels, trawlers, and invasion ships," an awestruck journalist wrote of the enormous convoy. "Lines of infantry landing craft swished silently through the water."

in the eastern part of the island. Once his weaker Italian field divisions had delayed the invaders, the Germans would pounce on them with their motorized infantry and 160 tanks. Kesselring preferred dividing the German forces, placing the bulk of the 15th Division in the west and the weaker Hermann Göring Panzer Division in the east and south. He expected a secondary invasion in the west and wanted German troops near enough to the shore to stamp out the Allies before they could establish a beachhead. As reports of stepped-up Allied naval activity mounted in late June, suggesting an impending invasion, Guzzoni gave in and agreed to Kesselring's plan—reluctantly and to his later regret.

Late on the afternoon of July 9, radio warnings started to stream into General Guzzoni's headquarters at Enna. Luftwaffe reconnaissance patrols reported spotting at least a half-dozen enormous Allied convoys steaming toward Sicily from south of Malta. The pilots did not exaggerate what they saw. The convoys were part of the largest amphibious force in history, a vast armada of some 3,000 vessels, ranging from battleships to small landing craft, bearing 600 tanks, 14,000 other vehicles, and nearly 180,000 British and American troops. Increased Allied air activity also warned the Axis of an imminent invasion.

At 7:00 p.m., less than an hour after the sightings, Guzzoni issued a preliminary alert. Three hours later, he ordered all garrisons to go on full alert. At midnight, the first news of an actual invasion reached headquarters. These frantic calls described tens of thousands of American paratroopers and glider-borne British soldiers landing all over southern Sicily. It was partly true. Fewer than 4,000 airborne troops had landed, but the air crews who delivered them had miscalculated so badly due to inexperience and strong winds that they were scattered in small, isolated groups far from the intended landing zones. There seemed to be more airborne invaders than there really were, which greatly increased Axis confusion.

Shortly after midnight, Guzzoni ordered demolition of pier facilities and alerted units near the beaches. In less than three hours, about 3:00 a.m. on July 10, droves of Allied troops started to storm ashore along a 100-mile front in southeastern Sicily. The invasion, Operation Husky, was under way. Four divisions of Montgomery's British Eighth Army struck on both sides of the Pachino Peninsula below Syracuse. Three divisions of the American

Italian soldiers operate a battery of defense guns on the coast of Sicily. Despite the defiant slogan *Vincere* (Conquer), crudely painted on the barrels, these weapons were no match for Allied bombers and warships. After inspecting shore fortifications, one Italian officer wrote, "I had shuddered at the sight of poor concrete defense works."

Seventh Army under Patton hit the southern beaches around Gela, approximately sixty miles to the west.

Almost all of the weak Italian coastal divisions caved in before the onslaught. British troops seized one battery while the crew, oblivious to Guzzoni's earlier alerts, slept beside their guns. During the early, chaotic hours of the invasion, Guzzoni tried desperately to gain control of his scattered forces. He ordered the return of the German 15th Division, the troops that on Kesselring's insistence had been sent westward, far from the landing sites. He ordered swift counterattacks against both the British and the American beachheads. But faulty communications and the lack of timely information plagued him at every turn. Orders failed to get through on a telephone system disrupted by Allied bombing and paratroopers' pliers. Only sketchy reports came through from confused ground units and the few reconnaissance flights the Luftwaffe could manage in the teeth of enemy air superiority.

One of the main threats beyond the old general's limited perimeter of information was developing in the British sector south of the ancient port city of Syracuse. During the night, a detachment of fewer than 100 British glider troops had seized the Ponte Grande, the key road bridge just below town, to await the arrival of infantry pushing up the coast from the Pachino Peninsula. The Italians counterattacked at 8:00 a.m., and after a furious seven-hour battle, they captured the fifteen or so surviving British troops and retook the bridge. Less than an hour later, as the Italians were replacing demolition charges the British glider troops had removed, British infantry arrived. They captured the bridge, crossed it, and marched into Syracuse. The Italian garrison there, in contrast to their countrymen whose bodies now littered the Ponte Grande, declined to resist and handed over the port city with its docks fully intact.

Erroneously assuming Syracuse to be well defended, Guzzoni had concentrated his main counterattack against the Americans to the west. His orders on the morning of the invasion called for a coordinated strike southward against the beachheads around Gela by the Italian Livorno Division and the Hermann Göring Panzer Division. With communications still disrupted, the divisions struck off on their own with no coordination. A battalion of Livorno infantry got off their trucks west of Gela and advanced in nineteenth-century parade-ground formation. American Rangers, employing captured Italian artillery pieces, decimated the battalion's closely ordered ranks. Another Italian unit, Mobile Group E, advanced on Gela from the northeast with three dozen or so small, outmoded tanks—some of them weighing no more than two tons and dating back to World War I. One column penetrated the town, but was repulsed by Rangers using

On July 10, the first day of Operation Husky, engineers from the 51st Infantry (Highland) Division of the British Eighth Army lug ashore mine detectors and other tools south of the city of Syracuse. The Highlanders met little resistance on landing.

317

bazookas as well as by salvos fired from American ships anchored offshore.

While these Italian attacks faltered, the Germans were preparing to strike at American beachheads east of Gela. Although Guzzoni's orders failed to reach the commander of the Hermann Göring Panzer Division, General Paul Conrath, he had learned of the invasion before dawn from his own patrols and from Kesselring's headquarters in Rome and had begun planning his own counterattack. Conrath himself was a hard-driving leader who had fought with distinction in France, the Balkans, and Russia. But his troops were green, his officers inexperienced, and his division a strange hybrid. Officially designated as a panzer division, it actually resembled the normal panzergrenadier division—equipped with 100 tanks but only one regiment of infantry instead of the standard two regiments.

Conrath split his unit into two task forces and sent them southward in two columns toward the beaches from their bases near Caltagirone, some twenty miles inland. He quickly ran into problems. Allied aircraft harassed his columns; narrow, twisting roads slowed them; inexperienced subordinates failed to keep them moving. In exasperation, he relieved the commander of his western column on the spot and took personal command.

It was 1:00 p.m., five hours behind Conrath's schedule, before his troops were finally in position for the two-pronged attack. At Piano Lupo, about ten miles east of Gela, Conrath's western column came under fire from the American cruisers and destroyers that were standing off the beaches as well as from dug-in American infantrymen and paratroopers. The Germans retreated, and not even their top commander's exhortative presence could rally them. About twelve miles farther southeast, Conrath's other column bogged down after the supporting Tiger I tanks got tangled up in terraces of dense olive groves.

Conrath sent his own chief of staff to unscramble the big Tigers and get them moving. Spearheaded by the tanks, the Germans renewed the assault and overran a battalion of Americans, capturing their commander and most of the surviving troops. But another Allied battalion moved into the breach, and Conrath's soldiers panicked and fled in disorder. That night, Conrath completed his housecleaning at the top by relieving the commander of the eastern task force as well.

Guzzoni sent orders to renew the attack. On the following morning, July 11, the Italian Livorno Division was to push down on the Gela beachhead from the northwest; the Hermann Göring Panzer Division was to converge on the beachhead in three separate columns from the northeast. Conrath, stung by the previous day's setback, led his troops in the attack at 6:15 a.m., only fifteen minutes late this time.

As the Axis forces opened their counteroffensive on a wide front, several separate battles developed into the most desperate fighting of the new campaign. In the west, on the Axis right, the Italian infantry approaching Gela once again faltered before a storm of fire, which included nearly 500 rounds of six-inch shells from the U.S. cruiser *Savannah.* American Rangers moving out from Gela to mop up accepted the surrender of nearly 400 Italian troops and found sickening sights. "There were human bodies hanging from the trees," noted an American captain, "and some blown to bits." With casualties of about 50 percent, the Italians took such a battering that the Livorno Division was finished as a credible combat unit.

The Germans, meanwhile, pressed the attack farther east, on the Axis left. Around Piano Lupo, six of their tanks broke through American lines but fell prey to a trick: The Americans let the panzers roll past their positions and then struck from the rear, disabling four of them. The Americans managed to hold the vital road junction there. Six miles farther east along Route 115, beyond the Acate River, 700 of Conrath's infantry confronted a much smaller scratch force of American paratroopers led by Colonel James Gavin of the 82d Airborne Division. The Germans were still paying the price for inexperience and lack of combat-tested officers. "The units were brought into the attack in confusion," wrote Colonel Helmut Bergengrün, a Hermann Göring Panzer Division staff officer. They failed to dislodge the Americans from a ridge, and when the outnumbered and outgunned Americans counterattacked late in the day, the Germans scattered.

It was near Gela, roughly in the center of the Axis counterattack, that the Hermann Göring Panzer Division gained the greatest penetration. Two powerful columns of about sixty panzers pierced the middle of the U.S. 1st Armored Division and converged on the treelined coastal highway four miles east of town. Awestruck Americans, peering through the smoke of battle from their shallow trenches, reported that hundreds of enemy tanks were about to overrun them. Before noon, the German vanguard punched through to the highway and began shelling landing craft in the water less than 2,000 yards away. Conrath, blinded by the apparent nearness of victory, somehow believed the enemy was starting to reembark. His message to that effect sent hopes soaring at Guzzoni's headquarters.

American resistance actually stiffened. Gunners poured in thousands of shells from both naval and field artillery. Four Sherman tanks struggled free of the soft sand on the beach and bolstered the line. Amphibious vehicles carried howitzers ashore and took them directly to the front, where crewmen lowered their barrels and fired straight at the advancing panzers 600 yards away. The combatants' lines so nearly verged that American naval gunners had to stop firing for fear of hitting their own men. Not a single panzer penetrated the wall of fire and crossed the strategic highway. About

On July 11, outside the village of Gela, German tanks churn up a dust cloud as they rumble toward American troops dug in at

the beach. The Tigers came within a mile of the Allied command center before shelling from warships drove them back.

2:00 p.m., Conrath called off the attack, and the Germans pulled back from the inferno, leaving the burning hulks of sixteen panzers. The surviving vehicles turned away and retreated swiftly northward under renewed shelling from the Allied naval guns.

Failure to break through to the landing beaches here and farther east cost Conrath dearly. He lost about 600 men, a third of his tanks, and all of his patience. On the retreat back to Caltagirone, he issued a blistering rebuke to his division for conduct "not worthy of a German soldier." He castigated officers who, "believing in false rumors, moved whole columns to the rear" and men who "came running to the rear, hysterically crying, because they had heard the detonation of a single shot." Conrath might also have been justified in scorning Kesselring's preinvasion decision to move the 15th Division to the western part of the island. The aid of these comrades, who had trained in this very region, might well have enabled Conrath to push the Americans off the beaches at Gela.

But Conrath could not complain about his air support. A preinvasion blitz by the Allied air forces had knocked out hundreds of Axis planes both in the air and on the ground, and more than half the surviving planes had been forced to fly to bases on the Italian mainland. During the first two days of the invasion, however, there was no American fighter cover, and Axis planes freely strafed and bombed the beaches and waters around Gela. They sank at least three ships, including an American destroyer, and set Allied sailors' nerves on edge.

Late on the evening of July 11, as Conrath's columns were retreating, American naval gunners saw planes flying low overhead and tragically mistook them for the Luftwaffe bombers that had attacked less than an hour earlier. They opened fire on them and destroyed twenty-three American transports that were carrying paratroopers to reinforce the Gela beachheads.

Disgusted by what he perceived to be the timidity of some of his men at Gela, General Paul Conrath, commander of the Hermann Göring Panzer Division, issued them a stern warning: "Withdrawal and cowardice will be punished on the spot, with arms if necessary."

By July 12, Guzzoni had abandoned any hope of throwing the Allies off their beachheads. He ordered his divisions to deploy in a defensive alignment designed to contain the Americans and British in the southeastern quadrant of the island—or at least to delay them until reinforcements arrived and he could retreat to a new line of resistance farther north. The 15th Division moved into place to oppose the American advance in south-central Sicily. The Hermann Göring Panzer Division started sidestepping eastward to link up with the Napoli Division and the German task force called Battle Group Schmalz, which opposed the British along the eastern coast. Even the usually optimistic Kesselring, who flew to Enna that morn-

DIVISION
HERMANN GÖRING
Wer zu uns gehören will
muß freiwillig kommen!

The division's recruiting booklet features the slogan "To join us, you must volunteer." Members wore the cuff title *(above, left)* on their uniforms and were eligible to receive the Luftwaffe ground combat badge *(above)*.

The Luftwaffe's Elite Tankmen

Although the Hermann Göring Panzer Division that was deployed in Sicily was an inexperienced outfit, its roots reached back to the earliest days of the Reich. Formed in 1933 by Göring himself, the division began as a special Nazi police unit, formed to suppress opponents of Hitler. As Göring's influence grew, so did his namesake organization. The original 400-member detachment soon expanded into a large state police force. After Göring became head of the Luftwaffe, the unit was transformed into an elite Luftwaffe ground regiment, then a brigade, and finally a division.

Because the unit was open only to volunteers, those who belonged to it were taught to think of themselves as a breed apart. They wore distinctive uniforms and lived in spacious new barracks.

After the Axis collapse in Tunisia in May 1943, the bulk of the division surrendered to the Allies. But the remnant of the Luftwaffe chief's namesake unit was not allowed to die. With fresh volunteers, it was reborn as a panzer division.

Enlisted men wore a black double-breasted jacket with matching trousers and forage cap. Their outfit was identical to that of panzer crews except for a few distinctive markings, notably the cuff title and the Luftwaffe eagle on the jacket and cap.

Although a visored cap was introduced in 1943 *(bottom),* many troops preferred the original forage model *(top).* Officers' caps, such as the two shown here, had aluminum piping as well as insignia made from aluminum thread.

The division in Italy wore Luftwaffe helmets daubed with tan camouflage paint *(top)*. Some officers wore the peaked tropical service cap *(bottom)* with removable sun flap.

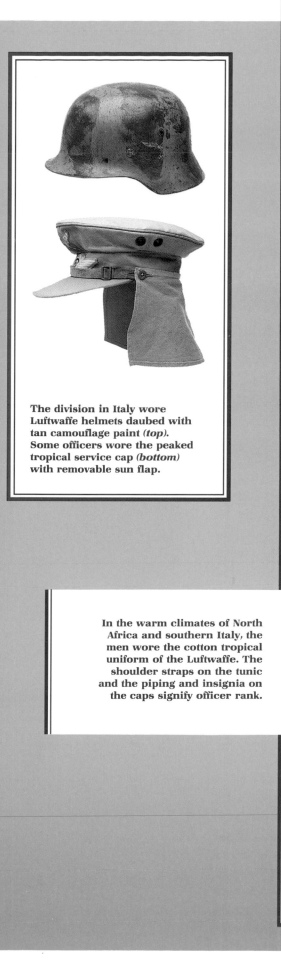

In the warm climates of North Africa and southern Italy, the men wore the cotton tropical uniform of the Luftwaffe. The shoulder straps on the tunic and the piping and insignia on the caps signify officer rank.

ing to meet with Guzzoni, could see no alternative to going on the defensive. "My flight to Sicily yielded nothing but a headache," he wrote later.

What most appalled Kesselring was the woeful performance—"total breakdown," he termed it—of the Italian units. Although some Italians fought bravely, others by the tens of thousands either threw down their arms at the sight of their enemy and surrendered or simply deserted and wandered off into the countryside. The Sicilians, unlike the Germans and mainland Italians, knew that the harder they fought, the more likely it was that their own homes would be destroyed. Conrath gave vent to the feelings of many Germans when he wrote, "The good intentions of some commanders and the good appearance of some officers and noncommissioned officers must not lead one to overlook the fact that 90 percent of the Italian army are cowards and do not want to fight." The Germans could not understand that their allies no longer had any stomach for the fascist cause—which had become the German cause only.

The Italian failures most damaging to Guzzoni's new defensive strategy occurred along the southeastern coast where the British were attacking. The two neighboring port cities there, Syracuse and Augusta, were so heavily fortified that Guzzoni had considered the area among his strongest defensive positions. But the abject surrender of Syracuse on the night of the invasion set the stage for even more scandalous behavior at Augusta, twenty miles to the north. That same night, a small German naval unit stationed at Augusta left the harbor and fled in its torpedo boats to the Italian mainland. Then, the following night, July 11, members of the Italian naval garrison began blowing up their big guns and torching fuel and ammunition dumps. Their commander, Admiral Priamo Leonardi, brazenly tried to justify these actions as the response to a local invasion from the sea, a landing that in fact never occurred. When British soldiers of the 5th Division assaulted Augusta the next morning, July 12, they found the fortress ruined and abandoned. Its garrison had fled north in disarray.

The loss of Syracuse and Augusta threw into jeopardy the defense of the Plain of Catania to the north. This coastal plain, a marshy lowland, begins around the port of Catania, about halfway up the eastern coast, and stretches to Messina at the island's northeastern tip. Only about twelve miles wide, it is wedged between the sea and the mountainous interior dominated by Mount Etna, an active volcano that towers to nearly 11,000 feet. Up the plain runs the coastal highway, Route 114, which hugs the shore all the way to Messina. The Strait of Messina served as the Axis lifeline to the nearby mainland. If the British could break through and race to Messina, only seventy-five air miles from Augusta, practically every German and Italian soldier on Sicily would be cut off.

British soldiers patrol the port city of Augusta in eastern Sicily. After entering the city on July 12, the British found that panicky Italian troops had abandoned it during Allied bombing raids earlier. A German officer later wrote of the Italians: "The will to fight comes from leadership, and the leaders no longer had complete control of the situation."

Between the British and such a breakthrough stood a single effective German force: Battle Group Schmalz. This task force consisted of an infantry battalion and two artillery batteries from the Hermann Göring Panzer Division and an infantry regiment from the 15th Division. The commander, Colonel Wilhelm Schmalz, was a skillful combat veteran whom his driver later described as "solid as a rock." Group Schmalz's Italian partner, the Napoli Division, had virtually disintegrated after the capture of its commanding general, but this loss was more than compensated for. As Schmalz fought a delaying action in the hills northwest of Augusta on the evening of July 12, German reinforcements began to arrive. Some 1,400 troops from the elite 3d Paratroop Regiment, flown in from France, floated down from the sky in an airdrop of admirable precision.

After landing about three miles south of the town of Catania, the paratroopers immediately were transported to the front. Two battalions moved down Route 114 to reinforce Schmalz south of Lentini; the third linked up with elements of the Hermann Göring Panzer Division to fill the gap on Schmalz's right. The following day, July 13, air transports carrying the 1st Paratroop Machine-Gun Battalion landed at the Catania airfield. These troops were sent down the highway to positions just south of the Simeto River, six miles below Catania. A 400-foot-long bridge, the Ponte Primosole, spanned the river there, and the commander of the 3d Paratroop Regiment, Lieut. Colonel Ludwig Heilmann, suspected the British might attempt to seize it with a surprise attack from the sea or the air.

On the same day, Montgomery felt so confident about the lack of opposition that he split his Eighth Army and began a double-barreled offensive. He sent two divisions west and north into the mountains toward Vizzini; this "left hook," as he phrased it, was designed to outflank the defenders of the Plain of Catania.

Montgomery's main blow, intended as the knockout punch, was aimed straight north toward Catania. It called for three simultaneous attacks on the night of July 13. Two of the planned strikes were directed toward bridges behind Axis lines. A seaborne regiment of commandos would come ashore and capture the Malati Bridge over the river, three miles north of Lentini. An airborne brigade would drop on both sides of the Primosole Bridge eight miles farther up the road and secure that span. At the same time, a third element, the 50th Division, would charge up Route 114 from their positions south of Lentini; around dawn, they would join their comrades at the Malati and Primosole bridges and then smash into Catania and the plain beyond.

In early July, Colonel Wilhelm Schmalz, commander of a battle group in the Hermann Göring Panzer Division, threw together a piecemeal force near Catania upon learning that the Italians had abandoned the area. His troops, standing alone, blocked the advance of the British Eighth Army until reinforcements arrived from Germany.

The commando phase of the British assault began at 10:00 p.m. with a landing on the coast. German paratroopers and infantry harassed the commandos all the way to the Malati Bridge, some five miles inland. But about 3:00 a.m., the British routed the handful of Italians guarding the bridge and removed the demolition charges. Dawn came without the scheduled relief from the 50th Division, which had been delayed south of Lentini by Battle Group Schmalz and its paratrooper reinforcements. The commandos then came under such intense fire from German tanks and mortars that they had to abandon the bridge during the afternoon. But it soon changed hands again, when the 50th Division infantry arrived in overwhelming strength and forced a German retreat. In their haste to withdraw, the Germans failed to reset the explosives, and the British took possession of the Malati Bridge intact.

Eight miles to the north, the Primosole Bridge had become the focus of intense fighting. Around the steel girders spanning the muddy Simeto raged one of the largest battles of the war between opposing airborne forces—and a key encounter in the battle for Sicily.

On the night of July 13, only a few miles south of where the German airborne regiment had landed a little more than twenty-four hours earlier, Allied C-47 transports arrived overhead carrying members of the British 1st Paratroop Brigade. A deadly reception awaited them. The German 1st Paratroop Machine-Gun Battalion was dug in at the edge of an orange grove just west of Route 114 and 2,000 yards south of the bridge with Heilmann's orders to hold the span at all costs.

Bad luck had dogged the British mission. On the flight from North Africa, antiaircraft fire from friendly ships had disrupted the C-47s' formations. Now it got worse. By happenstance, the Germans' flak batteries were zeroed in on the precise line of approach being taken by more than half of the transports. In just a few minutes, one German platoon shot down three C-47s; another destroyed three gliders attempting to coast down with their artillery loads. In the confusion aloft, fewer than 300 of the 1,850 paratroopers on the mission that evening were actually dropped in their target zones around the bridge.

The German gunners now turned their attention to their British counterparts on the ground. During the night, the Germans captured eighty-two of the Allied soldiers scattered by errant drops. After the sun came up on July 14, the Germans opened up with mortar and machine guns and drove the British off one of the small hills about a mile south of the bridge. Soon

Troops from Germany's 1st Paratroop Division dig in along the railroad line to Catania. These seasoned men bolstered the thin ranks of Schmalz's group and fought valiantly at Primosole Bridge, a critical crossing south of the city.

they had surrounded another hill. Some dry grass caught fire, and a sea of flames seared the British perimeter, driving back the troops. About 9:00 a.m., the British finally made radio contact with their cruiser *Newfoundland* standing offshore. The resulting salvos of six-inch shells staved off another German assault and created a stalemate.

Thus preoccupied to the south, out of sight of the Primosole Bridge, these Germans did not realize that it was already in British hands. Hours before, about 2:00 a.m., a detachment of fifty British paratroopers had attacked from the north bank. Then the Italian defenders fled in panic when one of the British gliders crashed into the bridge. The British were able to seize the span intact and dismantle the explosives strapped to its steel girders. They endured a strafing attack by a squadron of Focke Wulf 190s and some shelling by German 88-mm guns, then enjoyed a quiet time of it until shortly past noon.

Triumphant British soldiers in a Bren gun carrier charge across the Primosole Bridge after it was wrested from the Germans. To their credit, German troops relinquished Sicily only after bitter resistance. "They fought superbly," reported the *Times* of London. "They were troops of the highest quality, cool and skillful, Nazi zealots to a man."

Meanwhile, a German counterattack was gathering force. Up at Catania, a regimental staff officer, Captain Franz Stangenberg, learned of the British seizure of the Primosole Bridge and set about recruiting a battle group to recapture it. Except for the paratroop machine-gun battalion tied up just south of the bridge, all the rest of the combat troops—paratroopers as well as Battle Group Schmalz—were engaged against British infantry down near Lentini. Stangenberg desperately improvised a 350-man group consisting of the communications specialists of a signal company and every clerk, cook, mechanic, and driver he could scrape up.

Then Stangenberg enlisted a flak battery of 88-mm guns for artillery support and led 200 men down Route 114 toward the Primosole Bridge. At the same time, the 150-man signal company crossed the river east of the bridge. Stangenberg attacked the north bank shortly after 1:00 p.m. on the 14th, while the radio specialists prepared to assault the south bank.

Pushed at both ends and outnumbered nearly two to one, the British defenders gave ground. Across the river, the German radiomen inched forward and began to take prisoners. These members of the airborne elite from two opposing armies regarded each other with grudging mutual respect. The British were "splendid fellows," Major Rudolf Böhmler wrote later, perhaps overstating the spirit of camaraderie. "Really a pity that one had to fight against such spirited types so similar to our German paratroopers, and who did not seem to be annoyed that they had been captured by their German 'comrades in arms.' "

The beleaguered British waited in vain throughout the afternoon for the infantry force that had been scheduled to relieve them soon after dawn. They were running out of ammunition and had lost radio contact with their naval gun support. At 5:30 p.m., they pulled back from their positions on the north bank and huddled behind two concrete pillboxes at the south end of the bridge. Stangenberg moved a high-velocity 88-mm antiaircraft gun into place on the north bank, and it proceeded to pulverize the pillboxes. At 6:30 p.m., after holding the Primosole Bridge for sixteen hours, the surviving British withdrew to the hills to the south, where they would try in vain to link up with their comrades. Stangenberg's jumbled band of cooks, clerks, and radiomen swarmed over the bridge, joyously victorious.

Just before dusk, Stangenberg thought he had further cause for joy. A column of troops was reported moving up Route 114 from the south. Stangenberg had been expecting the arrival of two battalions of Heilmann's 3d Paratroop Regiment—some 900 desperately needed reinforcements. To his dismay, the sighting turned out to be the tank-supported vanguard of the British 50th Division. These men had seized the Malati Bridge, and now they relieved the British paratroopers who had been battling on the high ground south of the Primosole Bridge since the middle of the night. Exhausted after marching more than twenty miles that day in broiling heat, the relief force rested.

Stangenberg looked in vain for reinforcement by the paratroopers. Heilmann's men had been cut off and would not make it to the north bank of the Simeto River for nearly three days. But help did arrive that night, July 14. Some 450 men of the German 1st Paratroop Engineer Battalion air-dropped near the Catania airfield and moved south to relieve Stangenberg's improvised task force at both ends of the bridge. They were reinforced by members of the German 1st Paratroop Machine-Gun Battalion who were separated from their unit and managed to make their way up to the river.

At eight o'clock the next morning, July 15, the British Durham Light Infantry Regiment headed up Route 114 toward the bridge. They were backed by heavy artillery and accompanied by Sherman tanks. A British airborne officer described the attack: "The Germans held their fire until the Durhams were within some fifty yards, more or less point-blank range, then mowed the leading platoons down. They directed burst after burst of machine-gun fire at the tanks, which had the effect of forcing them to remain closed down and therefore unable to identify enemy targets. Without protection, the infantry attack just faded away."

During the afternoon, the German signal company that had served so ably returned from Catania to reinforce the Primosole Bridge—and just in time. Around midnight, two companies of Durhams forded the river about 400 yards west of the bridge. They surprised the Germans and seized a foothold at the northern end of the span. At dawn, a tank-led British force started across. A German 88 knocked out the first two Shermans and, before the day was over, destroyed three more tanks. Retreating to the cover of dense vineyards and a sunken track several hundred yards north of the bridge, the German defenders fought desperately through the day.

The British, trying to expand their shallow bridgehead on the north bank, renewed the attack early on July 17. Six regiments of artillery—160 guns in all—opened fire. Reinforcements forded the river. More tanks rolled across the wreckage-strewn bridge. The fighting was even more savage than on the previous day. The heroic German radiomen knocked out three British tanks, but much of the combat was carried on at closer quarters with bayonets and fists. A disarmed German paratrooper tried to hide in an olive tree. When British soldiers attempted to get him down, he spat on them—and died in a retaliatory blast of rifle fire. A wounded paratrooper dragged himself up to hurl a grenade, and was shot again. He rose up once more, shouted "Heil Hitler!" and killed himself with his own knife.

By daylight, the field was strewn with the dead and dying of both sides.

Under a blistering sun, German paratroopers trudge up a mountain road in eastern Sicily. The island's steep, narrow roads, which were scarcely more than mule tracks, were nearly impossible to negotiate in motor vehicles and hindered Axis and Allied troops alike.

The commander of the German signal company, Captain Erich Fassl, was so heartsick at the sight that he risked his life to recover the wounded. A captured British medic, waving aloft a white handkerchief, led Fassl between the lines to arrange a temporary truce. "Germans and British called out to each other to show where their seriously wounded lay," Fassl recalled. "Everything went well, and finally, two long columns of wounded, some supporting others and all bound up with emergency field dressings, left the battlefield and disappeared into the dusty, glowing landscape. I asked 'our' British medical orderly to call a few words of thanks to the British and then let him leave with the last group of wounded."

British pressure was too great that day for the Germans to hold their ground near the Primosole Bridge. Captain Paul Adolff, commander of the German engineers, tried to destroy the bridge, but repeated attempts to reach it with explosive-laden trucks failed. On the final try, Adolff himself was mortally wounded.

After more than eighty hours of fighting on and around the bridge, the Germans withdrew that afternoon—but not far. The surviving engineers, together with the remnants of the machine-gun battalion and signal company, fell back to prepared positions in the Fosso Bottaceto, a dry irrigation canal on the edge of the Catania airfield two and a half miles north of the bridge. The Germans had lost some 300 dead on the battlefield and 155 captured; the British Durham Light Infantry Regiment had lost 500 killed,

wounded, and missing. Such was the respect the German paratroopers had earned from the foe that as one of their officers was led away into captivity, a British battalion commander stopped him and quietly shook his hand.

The Germans held firm at the Fosso Bottaceto. Reinforced by newly arriving troops of the 4th Paratroop Regiment, Heilmann's 3d Paratroop Regiment, and elements of Battle Group Schmalz, they turned away every additional British attempt to reach Catania for a period of more than two weeks. The inability of the British to break through to the Plain of Catania was later variously explained: the strange lack of close air support; the cancellation of a planned sea landing behind the lines at Catania; and Montgomery's uncharacteristic failure to concentrate his forces at the point of attack. But there was also the lesson in courage and tenacity delivered by the German paratroopers, who gave the British some of the bitterest combat of the war. "To fight against them," said the *Times* of London, "was an education for any soldier."

In early August 1943, German Ju 52s laden with supplies and flying at wave-top level try to escape machine-gun fire from American B-25 bombers. Although German pilots hugged the surface in order to avoid detection, interference by Allied warplanes near the Strait of Messina thwarted a number of last-minute supply runs to hard-pressed Axis troops.

The stand at the Primosole Bridge and beyond bought time for the Germans to consolidate their defenses under a new commander. General Hans Hube, a one-armed World War I veteran who had proved to be one of the ablest panzer leaders on the Russian front, took command of German forces in Sicily on July 17, just as his eastern units were taking up new positions at the Fosso Bottaceto. His orders, handed down via Kesselring from Hitler, were to "delay the enemy advance as much as possible and to bring it to a halt in front of Etna."

Hube intended to make a stand at the Etna Line, which cut diagonally across Sicily south and west of the giant volcano, and thereby abandon the entire western part of the island to the Allies. Embracing the northeastern quarter of the island, the line extended from Catania to Santo Stefano, midway along the northern coast. It was manned by remnants of the Italian divisions, along with more than three German divisions including newly arriving units from the reconstituted 29th Panzergrenadier Division, built around cadres that had survived Stalingrad.

The Allies, confronted by the Germans' slow, fighting withdrawal to these new defenses, took dramatically different tacks during the latter half of July. Montgomery, with the eastern wing of his Eighth Army stymied at Catania, pushed his "left hook" toward Enna and Leonforte, fighting through the rough mountains of central Sicily. Patton, pushing out from the Seventh Army's beachheads in the south, decided on a sudden new turn. Fearing that Montgomery would finally break through at Catania, beat the Americans to Messina, and hog all the glory, Patton, with Alexander's permission, launched a spectacular end run on July 18.

He sent three American divisions on a dash into the feebly defended northwestern part of the island. One division, the 3d, marched up to twenty-five miles a day in the heat and tortuous mountain terrain with a pace known as the Truscott Trot, after the division commander, Major General Lucian K. Truscott. The Americans slowed up only long enough to accept the surrender of tens of thousands of Italians who were trying to withdraw eastward in their path. On July 22, Truscott's troops marched into Palermo, the ancient port city at the northwestern tip of the island. It was well past nightfall when Patton entered the city, to find his triumphant subordinates already in bed.

The fall of Sicily's largest city, though of little military importance, punctuated the political crisis gripping the Italian government. Failing physically and sick at heart over his country's war exhaustion, Mussolini had met with Hitler three days earlier, on July 19, at Feltre in northern Italy. Instead of heeding his top general's advice to be honest with Hitler about Italy's desperate need to drop out of the war, Mussolini sat mute while the

German dictator lectured him on Italian shortcomings. Only the news of the first Allied bombing of Rome temporarily interrupted the Führer's two-hour monologue. Hitler was undeterred by this disturbing report and determined to bolster his old partner's weakening resolve. To his staff's astonishment, Hitler even raised the possibility of sending enough German reinforcements to Sicily to "enable us ultimately to take the offensive."

Mussolini returned to Rome still flirting with the idea that he could somehow remove Italy from Hitler's iron embrace. But a conspiracy among his own associates that reached as high as King Victor Emmanuel III already had sealed the duce's fate. In the early hours of July 25, the Fascist Grand Council voted to strip Mussolini of his military powers. Later that day, the old king demanded and received the resignation of the man he had installed as dictator twenty-one years earlier. As the dejected Mussolini left the royal villa near Rome that afternoon, he was arrested and—"for your own safety," he was told—carted off in an ambulance to a secret location.

Hitler was shocked and confused. Although the new premier, Marshal Pietro Badoglio, proclaimed, "The war goes on," and promised to remain faithful to the Axis, Hitler suspected treachery in the form of imminent defection by the Italians. He was so angry at the ascendancy of Badoglio—"our bitterest enemy"—that he threatened to order an immediate German occupation of Italy and even the abduction of the king. Cooler heads prevailed, and Hitler's staff proceeded to revive and refine earlier contingency plans to seize Italy in the event the country collapsed. Meanwhile, even the Führer, who only a few days before had talked boldly of taking the offensive in Sicily, was now resigned to its loss. Once he was sure that Mussolini had really been ousted, Hitler decided he had to evacuate Sicily—a stroke of common sense that did not last long.

Orders to General Hube to prepare for the evacuation went out on July 27, two days after Mussolini's fall. With Guzzoni's consent, Hube already had taken unofficial command of both Italian and German forces on the island, and his troops were fighting fierce delaying actions all along the front. As elements of the 29th Panzergrenadier Division came over from the mainland, Hube sent them to the northern sector to prevent an American breakthrough along the coast near Santo Stefano. These troops, as well as the 15th and Hermann Göring divisions farther east, took advantage of the mountainous terrain to conduct stubborn delaying actions during the last week in July. As they withdrew slowly to the Etna Line, German engineers became particularly adept at planting land mines. The mines were unusually effective because the high iron content of Sicily's hardened lava misled the Allies' magnetic detectors.

A Fighting Withdrawal to Italy's Boot

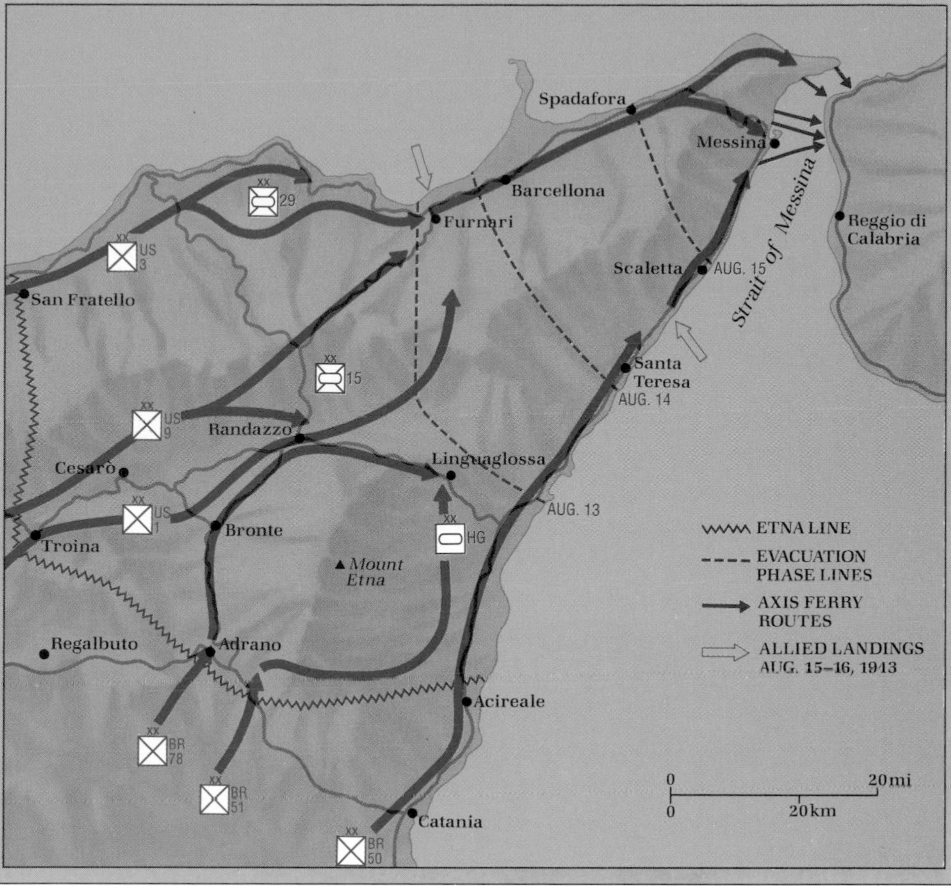

After falling back to the Etna Line in northeastern Sicily in late July, Hube, the German commander, waited anxiously for the order to evacuate. But the chaotic political situation culminating in the fall of Mussolini, and Hitler's reluctance to surrender territory, held up any decision to abandon the island. So the Germans fought on, digging in at San Fratello, Troina, and Adrano and beating back repeated Allied assaults until, stripped of reserves and threatened by amphibious landings in their rear, Hube ordered his divisions to withdraw. Finally, on August 8, Kesselring, on his own authority, gave the order. The Germans pulled back to Messina and then across the strait to Calabria.

Hube intended the central and northern sectors of the Etna Line to be a series of mountain strongpoints instead of a static, continuous array of defenses. Each was to be held long enough to permit a gradual and orderly withdrawal of German forces. By the end of July, the Americans were threatening the northern part of the Etna Line in parallel thrusts eastward along the coastal highway and along Route 120, some twenty miles inland. On July 30, the German 29th Division pulled back from Santo Stefano, the northern terminus of the line, to San Fratello. But to Hube, the key to delaying the Americans and preventing a British breakthrough in the central sector resided farther inland—at the mountainous ridge around Troina, which straddled Route 120 about twenty miles west of Mount Etna.

On July 31, General Eberhard Rodt's 15th Panzergrenadier Division was entrenched on a half-dozen hills north and south of Troina. His men, together with scraps from the Italian Aosta Division, were easily outnumbered by the approaching Americans. But the formerly dispersed 15th was operating as a unified division for the first time since the beginning of the campaign, and it was well prepared. Several days earlier, as his units slowly retreated eastward, Rodt had sent back engineers and other troops to sow the approaches with mines, dig redoubts along the Troina ridge, and install artillery. These hills rose to heights of up to 4,000 feet, and the guns on them commanded Route 120 and the barren, dusty, bowl-shape valley it traversed all the way to Cerami, some five miles to the west.

From Cerami late that afternoon, the Americans launched their first

Downfall of a Dictator

When Italian radio first announced the resignation of Benito Mussolini on Sunday night, July 25, 1943, ecstatic citizens throughout the country, some of them clad only in their pajamas, rushed into the streets to celebrate. "Finally we can say what we think," exulted one Roman. "We can breathe."

Recent Allied victories in Sicily and the bombing of Rome on July 19 had turned even many of the duce's most passionate supporters against him. For the majority of Italians, the dictator's downfall signaled the end of the war and the misery it had brought. Throngs shouting "Down with Fascism!" and "Death to Mussolini!" smashed statues and burned portraits of the erstwhile leader, beat up fascists, and ransacked government offices.

Two days later, their exhilaration turned to apprehension when the interim government, made up mostly of fascist and military leaders, clamped down. But the people would ultimately have their way: Less than two years later, in the waning days of the war, Mussolini would die ignominiously at the hands of Italian partisans.

Drawn by the headline "Long live free Italy," happy Romans read of Mussolini's downfall in the newspaper *Il Messagero*.

A mob of stick-wielding Italians batters a toppled statue of Benito Mussolini in the city of Milan.

attack on Troina. Their intelligence sources, anticipating a German stand farther east, reported that Troina was "lightly held." Although their force consisted of a full infantry division plus an additional regiment, the American commanders were so confident that they committed less than a full regiment to the first assault.

The fury of the reception stunned the Americans. They ran into a firestorm raining down from German artillery and machine guns on the heights. Day after day the Americans kept coming, in increasing numbers and backed by their own artillery firepower of no fewer than 165 guns. The American assault climaxed on the fifth day, August 4, when wave after wave of A-36 fighter-bombers—seventy-two in all—pounded the German positions morning and afternoon. There was no challenge from the Luftwaffe, which had fled Sicilian airfields more than a week previously and now mounted an average of only sixty sorties a day from the mainland. Temporarily dazed as the Allied infantry surged forward once more, the Germans rallied and lashed back. A battalion of Italians from the Aosta Division counterattacked and took forty prisoners. The Germans and Italians mounted at least twenty-four counterattacks at Troina that week.

On the sixth day of the battle, August 5, General Rodt realized it was time to end his division's dogged delaying action. A fresh regiment of Americans threatened to outflank him from the north; British and Canadian troops, forcing back the Hermann Göring Panzer Division, threatened to engulf him from the south. He was short of supplies—living "from hand to mouth," in the words of one staff officer—and almost out of troops. The fierce fighting had cost the division 1,600 dead. General Hube at first rejected Rodt's request for permission to withdraw, then relented a few hours later. When the Americans marched into the shell-ravaged town of Troina the next morning, the Germans were gone.

With the retreat from Troina, the Etna Line crumbled. To the east, the paratroopers and Battle Group Schmalz already had ended their extraordinary stand north of the Primosole Bridge, abandoning Catania under orders on the night of August 4. The Hermann Göring Panzer Division withdrew from Adrano, the fiercely contested strongpoint near the center of the line, on August 6. Up on the northern coast, the 29th Division was forced to leave San Fratello on August 7. The withdrawal was orderly all along the line, enabling the Germans to concentrate their defenses a few miles closer to Messina.

It was time to get out. On August 8, Field Marshal Kesselring sent Hube orders to initiate the evacuation, code-named Operation Lehrgang (Training Tour), which had been under preparation since shortly after the fall of

On the road to Nissoria in central Sicily, a military policeman from the American Seventh Army pauses for a cigarette with his two German captives. Thanks to the difficult terrain and efficient German rearguard action, the Wehrmacht lost few men during the orderly two-week retreat from Sicily.

Mussolini. Kesselring did so without consulting Hitler, who entered no objection when word reached the Reich the following day. Fearing that Allied amphibious landings might cut off the escape routes to Messina, Hube on his own initiative already had begun evacuating the wounded and able-bodied men who could be spared from the rearguard fighting. During the first ten days of August, 8,615 German troops, along with 4,489 wounded, were transported across the two-mile-wide Strait of Messina to Calabria, the toe of the Italian boot.

The plans for Lehrgang reflected German logistical thinking at its best. Combat units were to withdraw in phases. As units reached each of five successive defense lines, 8,000 or so troops would be released to make their way along one or both of the two coastal highways to the four designated ferry sites north of Messina. Awaiting them would be a flotilla of thirty-three naval barges, scores of landing craft and motorboats, and a dozen ingenious vessels known as Siebel ferries. Invented in 1940 by aircraft designer Fritz Siebel for the intended invasion of England, these craft consisted of a pair of large pontoons held together by steel girders overlaid with a platform and powered by two aircraft engines. The Italians organized their own separate but simultaneous evacuation from the Messina area, utilizing small steamboats, large motor-rafts, and a train ferry capable of carrying 3,000 men at a time. Protecting both German and Italian flotillas were some 500 guns—antiaircraft, naval, and dual-purpose pieces that could counter attacks from both air and ground. They lined both sides of the strait in a concentration that Allied airmen described as "heavier than the Ruhr"—a reference to Germany's heavily defended industrial heartland.

The Germans launched Operation Lehrgang on the night of August 11. Some units were still engaged in combat at distances of more than forty air miles from Messina. They had to pull back slowly, step by step, fighting to fend off the Allied advance, which was strongest along the two coasts, while units in the successive phases moved ever closer to the ferries. Engineers planted the last of their mines and blew up bridges and long sections of the coastal highways. On four different occasions, the retreating Germans eluded Allied attempts to make amphibious jumps behind their lines. The Allies did not have enough assault ships to do the job properly.

The withdrawal and evacuation exceeded the most optimistic expectations of the planners. Overwhelming Allied superiority in the air and at sea had given the Germans serious doubts. "We were all fully convinced," wrote a German colonel, "that only a few of us would get away from the island safe and sound." But the Allies made no serious attempt to intervene from the sea. In the face of formidable German firepower, Allied air attacks—an average of 250 sorties a day—proved notably ineffective, even though most of the ferry crossings were carried out in broad daylight. Concerted Allied air action over the Strait of Messina sank just seven Axis vessels and killed only a single Wehrmacht soldier.

It was a reprise of a familiar story when an American patrol entered Messina at 10:00 p.m. on August 16, beating the British to the tip of the island. The city was ruined and abandoned, the enemy gone. A few hours later, at 6:35 a.m. on August 17, General Hube reported from Calabria the successful completion of Operation Lehrgang. The Germans had evacuated 40,000 troops (26,000 of them in only six nights), nearly 10,000 vehicles, and most of their other equipment. The Italians had saved 70,000 soldiers and sailors, some equipment, and twelve mules.

The Allies, in capturing Sicily, had won much. They had breached the

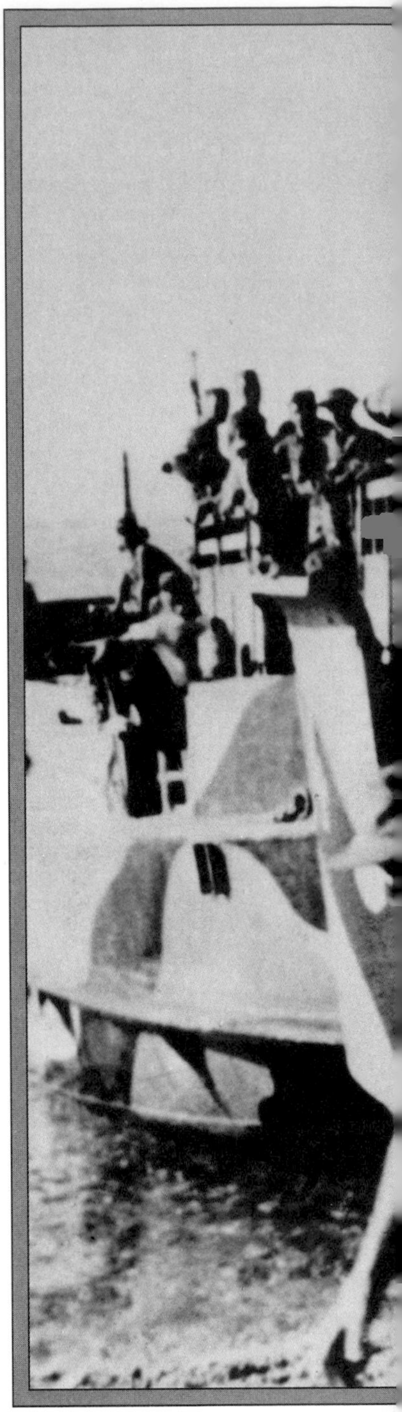

A German ferry prepares to carry a truckload of soldiers from Messina to Calabria on the Italian mainland. Sporadic shelling by warships and inaccurate nighttime air raids interfered little with the Axis retreat from Sicily. The officer directing the operation boasted, "We have not given up a single German soldier, weapon, or vehicle into enemy hands."

Axis empire, helped bring down Mussolini, and gained a substantial foothold at the brink of the Italian mainland. They had accomplished all this for a relatively moderate price in casualties: 20,000 Allies compared to 29,000 Germans and 144,000 Italians—almost all of the latter taken prisoner.

But the Germans, too, could take pride. In the face of Allied air and naval superiority and a peak troop strength that outnumbered them by seven to one, the Germans could claim a kind of victory. With only a little help from their Italian comrades, they had transformed a campaign that the Allied leaders expected to last a fortnight into a delaying action of thirty-eight days. And now, thanks to a brilliantly executed strategic withdrawal, three and a half German divisions stood on the Italian mainland—equipped, obdurate, and ready to keep on fighting.

Mussolini glances apprehensively around the cockpit of the tiny Fieseler Storch spotter plane that his rescuer Otto Skorzeny (*right*) has brought for the duce's escape. The former dictator asked to be taken to his villa in Romagna, but his rescuers denied the request.

Rescuing the Duce

When Adolf Hitler learned on July 25, 1943, that Benito Mussolini had been deposed and arrested, he lost no time in ordering a rescue mission for the Italian dictator, his "dear friend." Hitler rightly suspected that Italy's new government was negotiating to surrender to the Allies. In their hands, Mussolini would be a powerful propaganda weapon; he had to be safeguarded.

To carry out the rescue, Hitler picked Waffen-SS captain Otto Skorzeny, 35-year-old leader of a new SS special operations unit. In overall command was General Kurt Student, chief of German airborne troops.

After a month-long investigation, Skorzeny located the duce at a ski lodge perched six thousand feet up in the Gran Sasso d'Italia, the highest Apennine range. The resort could be reached only by a funicular railway, but Skorzeny's aerial reconnaissance showed a "triangular meadow" just below the hotel.

To surprise Mussolini's guards, Skorzeny proposed landing gliders in the tiny meadow. Student reluctantly agreed. At 2:00 p.m. on September 12, eight gliders coasted toward the Gran Sasso. Skorzeny's "meadow" proved to be a precipitous slope, impossible for landing; so the pilots daringly set their fragile craft down on a narrow strip almost at the hotel's doorstep. Some 70 paratroopers then seized the hotel from at least 150 members of the Italian paramilitary police force, the *carabinieri*, without firing a shot. That night, Skorzeny escorted the former dictator to safety in Vienna.

Mussolini himself called his rescue from Gran Sasso "the boldest, most romantic of all, and at the same time the most modern in method and style." Although much credit belonged to the Luftwaffe paratroopers, Skorzeny claimed it all—and Hitler concurred, awarding him a promotion to major and the coveted Knight's Cross of the Iron Cross.

Painstaking Rehearsals for a Daring Raid

General Kurt Student's paratroopers practice mock attacks from gliders as they train for the Gran Sasso landing. Their DFS 230 gliders were specially fitted with three braking rockets in the nose, as well as a drag parachute in the tail, to permit as short a landing as possible.

On the day of the raid, paratroopers buckle on their gear for the glider ascent. All had volunteered for the perilous mission, even though General Student's planners predicted casualties as high as 80 percent.

A Crash Landing in Punishing Terrain

This glider and six others landed safely on the rocky ledge surrounding the hotel. The boulders even helped bring the tubular steel, wood-and-canvas craft to a stop without wrecking them. But the eighth glider was smashed to the ground by a gust of wind, and all ten men aboard were severely injured.

An injured paratrooper from the glider that crashed is helped along by two soldiers. By this time in the mission, Major Otto-Harald Mors, with a paratroop battalion, had captured the lower station of the funicular railway and was using its cable cars to bring reinforcements to the top. The raiders would later escape by the railway, then disable it.

Snatching the Deposed Dictator

The duce was held prisoner on the second floor of the hotel. Within four minutes of landing, Skorzeny's party smashed the garrison's radio transmitter and burst into Mussolini's room. The guards capitulated, hanging a white bedspread out a window.

An unshaven Mussolini, in ill-fitting civilian clothes, displays none of his customary bravado as he is led from the hotel by Otto Skorzeny (wearing field glasses) and Luftwaffe paratroopers. Skorzeny had greeted his charge by announcing, "Duce, the Führer sent me! You are free!" Mussolini replied: "I knew that my friend Adolf Hitler would not desert me."

Gearing Up for a Perilous Flight

Skorzeny boosts the hesitant duce into the waiting Storch two-seater. The pilot, Captain Heinrich Gerlach, was dismayed to see Skorzeny climb in after Mussolini, overburdening the plane. Determined to accompany his charge to the final destination, Skorzeny chose "to share the danger with him, even though my presence added to it."

German paratroopers and Italian *carabinieri* salute as the tiny plane taxis down the makeshift runway, which they have cleared of the largest boulders. Twelve men held the plane back while Gerlach revved its engine to the maximum.

After a sickening lurch over the edge of a precipice and a long dive toward the valley floor, Gerlach manages to level the Storch and head toward the Pratica di Mare air base near Rome. There, Student had three He 111s waiting for the next leg of the duce's journey, to Vienna.

A Fearful Takeoff and Warm Reunion

At an airstrip near Rastenburg, East Prussia, a grateful Mussolini greets Hitler with, "Führer, how can I thank you?" According to Hitler's plans, the fallen duce was to show his gratitude by heading the Reich's puppet regime in the newly created fascist state in northern Italy.

THREE

Knocking on the Door of Axis Europe

Even as the last German and Italian troops were withdrawing from Sicily, Hitler and his armed forces high command (OKW) were urgently updating their defense plans in the Mediterranean. They had been impressed by the Allied amphibious capability in the Sicily operation. The Allies would obviously use it again—and soon. But where?

The list of potential targets was long: Greece, Albania, Yugoslavia, southern France, Sardinia, Corsica, and on the Italian mainland, the toe of the Italian boot, the heel, Naples, south or north of Rome, Leghorn, the Adriatic ports. Hitler still believed the next invasion would target the Balkans. Why, he argued, with the obvious strategic benefits in the Balkans, would the Allies settle for more island-hopping, perhaps to Sardinia and Corsica, or plunge into the Italian mainland, where terrain favored a determined defender and where, sooner or later, any offensive against Germany itself would founder at the rampart of the Alps?

Some German planners, however, believed that the Allies might opt for closer and presumably easier targets than the Balkans. The capture of Sardinia and Corsica, for example, would give them air bases closer to France and northern Italy. From the two big islands, they could launch air attacks on industrial centers and provide better air cover for additional amphibious landings in southern France or central Italy. The fall of Rome alone would be an immense psychological and political victory—the first Axis capital in Europe to be captured. A successful landing north of Rome would also force the Germans to withdraw all of their troops from southern and central Italy into a last defensive redoubt in the northern Apennines, where they would have to fight to keep the Allies out of the industrial areas of the Po Valley and block the way to Germany itself.

It also seemed logical to German strategists that the Allies might simply decide to step across the narrow Strait of Messina from Sicily to Calabria, the toe of Italy. Perhaps such an operation could be coordinated with a landing on the Apulian plain, along the southern Adriatic coast, aimed at capturing the airfields around Foggia. From there big bombers could reach the Rumanian oil fields as well as targets in southern Germany.

German sappers camouflage each other with straw before action against Allied forces on the Volturno River front north of Naples in October 1943. After weeks of rain, the raging floodwaters of the Volturno were the Germans' main ally as they tried to pin the British and Americans to the south bank of the river.

Kesselring, as an airman, felt certain that the Anglo-Americans would not attempt any landing in an area where they did not have superior air support. Since their available carriers alone would not provide that guarantee, any invasion site would have to be within range of their fighter bases in Sicily or North Africa. That, for him, immediately ruled out any direct invasion of the Balkans.

Complicating the planning process was another perplexity: What would Italy do now that Mussolini had been deposed and King Victor Emmanuel III was in command of all Italian military forces? On paper at least, the Italians still had a large army—about 1,700,000 men. Although poorly equipped and despondent, these troops in sheer numbers would burden the Germans if Italy surrendered. At the very least, the Italian soldiers would have to be disarmed and somehow confined. At worst, they might put up prolonged resistance. In either case, their defensive positions would have to be manned by German troops taken from other duties.

On the question of Italy's possible defection and duplicity, Hitler had no doubts. Even when Mussolini was in power, Hitler had never trusted the king and his court, the Vatican, or many of the duce's high-ranking military officers. On July 29, 1943, German intelligence had intercepted a transatlantic conversation between Roosevelt and Churchill that revealed they were expecting diplomatic overtures from the Italian government. OKW suspicions increased on August 14, when the Italians declared Rome an open city—an obvious prelude to an armistice. That was enough to convince Hitler that Victor Emmanuel and the new premier, Pietro Badoglio, were making a deal with the Anglo-Americans. He became increasingly angry with those of his top officials in Rome, including Kesselring, who were still willing to accept the king's and Badoglio's assurances that the Italians were not about to betray Germany. To the German high command (whom Kesselring regarded as Hitler's yes-men), Kesselring and his cobelievers in Italy's sincerity were naive Italophiles. "That fellow Kesselring," Hitler complained, "is too honest for those born traitors down there." He summoned Kesselring to his headquarters at 3:00 a.m. on August 23 and, in Göring's presence, told him that he had received infallible proof of Italy's treachery. "He begged me," Kesselring wrote in his memoirs, "to stop being the dupe of the Italians and to prepare myself for serious developments."

To prepare for those developments, Hitler sent Kesselring the 2d Paratroop Division from France. The additional troops were part of the plan, originally code-named *Alarich*, now called *Achse* (Axis), to handle an Italian surrender. If the Italians capitulated, the code would be broadcast, and German forces all over Italy would disarm their former allies, using whatever force was necessary.

With Sicily lost and the Italians maneuvering to drop out of the war, Hitler ordered his army to take over the defense of Italy. After an Anglo-American force landed at Salerno and the British came ashore at Reggio di Calabria and Taranto in September 1943, the Wehrmacht exploited the country's rugged mountains, steep-banked rivers, and narrow, winding roads to set up strongpoint after strongpoint, making their enemies pay in blood for every foot of ground taken. The Germans established two major redoubts: the Gustav Line, which the Allies were unable to breach before the winter of 1943 brought them to a four-month-long halt short of Rome, and the Gothic Line, north of Florence, where a year later the Germans again stymied their exhausted enemies, who had to settle in for yet another winter.

Grim Struggle for the Italian Peninsula

There was considerably less agreement at the OKW about how to defend against an Allied landing, especially since German intelligence sources had no firm information on where and how strong the major thrust would be. The argument over strategy was dominated by two field marshals with different defensive philosophies and personalities. From his headquarters at Lake Garda in northern Italy, Rommel argued that it made little strategic sense to try to defend southern or even central Italy, including Rome, especially if that meant committing more divisions there. Italy was, after all, only a secondary theater, and he feared that a strong Allied amphibious operation, combined with the possible defection of Italian troops to fight alongside the Allies, risked the destruction of German troops who could be used more effectively elsewhere. He argued for caution: As soon as any Anglo-American attack began, German forces in southern and central Italy should be withdrawn northward to a heavily fortified defensive line (later known as the Gothic Line) that would run from north of Pisa near the Ligurian coast across the Apennines to south of Rimini on the Adriatic.

Kesselring strenuously took the opposite view. Defending southern Italy, he felt, would deny the enemy bridgeheads in the Apulian plain from which they might later launch attacks against the vital Balkans. And defending central Italy would deny them the psychological victory of liberating Rome. Optimistic by nature, Kesselring insisted that with the eight divisions he had under his command (including the 40,000 men who had been salvaged from Sicily), he could fight a successful delaying action against an Allied landing in the south. He went further. If Hitler would detach two divisions from Rommel's northern command and send them to him immediately, he might do even better—drive the Allied invaders back into the sea.

When Hitler rejected his recommendations, Kesselring submitted his resignation; after all, under Rommel's scenario he would soon have no troops to command anyway. Hitler refused to accept the resignation; he regarded Kesselring as the best player he had in Rome in the duplicitous game the Axis partners were still playing. Instead, following the advice of the OKW, he hastily created a new Tenth Army out of troops that had fought earlier in Sicily and gave its command to General Heinrich von Vietinghoff, a veteran Prussian infantry officer who had considerable field experience, including the command of a corps on the eastern front and an army in France. Hitler personally gave Vietinghoff his orders: He was to withdraw his three mobile divisions and supporting troops in southern Italy to the Naples-Salerno area; defend the Foggia airfields with part of the 1st Paratroop Division; and conduct limited delaying action against a possible invasion of the Calabrian toe. For the time being, Vietinghoff's Tenth Army was to come under Kesselring's command.

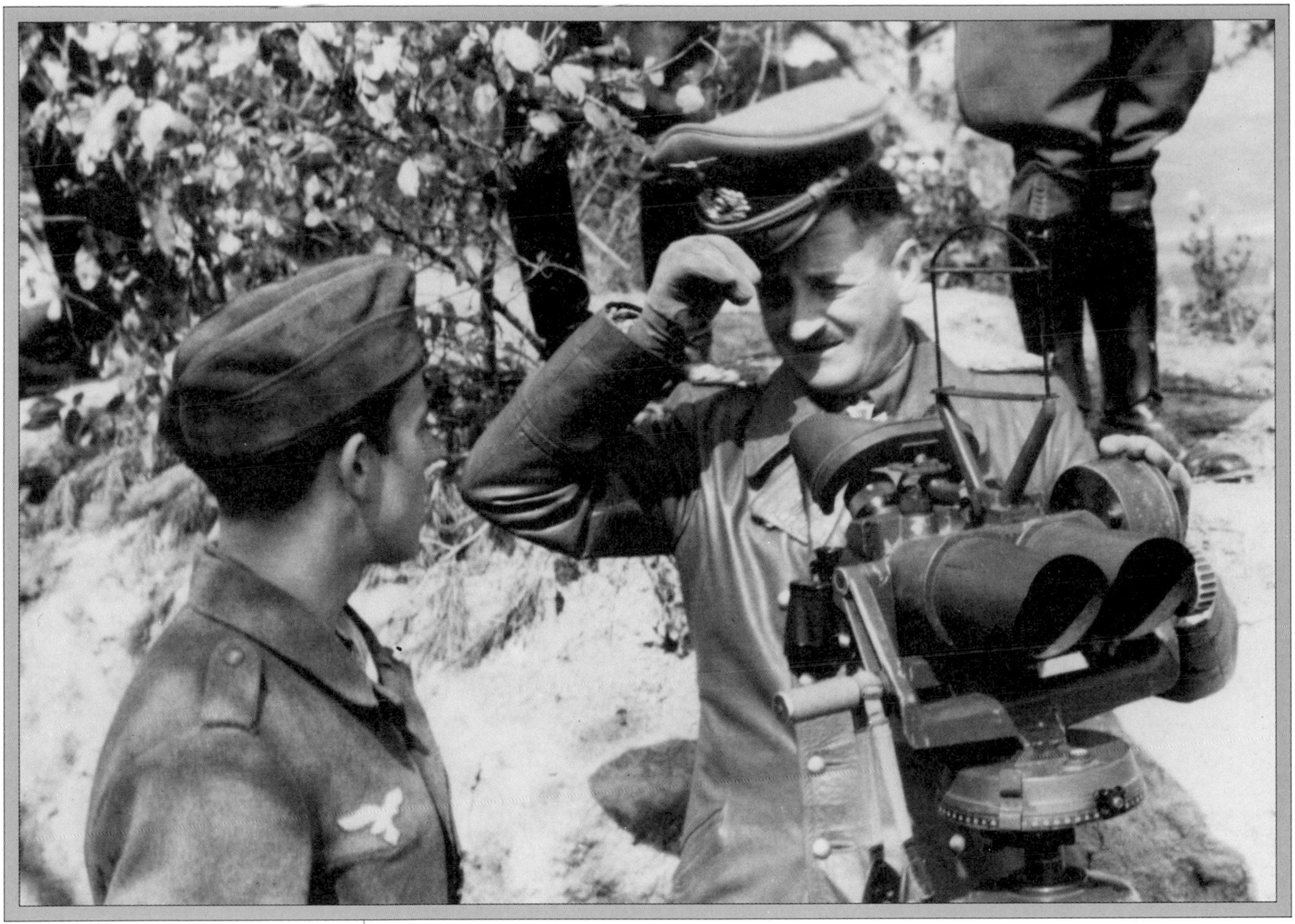

Looking every bit the friendly leader, General Heinrich von Vietinghoff, commander of the German Tenth Army, flashes an uncharacteristic smile at a soldier at a forward observation post near Naples. Vietinghoff, though accomplished militarily, actually had a reputation for being distant with the troops.

Hitler issued two other preinvasion orders: Mussolini was to be found and rescued; and every effort was to be made to bring German troops from Corsica and Sardinia to the mainland to help defend northern Italy.

As far as Kesselring was concerned, rightly or wrongly, what Hitler seemed to be saying was: If you can defend Rome with the troops you already have, fine. But if not, I'm willing to lose them—and you. "It still defeats me," Kesselring wrote after the war, "why Hitler chose to write off eight first-class German divisions (in the south) instead of sending me one or two divisions (from the north). Rommel's idea had apparently taken such firm root in Hitler's mind that he turned a deaf ear to even the most self-evident tactical requirements."

The Anglo-Americans and Italians were also making plans—separately and jointly. Given the limitations on the number of troops and amphibious craft at his disposal, Eisenhower had planned a relatively modest operation against the Italian mainland. Troops of Montgomery's Eighth Army were to cross the Strait of Messina. About a week later, simultaneously with another Eighth Army landing at Taranto on the heel of the Italian boot, Lieut. General Mark Clark's Fifth Army would invade Salerno, south of Naples. Montgomery was to take Foggia and link up with Clark at Salerno.

Kesselring had judged correctly: One reason Eisenhower had chosen Salerno as the landing site was that it was as far north as Sicily-based fighters could operate and still have time over the beachhead before they were forced to return home for refueling.

The Italians, meanwhile, had signed a secret armistice on September 3. It was not to be announced until September 8, at 6:30 p.m., by Eisenhower and Badoglio simultaneously. Right up to the last minute, however, Eisenhower could not be certain that the Italians would honor the agreement.

At 2:00 p.m. on September 7, Lieutenant Rocholl of the 16th Reconnaissance Unit of the 16th Panzer Division, which only one week earlier had been ordered to establish defensive positions in the Salerno area, received a phone call from his regimental operations officer. "Attention: *Feuerbrunst* (Firestorm). Be prepared for an early enemy attempt to land!"

Four days earlier the British Eighth Army had invaded Calabria, and the Germans were expecting another, heavier landing farther north. Since Rocholl had received many similar alarms before, he and his men did not interrupt their afternoon nap. But two and a half hours later, another urgent call came through from Operations. "Attention: *Orkan* (Hurricane). A large enemy convoy is now in sight, and a major landing is imminent!"

Rocholl and his men piled into armored cars and sped to an observation post atop a high ridge near the sea southeast of Salerno. From there they could see northwest toward Salerno and Vietri sul Mare and south along the entire coast and the Faiano plain. Nearby, a heavy-machine-gun unit had also taken up position. Together they looked out over the Gulf of Salerno and waited for the Allies to land.

For Kesselring the day had started badly. In the morning, a fleet of 130 B-17 bombers had dropped almost 400 tons of bombs on Frascati, just to the southeast of Rome. Kesselring's headquarters there was hit, but he was able to crawl out of the wreckage unharmed. A map recovered from a downed bomber marked the exact location of his office and that of Field Marshal Wolfram von Richthofen, commander of the German air forces in Italy. This indicated, Kesselring later wrote, "some excellent lackey work on the part of the Italians."

Still, hours after the raid, Kesselring discerned no new suspicious behavior on the part of Italian military commanders. The German ambassador had met at noon with King Victor Emmanuel and come away with no clues of a change in Italian policy. Early that evening, while Kesselring's chief of staff and the German military attaché were meeting with General Mario Roatta, Italian army chief, at Roatta's headquarters about coordinating their forces against Allied landings, the two German officers received a momentous call from their embassy: Washington had just announced an armistice with Italy! Roatta placidly assured them that the report was nothing but a ruse to create friction between the Axis partners, and the three generals resumed their deliberations. Shortly thereafter, at 7:45 p.m., more than an hour later than the time agreed upon with Eisenhower, Badoglio confirmed over Radio Rome that Italy had signed an armistice. Meanwhile, Eisenhower had released the news at 6:30 p.m.

Achse! The code was flashed to every German command in the Mediterranean. *Ernte einbringen!* (Bring in the harvest). Start immediately to disarm all Italian forces! Although the OKW for many weeks had been expecting both the invasion and the armistice, the actual timing caught them by surprise. In all their planning, they had never considered the possibility that both events might occur simultaneously.

In the first hours after Badoglio's announcement, Rome was in chaos. At the German Embassy, the ambassador and his staff, fearful of capture by Italian troops, rounded up as many German civilians as they could and caught the last diplomatic train heading north. So precipitate was their departure that they neglected to burn embassy documents or turn them

General Giuseppe Castellano (in civilian dress), a representative of the Italian high command, shakes hands with General Dwight D. Eisenhower, the Allied commander, after signing surrender papers at Allied headquarters in Sicily on September 3, 1943. General Walter B. Smith, Eisenhower's chief of staff, looks on.

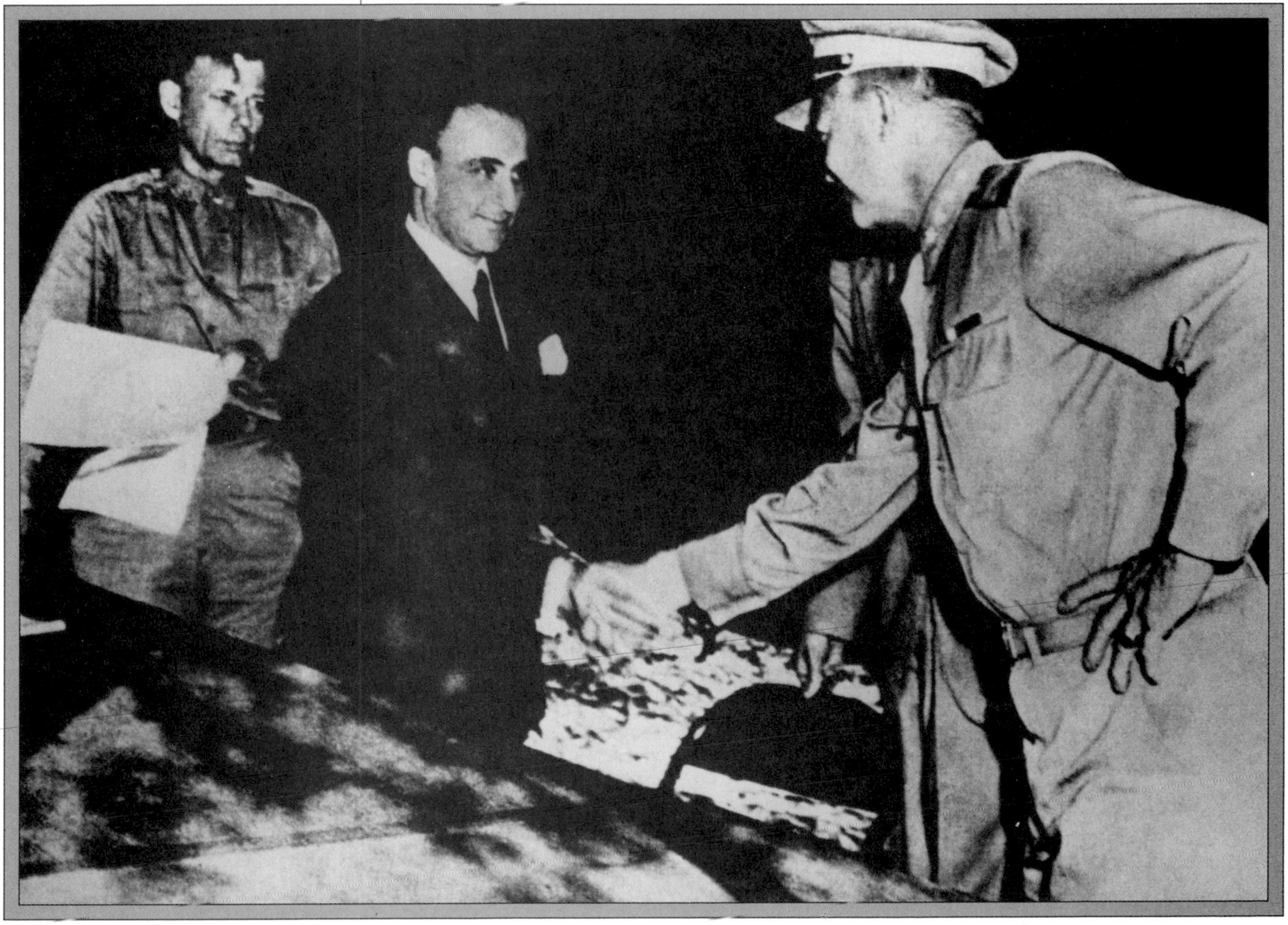

over to the German military. The Italian royal family and Badoglio, fearing capture by German troops, fled in an automobile at 5:00 a.m. the next morning for the Adriatic port of Pescara.

In the meantime, German military units were advancing on Rome. A battalion from the 1st Paratroop Division, dropping on Italian army headquarters at Monterotondo, arrived too late to catch Roatta, who wisely had also taken off for Pescara. The 2d Paratroop Division and the 3d Panzergrenadier Division moved to confront the five Italian divisions in the Rome area. There were brief skirmishes between the former allies, but by a skillful use of stick and carrot, Kesselring brought the situation under control. If Italian troops continued to resist the German takeover, he threatened, Rome would be bombed by the Luftwaffe and all its aqueducts blown up. The Anglo-American invading force, he pointed out, was too far away to save them. If, on the other hand, they gave up and surrendered their arms, they could simply go home and for them the war would be over. (At an earlier discussion on the subject, Hitler had insisted that Italians not be allowed to keep their weapons. Otherwise, he said contemptuously, "They'll sell them!" And Göring had added: "They'll sell the buttons off their pants for English pounds.")

Weary of the war, demoralized, their leaders in flight, the Italians gave in to Kesselring's ultimatum; they turned in their weapons and headed for home. Thousands of others on garrison duty had already thrown away their uniforms upon first word of the armistice and melted into the countryside. By the evening of September 10, Kesselring was master of Rome.

In the Balkans, in Crete, and in Rhodes, 600,000 more Italian soldiers were disarmed, after offering little resistance. The OKW's orders stated that Italians willing to fight in German units would be welcomed; all others would become prisoners of war and sent as forced laborers to Germany. Kesselring had simply ignored that order; he had enough to worry about without having to cope with thousands of prisoners. In northern Italy and occupied France, hundreds of thousands of Italian soldiers simply vanished. Rommel's men were able to round up only some 40,000 for transfer to Germany, a severe disappointment to Hitler, who had hoped that a great number of Italians, fired by the fascist spirit, would volunteer for combat duty with the Germans.

The Italian army and what was left of the air force opted out of the war. The Italian navy sailed expeditiously from Spezia and Taranto, but the German bombers attacked the vessels, sinking the *Roma*, the Italian flagship, and damaging another. Nevertheless, four Italian battleships, seven cruisers, and eight destroyers sailed safely into Allied ports.

Shortly before 3:30 a.m. on September 9, Allied troops began wading

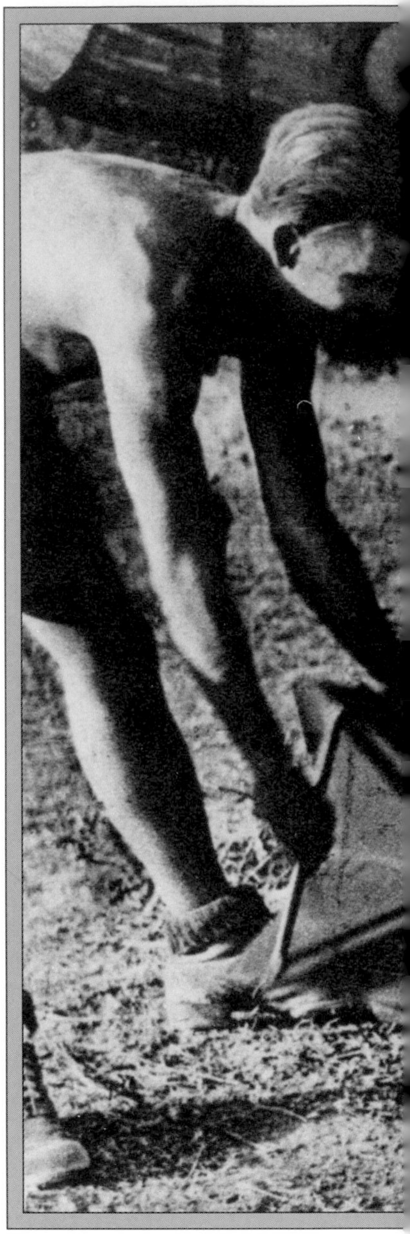

A Luftwaffe ground crew at an airfield in southern Italy prepares to load a 250-kilogram bomb into a waiting Stuka for a mission against Allied forces landing at Salerno in September. German planes flew more than 500 sorties in the first three days of the amphibious invasion.

ashore in the Gulf of Salerno. The beaches there curve like a scimitar from Maiori at the base of the Sorrento Peninsula, southward some thirty miles to the town of Agropoli. Inland from the beaches rises a fertile plain, which is crisscrossed by irrigation ditches and cut by streams and two sizable rivers, the Sele and its tributary, the Calore. Only sixteen miles at its greatest depth, the plain is encircled by steep mountains that Kesselring, when he inspected the defensive positions, hailed as "God's gift" to German artillery.

The defense of the Gulf of Salerno had been assigned by Vietinghoff to the 16th Panzer Division. Originally part of the German Sixth Army at Stalingrad, the 16th had lost 70 percent of its men there. Reconstituted in France, it now had 17,000 soldiers and more than 100 tanks, but it lacked one battalion of the new, heavy Panzer VI Tiger I tanks, whose crews were still training in Germany.

The coastal defenses had been hastily improvised. Engineers had built eight strongpoints of reinforced concrete near the beach to be garrisoned by infantry platoons supported by heavy machine guns, mortars, and artillery. The only other protection for the coast consisted of some mines, barbed wire, and six artillery batteries the Germans had seized from Italians during Operation Achse.

The officers of the 16th Panzer knew that defending thirty-odd miles of beach with one division was impossible for any length of time. Major Herbert Düppenbecker, in command of the 1st Battalion, 79th Panzergrenadier Regiment, could not help thinking how his army college instructors had emphasized that a battalion should never occupy a front more than a thousand meters long; now he had been ordered to defend nine miles of open coastline.

The northern flank of the Allied beachhead was to be secured by three battalions of American Rangers and two of British commandos. After landing on the narrow beach at Maiori, about six miles west of the port of Salerno, the Rangers moved quickly inland against little resistance to occupy the strategic 4,000-foot-high Chiunzi Pass, overlooking the plain of Naples. The British commandos captured Vietri sul Mare, a fishing village four miles east of Maiori, and despite stubborn opposition, seized the southern end of La Molina Pass, which dominated the road to Naples. The Rangers and commandos then dug in to await the main body of assault troops and prepare for German counterattacks.

To the south, the 16th Panzer, reacting vigorously against the main landings by the British X Corps' 46th and 56th divisions on the north and the U.S. VI Corps' 36th Division on the south, fought to disrupt the Allied landing schedules. Aided by small parachute flares that lit up the landing zones, German machine guns and mortars raked and pounded Allied soldiers as soon as they set foot on shore. Tank guns and 88-mm antiaircraft cannon fired point-blank at landing craft while heavier artillery at the base of the mountains pounded the invasion fleet, a vast armada containing more than 500 ships, that was anchored out in the Gulf of Salerno. Luftwaffe fighters roared back and forth, strafing the beaches.

As Major Düppenbecker had feared, however, the German defenses were too thin to prevent the Allies from forging a beachhead. Throughout the day, Allied soldiers and equipment continued to pour ashore. The 16th Panzer Division mounted small counterattacks, sometimes by tank-infantry teams, sometimes by groups of five to seven tanks operating independently. In the effort, the division lost almost two-thirds of its armor to Allied artillery, tank fire, rocket launchers, and naval and air bombardment; only thirty-five tanks remained in condition to fight again.

Help for the 16th Panzer might have arrived in time if higher-echelon commanders had reacted faster to the landings—and if they had been able to communicate more effectively. The Italians' civilian telephone network, which the Germans had been using, was no longer reliable or secure, and

An Allied Lunge at Salerno

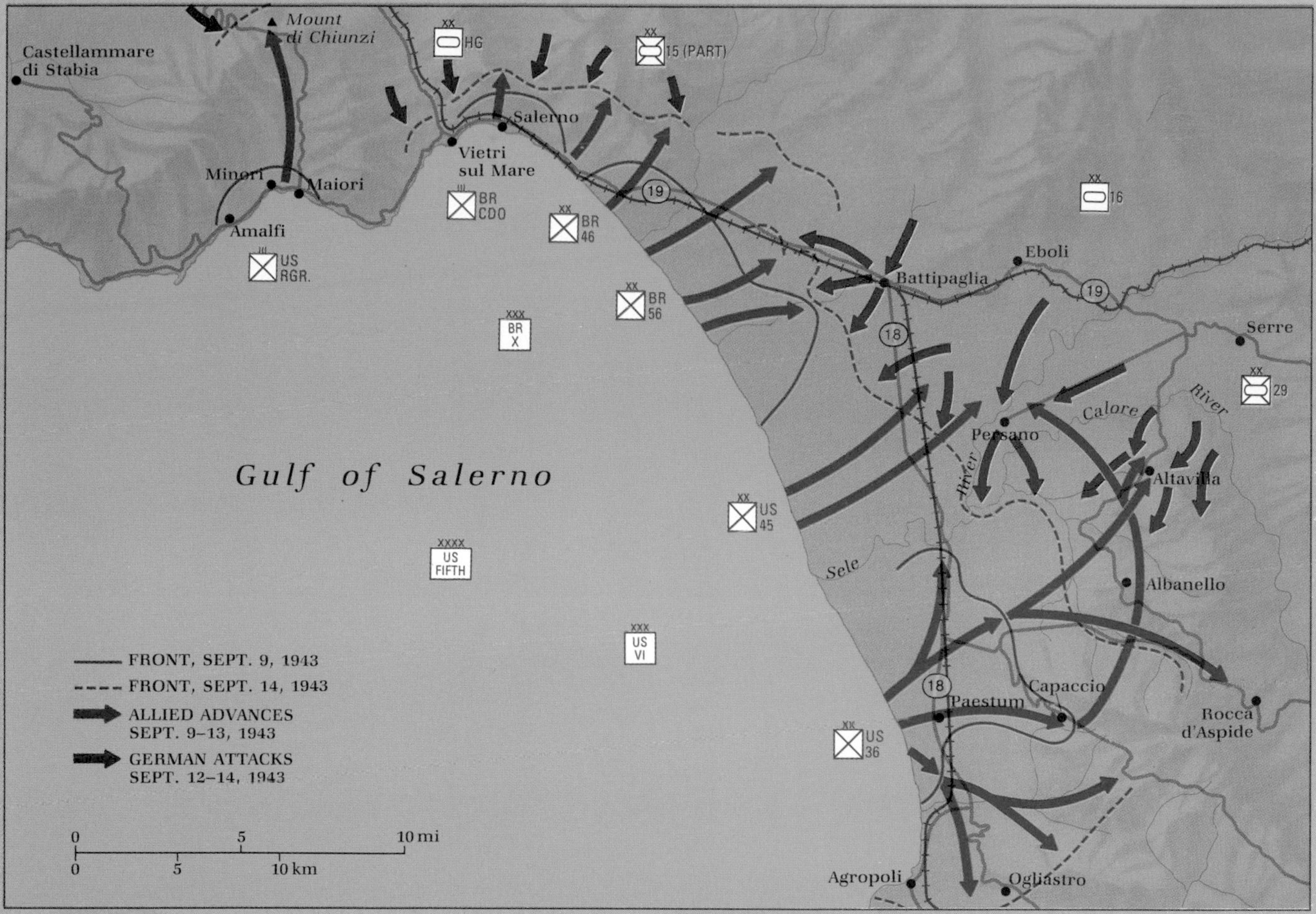

On September 9, the Germans had only a single division, the 16th Panzer, to confront the Anglo-American landing in the Gulf of Salerno. But reinforcements were quickly brought up. After first checking the Allied advance, the elements of four divisions, the 16th and Hermann Göring Panzer as well as the 15th and 29th Panzergrenadier, slammed into the fragile Allied line. The Germans launched their major attacks against the Allied center, into the gap between the British X and U.S. VI Corps. But after two days of fierce combat, the Germans were forced to fall back after being pounded by bombers and concentrated naval gunfire.

radio transmissions were subject to atmospheric disturbances. Lieut. General Hermann Balck, acting commander of XIV Panzer Corps, which was defending the Gaeta sector seventy-five miles northwest of Salerno, had no telephone communication with either Kesselring or Vietinghoff, and only uncertain radio contact.

Kesselring was still too busy with the Italian imbroglio to issue new instructions to Vietinghoff. When Vietinghoff decided on his own to defend the beachhead rather than withdraw to Rome, it took him several hours to contact Balck with orders to send all his troops immediately to the aid of the 16th Panzer. Balck, newly assigned and unfamiliar with the area, as well as fearful of other landings, was reluctant to strip his entire defenses. He dispatched only one reconnaissance battalion of the Hermann Göring Panzer Division to the sector under attack by the American Rangers, and it arrived too late to have any effect on the Allied assault.

The 16th Panzer, commanded by Major General Rudolf Sickenius, had

A German battle group in the Vietri hills above Salerno uses rifles, machine guns, and light antiaircraft and assault guns to pour fire down on the Allied troops who were trying to break out of their beachhead in mid-September 1943. These photographs, taken by members of a German propaganda company and published here for the first time, show the feverish activity of raw combat.

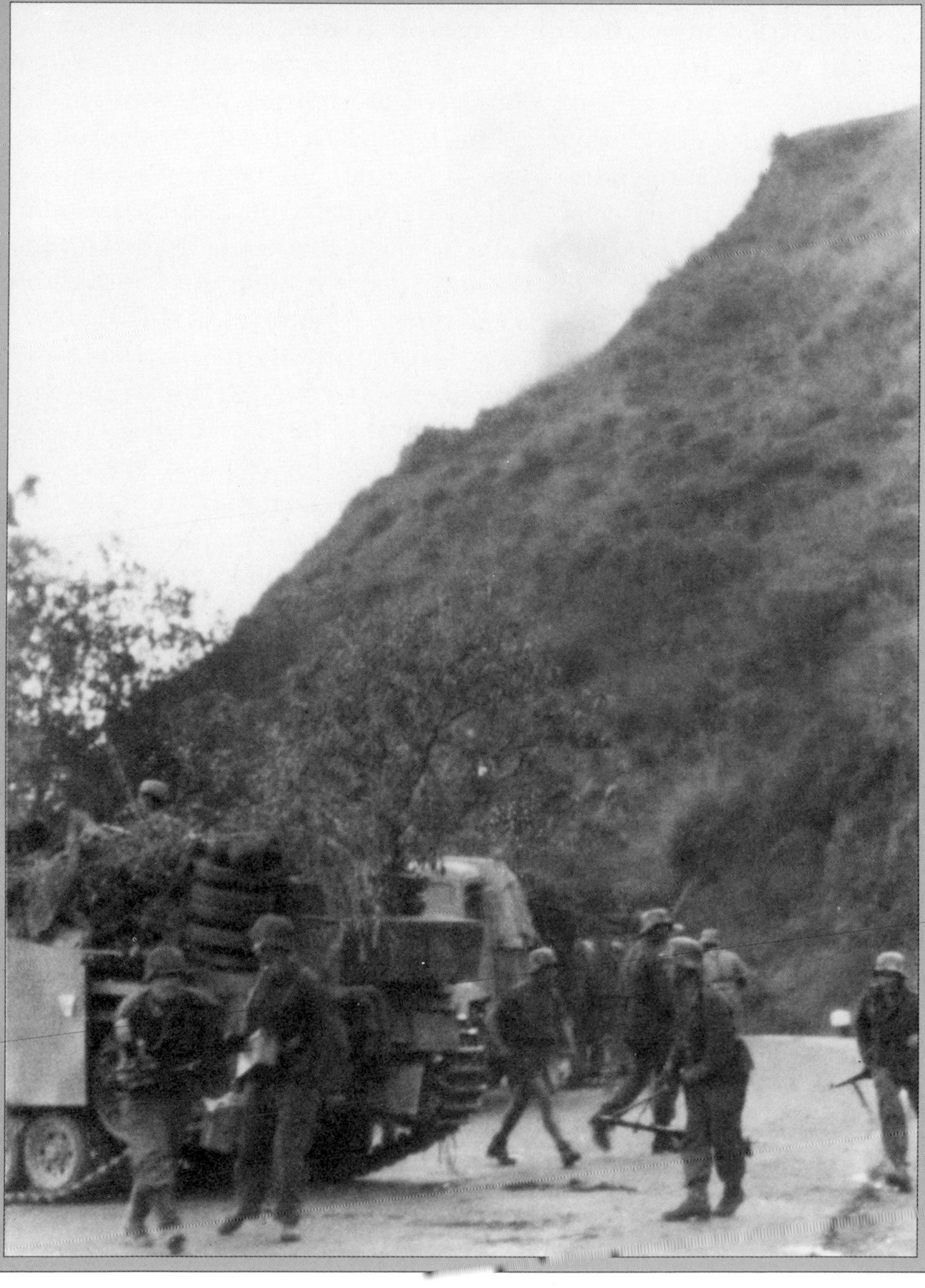

fought well on its own. At the end of the first day, the troops had contained the Allies' beachhead; nowhere had they penetrated deeper than six miles—only half of General Clark's territorial objective. And all the dominating mountains remained in German hands.

The beachhead was still to be won—or lost; the issue hung on which side could get reinforcements to the battlefield faster. At the beginning, Clark had about 70,000 troops, including reserves, waiting to go ashore. Vietinghoff had only about 17,000 on line to defend against them. But the German commander's reinforcements would come overland, and from shorter distances; Clark would have to get his to the beachhead by ship from as far away as Sicily and North Africa—or wait for Montgomery.

On the evening of September 9, the Hermann Göring Panzer Division in Naples and the 15th Panzergrenadier Division near Gaeta headed for the beach to become part of the XIV Panzer Corps fighting the British. Both divisions had been mauled in Sicily and were not yet at full strength; between them they had about 27,000 men, but only thirty-seven tanks and assault guns each. The 29th Panzergrenadier and the 26th Panzer divisions were ordered north from Calabria to join the 16th Panzer in the LXXVI Corps sector, facing the Americans.

The German buildup was hardly a textbook operation. Part of the 29th sat in Calabria for three days after their marching orders came. They had run out of gasoline. And the 26th Panzer, which had to march up through Calabria, where they had been holding up the British Eighth Army, were not only delayed by bad roads, but also by the need to leave the roads in even worse shape for Montgomery. Their last units straggled into the beachhead area the evening of September 12.

The Luftwaffe, meanwhile, had been stepping up its attacks on the invasion fleet. Responding to urgent appeals from General Balck that the Allies' devastatingly accurate naval fire must be stopped if German counterattacks were to have any chance of success, German fighters, fighter-bombers, and heavy bombers flew almost 550 sorties during the first three days. They scored eighty-five hits and sank four transports, one heavy cruiser, and seven landing craft. They also launched new weapons—radio-controlled glider and rocket bombs. (They had been available in Sicily, but were not used because Hitler wanted to keep them secret.) Containing 600 pounds of explosives and released from specially equipped high-altitude planes, they had a range of from three and a half to eight miles and a speed of 570 to 660 miles per hour. The bombs scored quick, dramatic successes. Two British warships and one American cruiser were put out of action, and others were damaged, forcing the Allied naval commander to call for reinforcements from Malta.

German artillerymen fighting the Americans near Salerno strain to load a rocket into a five-barreled launcher. The lethal weapon was labeled *Nebelwerfer*, or smoke thrower.

At the end of the fourth day, September 12, the Germans appeared to be in control of the beachhead. In the northern sector, their artillery fire was still denying the enemy the port of Salerno and the airfield at Montecorvino, two early Allied objectives. In the center they still held the heights at Battipaglia, and in the south the Altavilla heights, thus controlling the low flood plain that formed a V-shape corridor between the Sele and Calore rivers. The corridor was the rough dividing line between the British X Corps and the U.S. VI Corps. Ever since the landings, there had been an undefended gap between the two sectors; although the vulnerable area had now shrunk, it had still not entirely closed. A strong German attack there might punch all the way to the beach, split the defenses in two, and force the Allies to evacuate the beachhead.

When, on the morning of September 13, Vietinghoff confronted the existing gap, he could not believe that it was the result of tactical blunders; he felt instead, erroneously, that the enemy had voluntarily split into two sections in preparation for a withdrawal from the beachhead. He ordered an immediate attack to prevent them from escaping to their ships. From Battipaglia, Eboli, and Altavilla, about thirty tanks as well as infantry units of the 29th Panzergrenadier and 16th Panzer rolled down the corridor. They overran the thin defense, a single battalion of the U.S. 45th Division, and virtually destroyed it; the battalion lost more than 500 officers and enlisted men, most of them captured. By 5:30 p.m., Vietinghoff was so confident of victory there and elsewhere on the beachhead that he sent an exultant telegram to Kesselring: "Enemy resistance is collapsing." By 6:30 p.m., fifteen German tanks with supporting infantry had reached the juncture of the Sele and Calore rivers. Between the tanks and the gulf, two miles away, stood only a handful of American infantry troops and two battalions of 45th Division artillery.

The threat was so serious that Clark made hasty plans to move his beachhead command post, which was now only a few hundred yards behind the artillery, to the British sector. But the 45th Division artillery, guarded by an improvised infantry line of clerks, cooks, drivers, mechanics, and other noncombat troops, fired almost 4,000 rounds of ammunition into

A *Stürmgeschutz*, a 75-mm gun mounted on a tank chassis, blasts a British position above the Salerno beachhead in September 1943. Such self-propelled guns provided fearsome close-in artillery support for infantry units.

A British signalman *(left)* near Salerno hugs the earth as German shells explode nearby. The beach at Salerno, a stretch of flat sand in an otherwise craggy coastline, was such an obvious landing site for the Allies that the Germans were ready, and met them with fierce resistance.

the fields and woods where the German force had taken cover. By sunset the Germans were forced to withdraw.

Vietinghoff, however, was still confident that the Anglo-American beachhead was finished. "The battle of Salerno," the optimistic Tenth Army diarist wrote, "appears to be over."

Not quite. Late that night, in response to an urgent plea, General Clark—who had begun to despair that Montgomery's Eighth Army, still more than 100 miles away, would ever arrive in time to do any good—got help from another quarter. About ninety planes from Sicily glided low over the beachhead and dropped 1,300 paratroopers from the 82d Airborne Division to help plug gaps in the American lines and restore Allied morale. The next night, another 600 paratroopers were dropped behind German lines near Avellino to disrupt their communications, but that operation failed miserably. Dispersed over a wide area, the paratroopers were of little use in the battle, and 200 of them were taken prisoner.

Lieutenant Rocholl and the men of his reconnaissance company managed to capture more than their share of the paratroopers. On duty near Penta, a one-street village, Rocholl saw an "amazing sight, fifty to sixty paratroopers, still at the height of some 150 meters." Quickly overcoming the "moment of terror," he wrote in his diary, he roused the whole company: " 'To your arms! Prepare to fire!' Like cats the gunners sprang into the turrets, and soon fourteen 20-mm guns and some twenty MGs were firing on the descending enemy. This continued until the angle of fire became too small, and our men were in danger. 'Cease fire!' "

Then Rocholl and his men went through Penta searching house to house for the paratroopers. At the last house, Rocholl wrote, "I went up to the door and found it locked. Two of my men tried to force it and finally burst it open. At the same moment, three automatic rifles opened up from the house, and my men were lucky to escape injury. So that's where they were! One, two, three grenades were our prompt reply. A few bursts with our automatics, and we forced our way into the house. Pitch black! I risked it and flashed my torch round the room, calling out, 'hands up!' There were eight or ten paratroopers, apparently wounded, in the hallway. They blinked in the light and hesitantly raised their arms."

During the next two days, Rocholl's four-man foot patrols, their boots wrapped with rags to deaden their sound ("we did not have rubber soles like the Americans"), flushed another six paratroopers. That was the last entry in Lieutenant Rocholl's diary, which was found on his body after he was killed in action.

From September 14 to 16, Vietinghoff hammered at the perimeter of the beachhead. But now the Allies were throwing in the full weight of their superior air and naval power to support their beleaguered but strengthened ground forces. Hundreds of strategic bombers—B-25s, B-26s, and B-17s—were diverted to tactical use, plastering targets at Eboli, Battipaglia, and other key German positions. Even more than the aerial bombing, it was the volume and accuracy of naval artillery that proved crucial in breaking up German counterattacks, which had to be mounted in full view of battleships, cruisers, and destroyers. During the Salerno operation, Allied ships poured more than 11,000 tons of shells onto German targets. "With astonishing precision and freedom of maneuver," Vietinghoff marveled, "these ships shot at every recognized target with overwhelming effect."

Vietinghoff knew by September 16 that he could no longer dislodge the Allied forces. With Kesselring's reluctant permission, he began pulling his troops out two days later, satisfied that the Tenth Army had accomplished its mission. They had suffered about 3,500 casualties, but they had inflicted about 9,000 on the Allies. And they had certainly disrupted the enemy timetable for the capture of Naples. "Success has been ours," Vietinghoff proclaimed to his troops. "Once again German soldiers have proved their superiority over the enemy." Hitler agreed: He promoted Vietinghoff to the rank of colonel general.

As their units withdrew northward to new defensive positions, many German soldiers took one last look. "On the right in the mist," one wrote, "the towers of Salerno; in the center the gleaming gray strip of Montecorvino; the asphalt highway and railway near Battipaglia. Eboli down in the plain—and in the distance the sea. A warm wind blows up from the shore, taking no heed of the fresh graves lying in the shade of the olive trees."

Back on September 10, one day after the landings at Salerno, Kesselring had already mapped out his defensive plans north of the beachhead to deny the enemy Foggia, Naples, and, above all, Rome as long as possible. He ordered Vietinghoff to conduct a phased withdrawal to the north. The Tenth Army was to fight a series of delaying actions, using men and matériel as economically as possible, inflicting the maximum number of casualties, and giving ground slowly and only when confronted by overwhelming force. The object was to buy enough time to enable German engineers working with Italian crews to complete a series of fortified defensive lines that stretched all the way across Italy to the Adriatic. About eighteen miles north of Naples, the first of these lines, the Viktor, was thrown up along the Volturno River. Next came the Barbara, stretching from Mount Massico near the coast to the Matesian Mountains. Ten miles farther north was the Bernhardt Line, anchored on the mouth of the Garigliano River and running to the hulking mass of Mount Sammucro. Some twelve miles beyond the Bernhardt loomed the Gustav Line, the strongest of all, based on the Rapido River and the natural fortress of Monte Cassino. If the Tenth Army could buy enough time as it withdrew, Kesselring believed that the Gustav Line could be rendered so nearly impregnable that the enemy could be denied Rome for many months.

Kesselring had in his favor two formidable natural allies—terrain and weather. Below the Po Valley in the north, Italy is mostly one long range of mountains, the Apennines. Running like a jagged spine down the center of the country, the range forms a barrier separating east from west. Altitudes range from 2,500 to 6,000 feet. A series of ridges and river valleys fan out like fishbones toward narrow strips of coastline—only twenty-five miles wide on the west, ten miles on the east. Even in dry weather, the network of roads in southern Italy was barely adequate for modern divisions with motorized artillery and supply trains. In the fall and winter, snow and rain would turn dirt roads into quagmires, rivers into raging torrents. Tanks would be virtually useless except as stationary artillery, and air operations would be severely hampered.

The campaign, then, would be fought essentially by foot soldiers. The British Eighth Army on the Adriatic and the Fifth Army in the west, separated by steep mountains, would have to grind it out ridge by ridge, river by river, mile by muddy mile. In those conditions, the tactical advantage was with the resourceful defender, especially if there was time to prepare strongpoints. It would be the defender who dictated not only where the battle would be fought but also its pace. Kesselring's main worry was the Allies' potential for amphibious end runs around his defensive lines.

Kesselring had given Vietinghoff a tricky, difficult assignment. He had to break off close contact with the Allies at the beachhead, yet maintain enough rearguard fighting capability to ensure his retreating troops would not be overrun. At the same time, he had to extend his front eastward to link up with, and reinforce, the 1st Paratroop Division; reduced to only 8,000 men, it was the sole defense against the Eighth Army. To prepare for the expected main offensive against Naples, Vietinghoff had marshaled the bulk of his forces opposite the Fifth Army. Holding the Sorrento Peninsula north of Salerno as the pivot of the entire withdrawal line was the XIV Panzer Corps, made up largely of the Hermann Göring Panzer Division, two detached battalions of the 1st Paratroop, and the 3d and 15th Panzergrenadier divisions. The 15th and 16th Panzergrenadier were dispatched twenty miles north of Naples to prepare defensive positions along the Volturno River, the next defensive line in the withdrawal plan. Kesselring had ordered Vietinghoff not to allow the enemy to cross the Volturno before October 15. He also told him to wreck Naples harbor before he pulled out.

On September 17, the Tenth Army began pulling away from the beachhead. The 29th Panzergrenadier withdrew north and northeast, behind strong rear guards; two days later, the 26th Panzer moved out of the Battipaglia area. Both divisions were to link up by the end of the month with the 1st Paratroop as part of the LXXVI Corps defending the eastern flank.

The efficiency of Vietinghoff's defense became frustratingly apparent to the Fifth Army as soon as it began its attack on September 20. The 45th Division's first target was Oliveto Citra, ten miles northeast of Eboli; the 3d Division was to take Acerno, twelve miles away. The mountains were negotiable only over steep secondary roads with countless hairpin curves and narrow bridges. The retreating Germans had blown up more than twenty-five bridges between Paestum and Oliveto Citra alone, a road distance of about twenty miles. Repairing them or building bypasses with prefabricated steel bridges was time-consuming and dangerous. Often the Germans had small, well-concealed machine guns and artillery zeroed in on the blown bridges and other crossings. To bypass such roadblocks, small American infantry units, operating with little artillery support, had

Rain-soaked Germans lead pack mules along a muddy trail in southern Italy. Holdovers from past wars, always in short supply, mules provided practical transport through the rugged mountains that dominated the contested territory.

to climb up mined mountain slopes to drive out the German rear guards.

In front of the U.S. 3d Division sector, the Germans had blown the only bridge spanning a wide, deep gorge south of Acerno; dug in on the far side of the gorge to prevent engineers from erecting a temporary bridge was a rear guard of riflemen and machine gunners. The Americans would have to overcome them before they could capture the town. It took the leading regiment of the 3d Division, marching cross-country through the mountains, the better part of a day to do it.

Occasionally, the Allies would catch a glimpse of the German rearguard units through binoculars. According to one observer, they appeared to be "gaunt, unshaven men in shabby gray uniforms slinking away defiantly to repeat the same tactics a few miles back; the machine gunners carrying their much-feared MG 42 'Spandaus' over their shoulders and swathed with cross-belts of reserve ammunition, each rifleman similarly decorated and a stick grenade thrust handily down the leg of a muddy jackboot."

A scuttled vessel leans at a crazy angle against a pier littered with wreckage at the port of Naples in October 1943. In order to slow the Allied offensive, the retreating Germans methodically destroyed ships, warehouses, and dockside cranes. They even destroyed the waterworks and pasta factories of the city.

German paratroopers supported by a self-propelled gun *(left)* withdraw through Naples toward the end of September, pressured by the Allied advance from Salerno. The Allies captured Naples on October 1.

On the western flank of the Salerno front, meanwhile, the British X Corps launched the main Allied drive for Naples. The 46th and 56th divisions and American Ranger battalions attacked through the two major passes in the Sorrento hills. Once through the passes and onto the plain of Naples, the road to the city would allow the deployment of the British 7th Armored Division. Despite heavy artillery support, however, the offensive made little progress during the first three days. Troops of the Hermann Göring Panzer Division, who were dug in on heights flanking the passes, turned back every thrust. Not until October 1, ten days after the drive began, did the first armored patrols, from the King's Dragoon Guards, enter the city. By then, the Germans were already moving toward their first major defensive position, the Viktor line, anchored on the Volturno River.

The Germans in Naples had used the ten days that they had gained by their defense with ruthless efficiency. Following Kesselring's specific instructions, they did not touch historic buildings, museums, churches, monasteries, or hospitals. But everything else that could not be shipped north was demolished, booby-trapped, or mined—power plants, bridges, railroad tracks, radio stations, sewer and water lines, petroleum storage tanks, even wineries and breweries. The port, the primary Allied objective, was rendered useless.

When Fifth Army troops entered Naples, they found a shattered, ghostly city. Half the population of 800,000 had fled to the countryside; those who remained had had little to eat for more than a week, another burden the

Anglo-Americans had to assume. So thorough had been the German demolition that, although engineers took only about two weeks to partially restore the port facilities, it would be three months before the Allied military government could restore normal city life.

Even before the capture of Naples, Eisenhower had decided to reach for the gold ring—Rome. His intelligence reports, bolstered as usual by Ultra, up to then had indicated that the Germans would make a major defensive stand only north of Rome. What he did not anticipate was that Hitler would change his mind. On October 1, Hitler too decided that Rome was worth fighting for. Encouraged by Kesselring's successes in delaying the enemy advance and temperamentally loath to surrender *any* territory without a fight, he ordered that the main defense was no longer to be made in the northern Apennines, but south of Rome, at the Gustav Line. To bolster defenses there, he would send Kesselring three fresh divisions from Rommel's northern command by mid-October. Although Hitler was still worried about the possibility of amphibious landings north of his troops (he and the OKW continued to overestimate Allied capability in that field), he felt that the approaching winter made such attacks less likely. Both Hitler and Kesselring thought that the Allies, having secured the excellent airbase complex at Foggia on September 27, would halt their advance in Italy and prepare for an attack across the Adriatic into the Balkans.

In the west, German Tenth Army forces continued their slow, tenacious withdrawal; in the seven days since the loss of Naples, they had retreated only about twenty miles, to the Volturno area. In the east, however, General Richard Heidrich's 1st Paratroop Division had been hard pressed to fend off Montgomery's Eighth Army. After violent fighting, the Germans had been forced to withdraw from the Foggia area to higher ground north of the Biferno River. Meanwhile, on October 2, the British 78th Division was preparing an amphibious assault on the small port of Termoli, about two miles northwest of the mouth of the Biferno. The next morning, when a British force of 1,000 came ashore at Termoli, General Heidrich, fearful that an end run was about to envelop his men, ordered a withdrawal. About 130 German paratroopers were killed, and 200 taken prisoner. Heidrich hastily slipped out of town on foot, "kindly leaving behind," a ranking officer of the 78th later wrote, "his car, a 1939 Horch, long, low, black, and very fast."

When reports of the British commando landing reached Kesselring, he immediately ordered the 16th Panzer to Termoli to contain the beachhead. Since its ordeal at Salerno, the division had been reorganizing in a rest area north of the Volturno, but it was the only reserve unit available. Vietinghoff disputed the wisdom of Kesselring's order; he believed the 16th Panzer could be of much more use in helping to defend the Volturno when the

A Succession of Bristling Defensive Lines

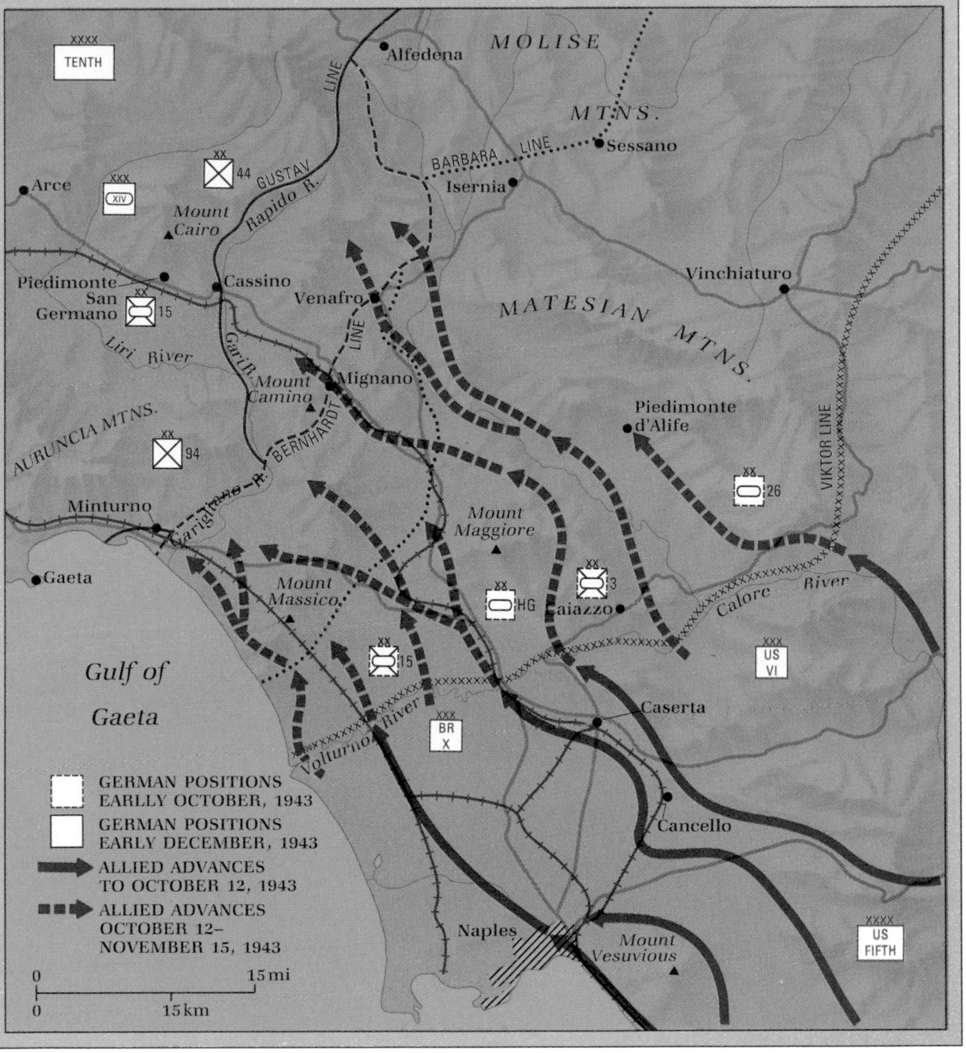

After falling back from Salerno, the retreating Germans turned every topographical impediment into a hornet's nest for the oncoming Allies. Moving slowly northward, the outnumbered German Tenth Army first dug in along the Viktor Line, where they hammered the Allies who were struggling to cross the Volturno River. Then the Germans moved on to the hastily developed Barbara Line, anchored on Mount Massico, where they held for two weeks before retreating to the Bernhardt Line, which guarded the Mignano Gap and the road to Rome. Only in early December did the Germans finally give way again, falling back to the even more formidable Gustav Line for the winter.

time came. The argument between the two officers caused the tanks and infantry to start off four hours behind schedule. After a forced march of ninety-five miles, the units were committed to battle piecemeal and inefficiently, and although the Luftwaffe made one of its increasingly rare appearances in support, they were unable to oust the British from the Termoli beachhead. The Germans were forced to withdraw to a new defensive line at the Trigno River on October 7.

The contending armies now faced each other on a broad front across two river barriers—the Volturno on the west, the Trigno on the east. To block Fifth Army attempts to cross the Volturno, Vietinghoff had 35,000 XIV Panzer Corps troops entrenched on the north bank. In the Adriatic sector, to hold off the British Eighth Army, were 25,000 men of the LXXVI Panzer Corps.

The Volturno, 150 to 300 feet wide, meanders almost 100 miles between banks 10 to 25 feet high. Its depth, normally 1 to 6 feet, would allow fording at some points. Recent rains had so swollen the river and increased the speed of its current, however, that at many points, crossing was possible only in assault boats. Levees, 10 to 15 feet high, provided excellent machine-gun and mortar positions for the XIV Panzer Corps. It was an almost ideal defensive line. But Vietinghoff had a big problem: His front-line troops were stretched so thin, and his reserves for counterattacks were so few, that he would be unable to hold the line very long.

Fortunately for him, the rains had forced Fifth Army commanders to postpone the attack for three days. Not until 2:00 a.m. on October 13 did units of the U.S. 3d Division, crossing on foot, in assault boats, and on improvised log rafts, begin clambering up the muddy slopes of the north bank in the central sector. The site of the crossing and the force of the attack so surprised soldiers of the defending Hermann Göring Panzer Division that they were badly bloodied and had to give ground. By the next morning, the 3d Division, suffering only 300 casualties, had carved out an unassailable, four-mile-deep bridgehead. Vietinghoff, who up to that point had not

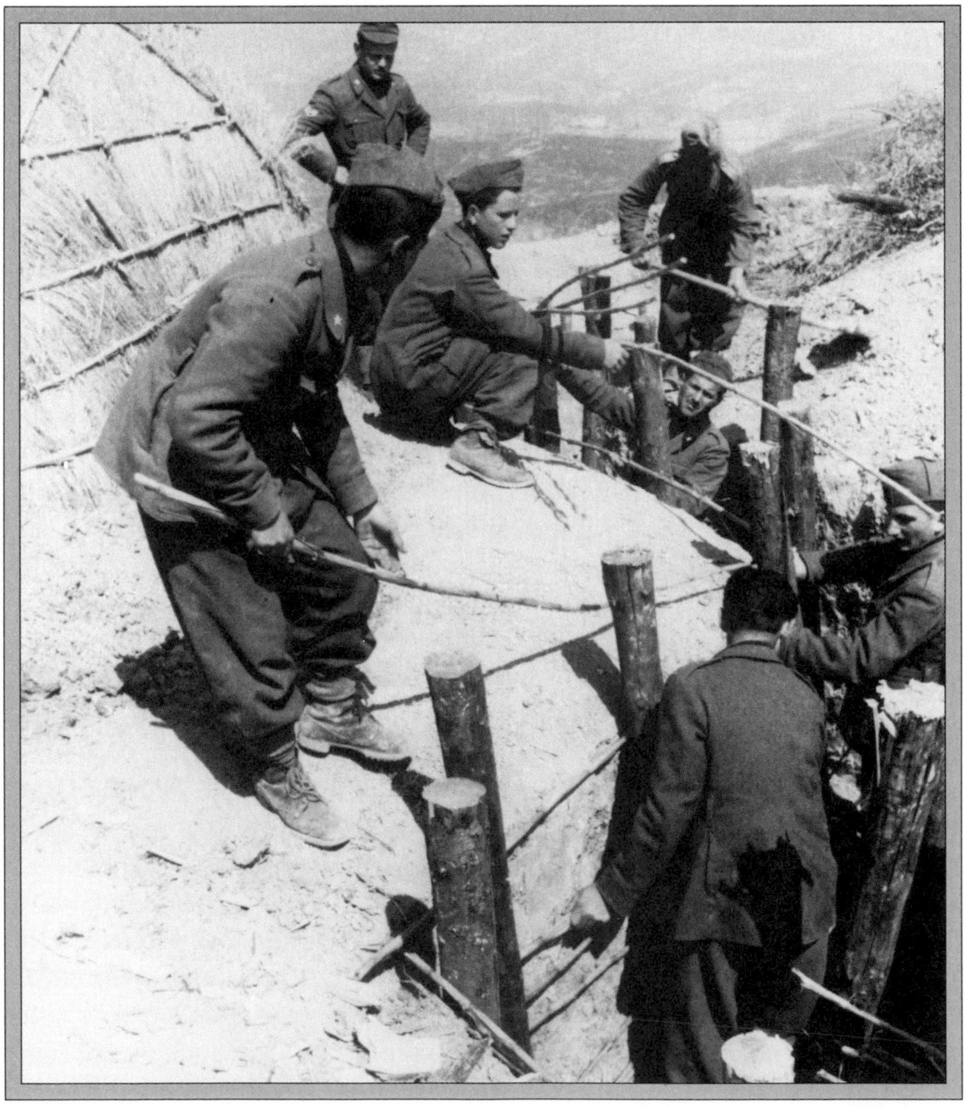

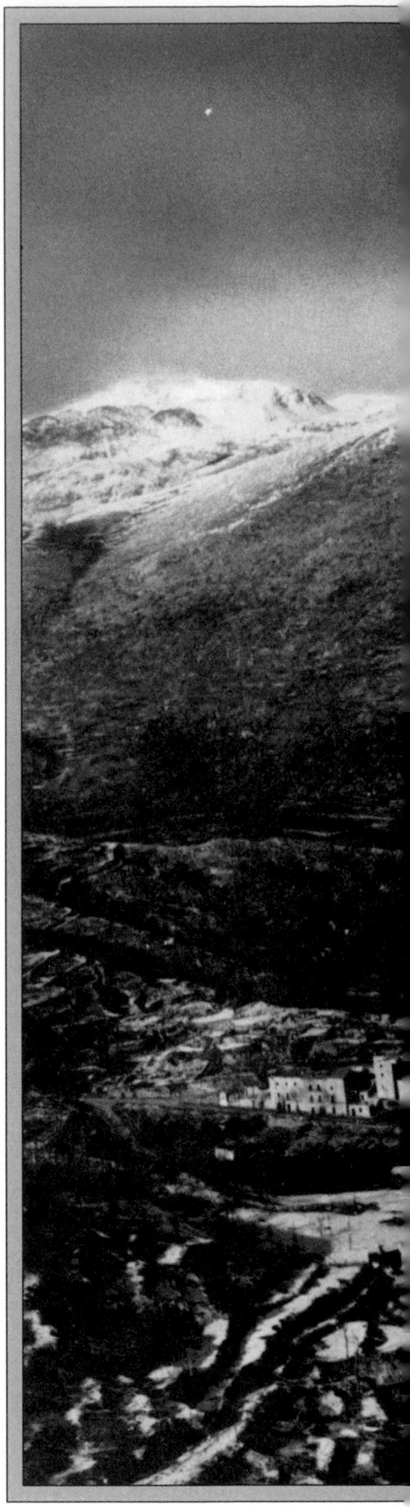

The formidable Gustav Line ran along these snow-clad peaks above the hill village of Acquafondata, in the foreground.

High in the Apennines *(left)*, German soldiers supervise Italian prisoners of war at work building fortifications in the Bernhardt Line at the village of Monte Trocchio. The site dominates the valley of the Rapido River, far below.

been much impressed by either the generalship or the fighting abilities of the Allies, was prompted to acknowledge the "very cleverly planned and forcefully executed attack."

On the Hermann Göring Panzer Division's left flank, units of the 3d Panzergrenadier, who had just arrived and barely settled into their defensive positions when troops of the U.S. 34th Division crossed the river, withdrew in disarray, offering little resistance. However, German artillery thwarted American attempts to build bridges, which were necessary to move tanks and artillery forward.

On the Germans' right flank, the 15th Panzergrenadier repulsed initial attempts by three divisions of the British X Corps to establish a foothold on the north bank of the Trigno River, hitting again and again to force them back to the south bank. During the first day of the fighting, the grenadiers killed or wounded 400 British soldiers and captured more than 200.

By October 15, still on Kesselring's timetable, Vietinghoff ordered a withdrawal along the entire Tenth Army line. In the Adriatic sector, the LXXVI Panzer Corps disengaged from the Eighth Army and fell back to another river, the Sangro. There, the 65th Infantry Division was already building field fortifications that would become the eastern end of the Gustav Line.

Like punch-drunk fighters, pursuer and pursued resumed their slugging match in the jagged terrain that lay between the Volturno River and the Barbara Line. As the Germans moved behind that line, their resistance grew even more stubborn. They had refined their tactics and made them deadlier. Portable pillboxes containing machine-gun crews and hauled from place to place by tractors were shielded with five inches of armor. Tanks used as artillery were buried up to their turrets to offer smaller targets.

Gun positions and command and observation posts were situated in mountain caves blasted out of solid rock. Sometimes the frustrated attackers could actually see their tormentors observing them from on high. An American sergeant with the Fifth Army recounted his experience with a German observer he called Rudolph. The German spotter lived "in an impregnable cave atop a mountain commanding all the valley approaches. He could be seen easily on occasion—whenever the sun came out, he would sun himself—but hit, never. The 4.2s (mortars) tried it almost daily, and when they wearied, they would mark it for nearby TDs (tank-destroyers) that came up every afternoon for a crack; 57s shot at him and 105s and doubtless many other caliber weapons. But after all the shooting was over, Rudolph could still emerge for his sunbath; not until his position was outflanked did he pull out."

The Tenth Army's delaying tactics had also allowed German personnel in the rear sufficient time to lay extensive minefields. Some 75,000 mines were strewn in the approaches to the Bernhardt Line. There were two kinds—equally feared by foot soldiers. One was the Bouncing Betty, which would leap several feet into the air before exploding and hurl shrapnel in every direction. Also vicious was the little *Schu* mine, whose wooden case could not be located by conventional mine detectors, which responded only to metal. Set off on contact, it seldom killed a soldier outright; it blew off a foot or tore open his groin.

Vietinghoff was still on schedule when he withdrew from the Barbara Line on November 1. But instead of a hearty "well done" from Kesselring, he was dressed down for failing to hold the line longer. Stung by the

Two German soldiers look down on the body of a comrade as a warrant officer makes out the required record of the details of his death. The infantryman was killed in the bloody defense of the Volturno River.

criticism, Vietinghoff asked for, and was granted, a six-week sick leave. During his absence, the Tenth Army would be commanded by Lieut. General Joachim Lemelsen.

The Bernhardt Line had been designed to guard the Mignano Gap, a winding six-mile corridor through which Highway 6 ran en route to the Liri Valley—and the city of Rome. Dominating the gap on both sides were steep mountains—Camino, La Difensa, Maggiore, Sammucro—rising as high as 3,000 feet. German engineers had created a wide belt of defensive positions linking the mountains and the Garigliano River to the west. Vietinghoff had ordered that command posts be put underground and that the main entrenchments be dug in on the rear slopes in order to avoid the direct impact of enemy artillery. Only outposts were to guard the crests and forward slopes.

To get through the Mignano Gap, the Fifth Army would first have to take the dominant mountains one by one, in terrain so steep that even pack mules often could not carry food and ammunition to the troops; where carrier pigeons at times were the only means of communication; where flocks of sheep and goats had to be driven first through minefields to clear passage for foot soldiers. For eight days in cold, wet weather, the 15th Panzergrenadier, still wearing the light summer uniforms they had originally been issued for Italy, repulsed every attack by the British 56th Division. Nearby, the U.S. 3d Division fought for ten days trying to take Mount La Difensa, suffering heavy losses on slopes so steep and rocky that it took six hours to get wounded men down from the mountain. The Allies finally had to call off the offensive.

By then, November 15, General Clark realized that his exhausted divisions, five of which had been on line since Salerno, could go no farther. He called a halt to all Fifth Army offensive operations for two weeks, to rest and regroup. It rained on them heavily every day of the pause.

On the Adriatic front, the British Eighth Army had bogged down before the Sangro River; in five weeks it had advanced only 30 miles. When it resumed its offensive on November 20, its new objective was Pescara, 150 miles up the coast to the north. The capture of that key port and road junction, Allied planners hoped, might force Kesselring to give up the Gustav Line and withdraw north of Rome to avoid being outflanked. Facing the Eighth Army were three German divisions: the untested 65th; the experienced but understrength 16th Panzer, awaiting transfer to the Russian front; and the tough 1st Paratroop. In the first two days of the attack, the 65th was virtually annihilated. Kesselring hurriedly sent help: The 26th Panzer raced over from the Bernhardt Line, and the 90th Panzergrenadier moved down from northern Italy. After more than two weeks of bitter fighting, Montgomery's advance ground to a halt on impassable roads, in mountain passes deep in snow. In spite of heavy casualties, the Germans had held—fifteen miles south of Pescara, blocking the back door to Rome.

In the west, the Fifth Army had resumed its battering against the front door. On December 1, the Americans began an all-out offensive against the mountains guarding the Mignano Gap, accompanied by such massive artillery bombardment that General Frido von Senger und Etterlin, who was now in command of the XIV Panzer Corps, was "astounded and dismayed. I had not witnessed such since the big battles of the First World War." The few battalions of the Hermann Göring Panzer Division he had in reserve could do little to hold back the Allies. On December 6, survivors of the undermanned 15th Panzergrenadier defending the summit of Mount Camino pulled out. On the same day, German-organized resistance also ceased in the La Difensa-Maggiore mountain complex.

The Fifth Army now controlled the entrance to the Mignano Gap. But in the middle of the corridor, two mountains—Luongo and Sammucro—still blocked the road to the Liri Valley. Hitler, who now insisted on approving every major military decision in Italy, countermanded an earlier order for a general withdrawal from the Bernhardt Line and ordered that San Pietro Infine, a village on the lower slopes of Mount Sammucro, be held at all costs by the 29th Panzergrenadier. In ten days, they turned back three attacks by the U.S. 36th Division; they finally withdrew on December 16.

German rear guards would hold up the Fifth Army for almost another month before withdrawing, at last, to the main defensive position at the abbey of Monte Cassino on the Gustav Line. In the six weeks since the

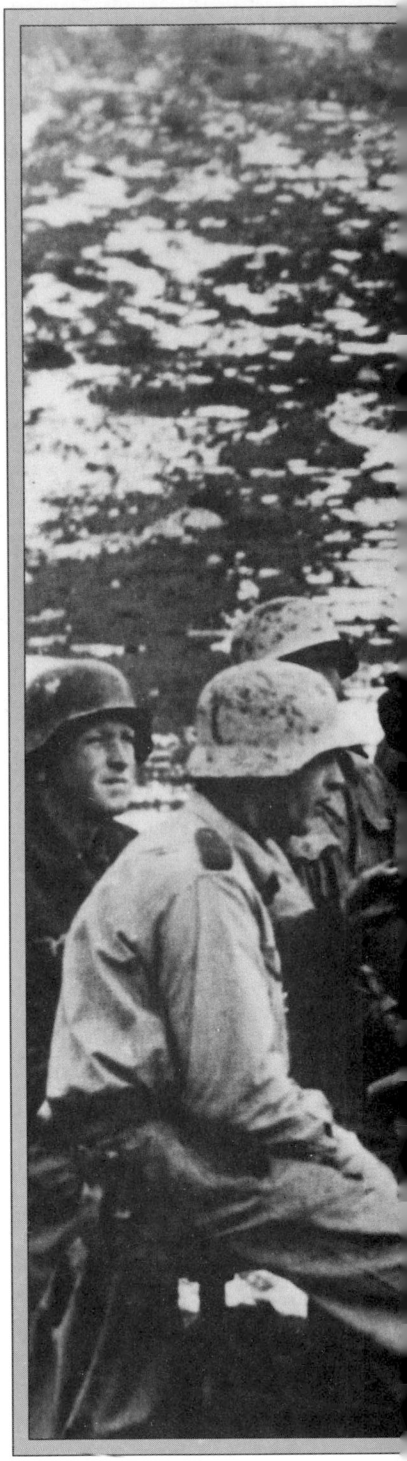

Braced for the arrival of Allied warplanes, the German crew of a four-barreled antiaircraft gun watches the skies above snow-covered Mount Camino and the Bernhardt Line in December 1943. The Allies mounted 886 bombing sorties against Mount Camino in only two days.

beginning of their December offensive, the Americans had managed to advance only seven miles in the central sector. For Kesselring, it was the vindication of his optimism and his defensive strategy. On November 21, Hitler put his personal cachet on both by finally choosing Kesselring over Rommel as commander of all forces in Italy. For the first time in the campaign, Kesselring had roughly the same number of ground troops as the Allies, in a tactical situation where normally the attacker should have a three-to-one superiority. He lacked air and naval support, but the terrain and the weather were greater friends than ever. And by now, the Gustav Line was so strongly fortified and defended, he believed, that the "British and Americans would break their teeth on it." ✚

The Destruction of Monte Cassino

In the winter of 1943-1944, Allied troops advancing on Rome found their route of attack blocked by an imposing eminence called Monte Cassino. Situated seventy-five miles southeast of the Eternal City, this rocky spur of the Apennines soared 1,700 feet above the surrounding Liri Valley. Nestled at its foot was the town of Cassino with 25,000 residents. At its crest was the abbey of Monte Cassino, a complex of buildings, courtyards, and crypts surrounded by the thick stone walls of a four-story dormitory. Founded in 529 by Saint Benedict of Nursia, the monastery was the birthplace of the Benedictine order, indeed, of Western monasticism. It was leveled twice by invading armies and once by an earthquake, but the monks stubbornly rebuilt it after each disaster. The abbey was not only a center of Christian study but also a storehouse for the treasures of the Benedictine order. Priceless paintings by Titian, Goya, and El Greco adorned its walls, and manuscripts by Ovid, Horace, and Cicero lay among the 70,000 documents stored in its archives.

Although Allied and Axis leaders had agreed not to wantonly destroy cultural and historic monuments, some Allied commanders suspected the Germans had seized and fortified the abbey, thereby making it a valid target. In fact, however, General Frido von Senger und Etterlin, head of the XIV Panzer Corps, realized that a landmark as conspicuous as the abbey would attract fire and had ordered his men to dig in farther down the mountain and on neighboring ridges. The monastery was still off-limits to German soldiers when Allied bombers blasted it on February 15, 1944, killing scores of civilian refugees sheltered inside.

In early 1944, the abbey of Monte Cassino sits unscathed atop its rocky peak while bombs explode on a hill above the town of Cassino *(foreground)*. Most of the abbey, including its central courtyard *(inset, top)* and its basilica *(inset, bottom)*, dated from a seventeenth-century restoration by baroque artisans.

Shipping Relics to Rome

In October 1943, as Allied bombs exploded at his doorstep, the seventy-nine-year-old abbot Gregorio Diamare accepted German offers to truck his monks and Monte Cassino's treasures to Rome. A German film crew recorded the chaos as Germans, monks, and civilian refugees packed chalices, scrolls, paintings, and other precious objects into crates and then loaded them onto trucks.

To prevent theft, Diamare insisted that two monks accompany each truckload of property. By mid-November, most of the monks and more than 100 truckloads of treasure had safely reached two monasteries in Rome, Saint Anselm's and Saint Paul's. Some items sent to Monte Cassino for safekeeping by state museums in Naples were pilfered at the Hermann Göring Panzer Division's Spoleto headquarters. Most of the state's property, however, was turned over to Italian authorities in Rome.

For men who had vowed to spend their entire lives at Monte Cassino, leaving was a wrenching experience. Abbot Diamare, his young secretary, Martino Matronola, and eight other monks stayed behind to look after their home and to comfort the hundreds of distraught civilians who had flocked there from nearby villages.

In October 1943, German soldiers, many of them carpenters, hammer together packing crates for Monte Cassino's valuables.

Abbot Gregorio Diamare *(wearing a crucifix)* sadly turns over a reliquary to a German officer, Lieut. Col. Julius Schlegel, for transport to Rome.

In December 1943, trucks loaded with abbey valuables lumber toward Castel Sant'Angelo in Rome.

Amici italiani,

ATTENZIONE!

Noi abbiamo sinora cercato in tutti i modi di evitare il bombardamento del monastero di Montecassino. I tedeschi hanno saputo trarre vantaggio da ciò. Ma ora il combattimento si è ancora più stretto attorno al Sacro Recinto. E venuto il tempo in cui a malincuore siamo costretti a puntare le nostre armi contro il Monastero stesso.

Noi vi avvertiamo perché voi abbiate la possibilità di porvi in salvo. Il nostro avvertimento è urgente: Lasciate il Monastero. Andatevene subito. Rispettate questo avviso. Esso è stato fatto a vostro vantaggio.

LA QUINTA ARMATA.

Italian friends,

BEWARE!

We have until now been especially careful to avoid shelling the Monte Cassino Monastery. The Germans have known how to benefit from this. But now the fighting has swept closer and closer to its sacred precincts. The time has come when we must train our guns on the Monastery itself.

We give you warning so that you may save yourselves. We warn you urgently: Leave the Monastery. Leave it at once. Respect this warning. It is for your benefit.

THE FIFTH ARMY.

Black smoke envelops Monte Cassino during the Allied bombing on February 15. The previous day, American howitzers had

fired twenty-five rounds of shells stuffed with leaflets warning of the attack *(inset)*.

A Lethal Rain of Allied Bombs

From late January until early February, shelling of the town of Cassino and the surrounding region increased as the Allies launched a major ground assault against German positions. Although the monastery was still off-limits for both sides, stray shells slammed into it with such frequency that the monks were forced to take shelter in underground rooms and passageways. Subterranean space was available for a handful of refugee families, but most of the townspeople had to find what shelter they could aboveground.

After weeks of bloody fighting ended in a stalemate, General Sir Harold Alexander, head of the Allied forces in the region, gave the order to destroy the monastery, despite bitter opposition from many of his senior officers. After Allies dropped leaflets on February 14 warning of the imminent bombing, Diamare announced to all in the abbey that they were on their own. The monks chose to stay and look after the sick and injured. Some refugees who tried to flee were stopped at the gate by German soldiers, who feared the escapees would divulge precious information to the Allies. In eight attacks, 239 bombers dropped 576 tons of bombs on the monastery during the daylight hours of February 15. Upon hearing the blasts from his headquarters at Castel Massimo to the north, Senger muttered to himself, "The idiots! They've done it after all. All our efforts were in vain."

Two days after the Allied bombing, refugees leave the abbey. Despite a monk's warning that they made an easy target for planes, the frightened survivors refused to spread out as they headed down the mountain.

General Frido von Senger und Etterlin, a devout Catholic and member of a Benedictine lay organization, helps Abbot Diamare into the car that took the elderly monk to Rome.

Flight to Safety

For two days, the Benedictines huddled in their underground chapel and clung to the hope that Vatican pressure on the Allies would achieve at least a temporary truce. Above them, bombs burst, buildings collapsed, and cloisters crumbled, crushing men, women, and children under heaps of masonry. Most survivors, including four monks, escaped during lulls in the assault by descending the mountain along a rocky mule path that led away from the fighting.

On the morning of February 17, before the Allies renewed their assault, Diamare took matters into his own hands. At 7:30, the abbot, his frail frame stooped by a large wooden cross slung over one shoulder, began to lead his monks and forty other survivors down the mountain path. They walked for some three hours before stopping for rest and food at a German first-aid shelter. An ambulance arrived late that afternoon and drove Diamare and Matronola to Senger's headquarters. The next morning, Diamare, with Matronola at his side, denounced the bombing during an interview with German radio. After reaching Rome later that day in a car provided by Senger, the two men were reunited at Saint Anselm's with their fellow monks from Monte Cassino.

Holding Out in the Rubble

Not long after Diamare and his charges left the monastery, German troops of the 1st Paratroop Division moved in. The bombing had turned the abbey into an excellent defensive position. Piles of rubble transformed courtyards into obstacle courses, while cellars and underground corridors of destroyed buildings now served as trenches. The paratroopers defended their stronghold until May 18. Polish troops who reached the monastery the next morning found that most of the Germans had slipped away. The bodies of dozens of civilians lay buried beneath the rubble.

A German major briefs his troops amid the abbey ruins.

In April 1944, German paratroopers man a machine gun amid the jumbled stones of bombed-out Monte Cassino.

Two German soldiers pick their way through the rubble-filled courtyard of the monastery.

The Long Road Back

Immediately after the Allied attack, the Nazi propaganda machine launched its own offensive. A German news agency trumpeted, "The monastery has been destroyed several times by barbarians. Today, these barbarians are called British and Americans, whose wish is to exterminate these phenomena of superior European civilization." For decades, the Allies stubbornly justified the bombing by insisting that the monastery was being held by Germans at the time. Not until 1969 did the U.S. Army quietly admit that the abbey was actually unoccupied by German troops.

Even before the war had ended, the Benedictines, with manpower supplied by Italian soldiers and German prisoners, painstakingly began to rebuild their abbey for the fourth time in its history. Forty years later, the restoration was nearly completed.

One year after the bombing, a Benedictine monk trudges up a rock-strewn road leading to the main gate of Monte Cassino. Although the monastery lay in ruins, many monks returned in 1945 and, in hastily improvised quarters, reestablished their lives while reconstruction of the abbey took place around them.

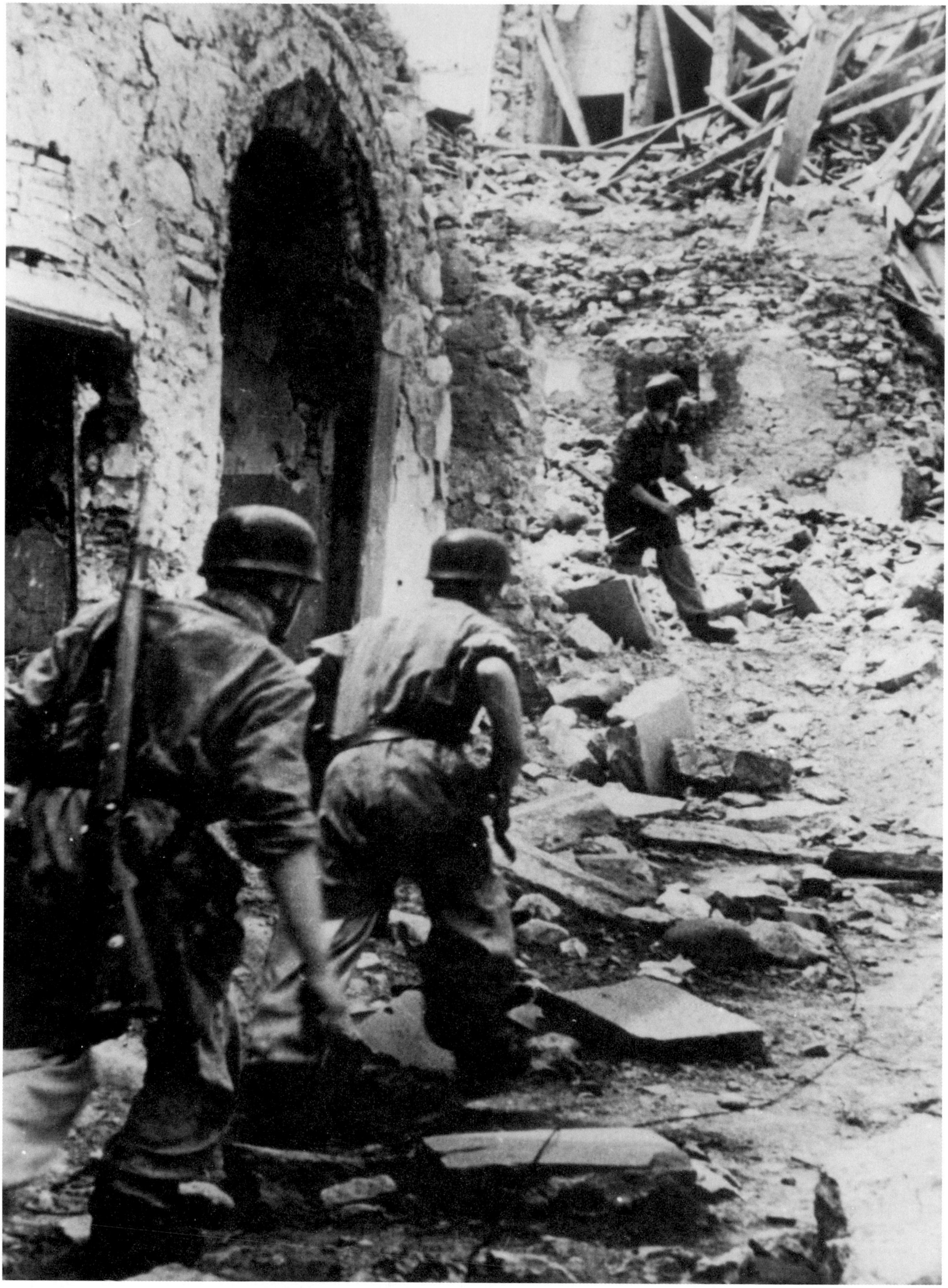

FOUR

The Eternal City and Beyond

After a brief lull in late December of 1943, the 15th Army Group commander, General Sir Harold Alexander, ordered a resumption of the drive on the Gustav Line. The U.S. II Corps, led by Major General Geoffrey Keyes, launched the main assault, attacking German strongpoints blocking the direct approach to Cassino on either side of Highway 6. The Americans were supported on the left by the British X Corps and on the right by the newly arrived French Expeditionary Corps. The French force, led by General Alphonse-Pierre Juin, provided the Allies with a welcome infusion of fresh troops. It consisted of the Algerian 3d and the Moroccan 2d divisions, tough colonial troops skilled in mountain warfare. As the first French soldiers to face the Germans since the humiliating defeat of France in 1940, the newcomers were spoiling for a fight.

During two weeks of combat in freezing weather, the Allies clawed their way forward several miles, to the Rapido and Garigliano rivers. Ordered to avoid heavy casualties, the German 44th Division and units from the 15th Panzergrenadier Division bought time for their comrades to strengthen the field fortifications along the swift-flowing rivers and amid the craggy mountain peaks and ravines. Then they pulled back.

The German engineers had made the most of the opportunity. They had created an ingenious and lethal defensive network, enlarging caves and blasting holes in the rock for gun emplacements, building hundreds of bombproof bunkers, mortar pits, and machine-gun nests, leveling houses and trees to improve fields of fire, strewing hillsides with thickets of barbed wire, and sewing mines everywhere. According to General Siegfried Westphal, Field Marshal Albert Kesselring's chief of staff, "The troops were told emphatically that the time of delaying actions was over, and that now rocklike defense was needed."

Kesselring was under enormous pressure to stop the Allies here. Since mid-December, the German high command had demanded that he submit daily progress reports on defenses in the Cassino sector. The Führer himself was monitoring the situation closely. The entire area, including the

Soldiers of the crack 1st Paratroop Division scramble through the wrecked town of Cassino in March 1944. After taking over the defense of the town and nearby Monte Cassino in late February, the German paratroopers held on tenaciously for more than two months.

world-renowned Benedictine monastery atop Monte Cassino, was about to become a bloody battlefield contested in increments of feet and inches.

At his headquarters in Frascati, a resort town in the Alban Hills southeast of Rome, Kesselring interpreted the Allied movements as a prelude to another amphibious invasion. "The hard fighting of recent months had convinced me that the Allies' reckless expenditure of troops must conceal some ulterior objective," he wrote. "I did not believe that Alexander could be satisfied for much longer with the slow and costly way the Allied front was edging forward. Sooner or later he must surely end it by a landing." The questions were—when and where? To counter the threat, Kesselring overrode the protests of General Heinrich von Vietinghoff, the Tenth Army commander in charge of the Gustav Line defenses, and withdrew the veteran 29th and 90th Panzergrenadier divisions, numbering about 25,000 men, and placed them in reserve outside Rome.

Naples was the obvious base for launching an Allied amphibious operation. Kesselring knew from intelligence reports that American engineers had repaired the damage inflicted on the port during the German pullout the previous September and that the harbor currently held about 350,000 tons of shipping. But with the Allies controlling the skies, reconnaissance flights could not get through to determine the whereabouts of Allied aircraft carriers, warships, and landing craft, or to locate other evidence of an imminent assault from the sea.

The appearance at Frascati of Admiral Wilhelm Canaris, head of the Abwehr, failed to clarify the picture. The high command's intelligence chief advised that while there was sufficient shipping in the Naples harbor to launch an expedition, there was "not the slightest sign that a new landing will be undertaken in the immediate future." Kesselring was not wholly convinced, but Westphal informed the field commanders that a landing was "out of the question for the next four to six weeks."

Allied leaders had been debating the wisdom of an additional amphibious invasion of Italy's west coast for months. Winston Churchill, the most forceful advocate of the idea, wanted to break the stagnation on the Italian front and seize Rome with a single bold stroke. The Americans were less enthusiastic. They reminded the British prime minister of the promises given to Stalin at the Tehran Conference in November of 1943. The Allies had assured the Soviet dictator that they would open a second front in the spring of 1944 by launching Overlord, a cross-channel invasion of northwestern France, and Anvil, a secondary invasion of southern France near Marseilles. Given the limited supply of landing craft and the need to build up for those operations, yet another seaborne invasion seemed impossible.

Armed with a *Panzerfaust* antitank weapon, a panzergrenadier awaits an Allied attack near Cassino. The *Panzerfaust* consisted of a simple steel tube and an armor-piercing charge.

The final decision had come only on December 28, when President Franklin Roosevelt gave his approval. To ensure the necessary shipping, Roosevelt agreed to delay until early February the departure of nearly five dozen landing craft from the Mediterranean theater to Britain for use in Overlord. Churchill's hope was that the Allies would seize Rome well before the cross-channel attack was due to begin.

Alexander and General Mark Clark, the American Fifth Army commander, gave Major General John Lucas of the U.S. VI Corps the responsibility for directing the invasion. He would command an Anglo-American force that would come ashore at the ancient town of Anzio, thirty-five miles south of Rome and about sixty-two miles behind the western end of the Gustav Line. Separated from Rome by the Alban Hills, Anzio lay in open, low terrain favorable to amphibious invaders and possessed a sheltered anchorage for supply ships. Alexander and Clark hoped that by landing in the rear of Kesselring's forces, they could cut his communications and make him evacuate the Gustav Line. Several days prior to the landing, the remainder of the Fifth Army would attack along the Gustav Line to draw in the German reserves and pin down Vietinghoff's entire army.

Each of Clark's four corps faced unenviable tasks. On the Allied left, the British X Corps was to cross the lower section of the fast-flowing Garigliano River. On the right, Juin's French colonial troops were to seize the steep mountains along the tangled upper reaches of the Rapido River, north and northwest of Cassino. The culminating effort was to take place in the center, where the U.S. II Corps would cross the Rapido at Sant'Angelo, two miles southeast of Cassino. A successful assault would open up the entrance to the Liri Valley, the conqueror's route to Rome from the south. If everything worked perfectly, Lucas's troops would break out of the Anzio beachhead and join the other Fifth Army troops for the march on Rome.

The British attacked on the moonless night of January 17, 1944, five days after the French corps had begun its mission in the mountains. Supported by heavy air, naval, and artillery bombardments, the troops crossed the Garigliano near its estuary in assault boats and tank landing craft. The German positions, held by the untested 94th Infantry Division, were widely dispersed. Vietinghoff had hoped that the swift current and the 24,000 mines that had been sown along both banks would discourage a crossing. But in the first twenty-four hours, the British ferried ten battalions to the opposite shore. They advanced three miles to the town of Minturno on the left of their line and two miles into the hills on the right—a few more miles, and they would outflank Monte Cassino.

General Frido von Senger und Etterlin, commander of the XIV Panzer Corps defending the western section of the line, quickly realized the danger. With no time to consult Vietinghoff, he telephoned Kesselring, urging him to commit the reserve divisions. When apprised of the crisis, Vietinghoff supported Senger's request.

Kesselring now faced a difficult decision. If he ordered the reserves to the front, Rome would be virtually undefended against an amphibious landing. An argument ensued at his headquarters. His chief of staff, Westphal, opposed the move. He interpreted the British attack as a feint to draw troops away from the beaches. Perhaps, Kesselring agreed. But an Allied landing had not materialized, and the threat to the Gustav Line was a reality. The field marshal sided with his field commanders. He dispatched the two divisions to the front. "The fate of the Tenth Army's right wing hung by a slender thread," Kesselring later explained. "If I let down the Tenth Army commander, his right wing might be driven in, and no one could tell where the retreat might stop."

Kesselring's action paid quick dividends. On January 19, the British tried to get a brigade across the river several miles upstream to protect the left flank of the Americans, who were scheduled to attack the next day. This time the German 94th Division, stiffened by the reserve units, stopped the British, and a counterattack the next day regained some of the lost ground.

Despite the German success in checking the British, Clark ordered Keyes to proceed with the Rapido River crossing at Sant'Angelo on January 20. Keyes had assigned the task to the U.S. 36th Division, the Texas National

An Allied Surprise at Anzio

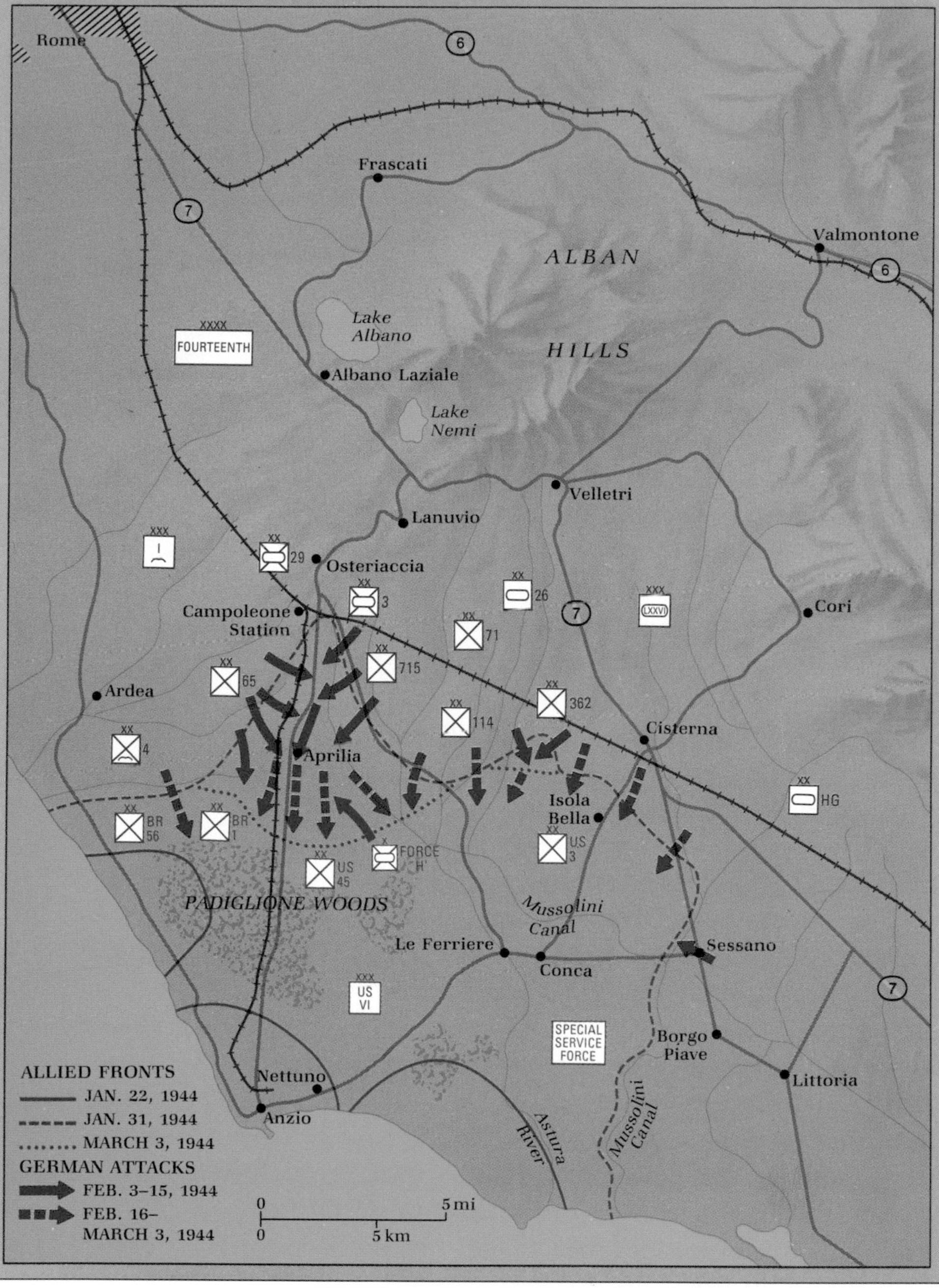

On January 22, 1943, the U.S. VI Corps came ashore at Anzio on Italy's west coast, catching Kesselring off guard. He had just sent off the bulk of his reserves to counter a fresh Allied offensive against the Gustav Line, leaving the coast south of Rome virtually undefended. But the Allies advanced cautiously, giving Kesselring time to assemble a powerful force drawn from no less than eight divisions and placed under Mackensen's Fourteenth Army. The Germans struck in the first week of February, driving in the flanks of the enemy salient along the Anzio-Albano road. After several days of heavy fighting, they retook Aprilia and beat off a series of strong counterattacks. Now less than ten miles from the coast, Kesselring launched his final push. On the 16th, the Germans renewed their attacks down the road toward Anzio while staging strong diversionary actions on the flanks. But now the Allies, fighting for their lives and with heavy air and naval gunfire support, held after initial German successes. By early March, the two fought-out armies settled down to a months-long stalemate.

Guard unit that had distinguished itself at Salerno. Both generals expected heavy casualties but nothing like the terrible slaughter that ensued.

Allied warplanes and artillery delivered a preliminary bombardment, but the German troops struck back immediately. Withering artillery, mortar, and small-arms fire from the crack 15th Panzergrenadier Division, Senger's favorite unit, mowed down the Americans as they slogged over an exposed mud flat and attempted to cross the narrow, fast-moving, high-banked river in unwieldy assault boats. The Germans destroyed one-fourth of the bridging equipment before the Americans even reached the crossing sites, and the few companies that made it to the opposite shore quickly found themselves caught in a deadly cross fire.

The Germans smashed a second assault the following night. This time,

the Americans managed to get a battalion across on two improvised footbridges, but the result was the same—they were pulverized by entrenched German guns and riddled by machine gunners. Those who could do so, escaped by recrossing the river. The message the panzergrenadiers dispatched to Senger crisply summed up the action: "Strong enemy assault detachments that have crossed the river are annihilated."

The lopsided battle cost the Americans 143 dead, 875 missing, 663 wounded—and prompted a congressional inquiry after the war. German casualties were virtually nil.

While the Germans were snuffing out the last American resistance on the Rapido, the amphibious assault that Kesselring feared was unfolding at Anzio. He had placed all troops on emergency alert on January 18, the day after the British crossed the Garigliano But on January 21, he yielded to pleas from his staff that the continuous stand-to was exhausting the men. Kesselring lifted the alert one day too soon.

In the predawn of January 22, an armada of more than 200 American, British, Dutch, Greek, Polish, and French ships, under Rear Admiral Frank Lowry, began disgorging troops on either side of Anzio. About 36,000 men and 3,200 vehicles came ashore. The only German fire came from scattered coastal artillery and antiaircraft batteries, which the Allies quickly destroyed. By midmorning, the U.S. 3d Division had moved three miles inland from the beaches south of the city. The American Rangers took the Anzio port while the 509th Parachute Infantry Battalion captured the neighboring town of Nettuno. North of Anzio, the British 1st Division, reinforced by commandos, carved out a beachhead two miles deep.

Lucas called the operation "one of the most complete surprises in history." All that stood between the Allied landing force and Rome were two German battalions. A bold dash might have seized the city. But Lucas did not know that, and even if he had, he lacked the armor for such a move.

News of the landing spread dismay at Kesselring's headquarters. The German field marshal hastily implemented a prearranged "alarm" plan that his staff had worked out to confront such an emergency. Code-named *Richard,* it brought special mobile detachments hurrying to the battle zone. The German high command also helped by dispatching the 715th Division from southern France, the 114th Division from the Balkans, and the 65th and 362d divisions from northern Italy.

Kesselring then scrounged up various units to block the roads leading from Anzio to the Alban Hills. The stopgap force included a wide assort-

An Allied LST carrying trucks heads for the low, sandy shore near Anzio as a destroyer lays down a protective smoke screen. The grisly German propaganda leaflet *(inset)*, one of many scattered over Anzio, was calculated to frighten invading troops.

ment of units: antiaircraft crews of Luftwaffe General Ritter von Pohl; a battalion of the 29th Panzergrenadier; part of a tank regiment and some artillery from the Hermann Göring Panzer Division that had been pulled out of the line; elements of the 3d Panzergrenadier and 4th Paratroop divisions; and a regiment of the 15th Panzergrenadier from Cassino.

By the end of the second day, the Allies had only slightly increased the size of the beachhead—to an area about seven miles deep and sixteen miles wide. The makeshift German force, on the other hand, had built up a substantial front, and more troops were racing to join them. A tour of the area encouraged Kesselring. "I had the confident feeling," he said, "that the Allies had missed a uniquely favorable chance of capturing Rome." He called Vietinghoff to tell him there was no need to send reinforcements to Anzio, let alone consider a retreat.

When General Eberhard von Mackensen of the Fourteenth Army arrived from northern Italy to take command of what Kesselring described as a "higgledy-piggledy jumble" of units, elements of eight German divisions were in place and five more were on the way. The entire beachhead was in reach of their long-range artillery, and the Luftwaffe had begun bombing runs. Kesselring gave Mackensen two tasks: tighten the noose around the enemy; then drive him into the sea.

General Lucas, warned by Clark not to take unnecessary risks, focused on getting the remainder of his corps ashore and on establishing a strong beachhead position. By the fourth day of the invasion, January 25, his only forward progress was a four-mile advance by the British that resulted in the capture of Aprilia, a village on the road to the Alban Hills. Clark, who also feared a German counterattack, praised Lucas's caution. But he told his corps commander that he needed to be more aggressive to relieve the pressure on the Fifth Army at Cassino.

On January 30, Lucas finally launched a two-pronged attack. The British 1st Division pushed north from Aprilia and took the town of Campoleone, four miles beyond. But a planned follow-up by the U.S. 1st Armored Division bogged down in the mud. On the right, the U.S. 3d Division, led by three battalions of Rangers, was to move northeast on the town of Cisterna to cut Highway 7, the ancient Appian Way running between Rome and Capua, then move into the Alban Hills from the east. A half-mile short of Cisterna, the Rangers walked into an ambush by troops of the Hermann Göring Panzer Division and the 715th Division, newly arrived from France. Only 6 of 767 Rangers returned. The rest were either killed or captured.

Halted along a semicircular line short of the Alban Hills and Cisterna, the VI Corps shifted to the defensive. Lucas had built up a force of 70,000 men and 356 tanks. But they were now surrounded by about 90,000 Germans.

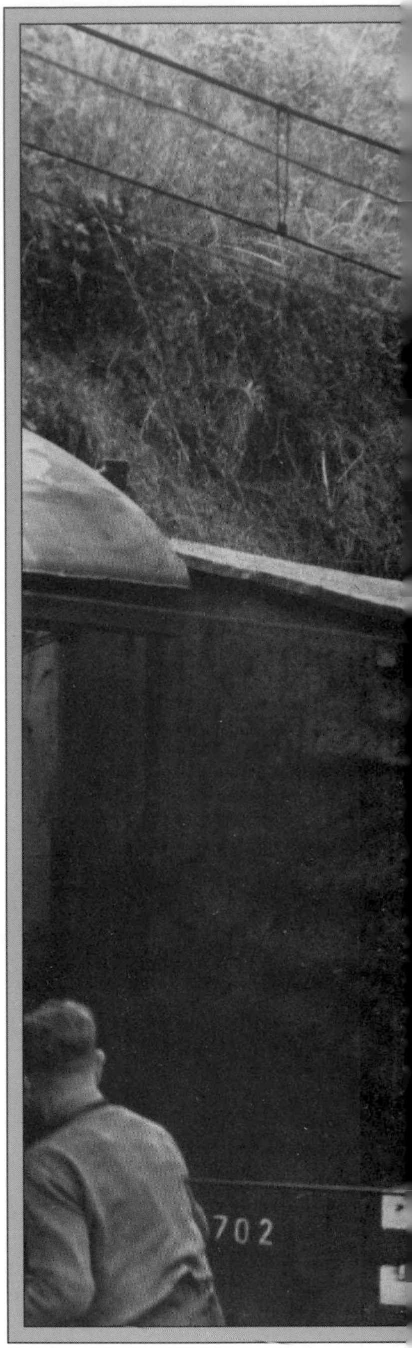

Artillerymen clean out the barrel of the huge 280-mm railroad gun with which the Germans bombarded the Anzio beachhead. When it was not firing its 561-pound shells, the powerful gun was kept safe from air attack in a rail tunnel near Velletri, located sixteen miles inland.

Convinced that the battle looming at Anzio would be one of the most crucial of the war, Hitler pressed Kesselring to counterattack. The Führer graphically called the beachhead that "abscess south of Rome," and he viewed it not only as a threat to his Fortress Europe but also as an opportunity to end the grim series of setbacks that the Wehrmacht had suffered since the fall of 1942. A smashing victory might make the Allies think twice before invading northern France and buy time for the production of Germany's *Wunderwaffen* (superweapons)—jet aircraft, long-range rockets, and improved U-boats—which could turn the tide of the war. The coming "battle for Rome," he said in a message to his commanders in Italy, "must be fought with bitter hatred against an enemy who wages a ruthless war of annihilation against the German people."

Meanwhile, the Allies had continued hammering at the Gustav Line. On January 24, two days after the U.S. 36th Division's debacle on the Rapido

River, Clark ordered Keyes to try again with his other infantry division, the 34th. The Americans were to cross north of Cassino where the river was shallow enough to wade. One force would attempt to take the town, the other would drive west into the mountains overlooking the Liri Valley.

The Germans had destroyed a dam on the upper reaches of the river, forcing the Americans to cross a waterlogged field before they reached the icy river. Twenty tanks sank so deeply into the quagmire that they had to be abandoned. On the far side, the Germans laid down curtains of fire from concealed positions in the mine-studded lower slopes of mountains. The Americans finally captured their first objective, a former Italian barracks that the Germans had converted into a strongpoint. One infantry battalion, supported by tanks, moved toward the northern outskirts of Cassino but was halted by machine-gun and antitank fire. During the first week of February, another American battalion inched up Hill 445, a round-topped peak just 400 yards below the abbey, only to be driven off by the Germans.

Two miles to the north, the French colonial troops under General Juin took Monte Belvedere and attempted a turning movement to link up with the Americans in the mountains. But the Germans stopped them too.

The cold, wet weather made life miserable for the soldiers. Countless men came down with respiratory illnesses and trench foot. The U.S. 34th Division had to employ more than 1,100 mules and 700 stretcher-bearers to supply the troops and evacuate the wounded over mountain trails that were little more than goat paths. The German units also suffered. "The artillery fire is driving me crazy," one German soldier wrote in his diary. "I am frightened as never before and cold. Rations are getting shorter—fifteen men, three loaves of bread, no hot meals."

A German cartoon portrays Monte Cassino and its adjacent heights as ravenous monsters gleefully gobbling up British and American troops. The cartoon was grimly accurate; in the succession of battles around Cassino, Allied forces suffered more than 100,000 casualties.

By the time a blizzard ended the battle on February 11, the two divisions of the French corps had suffered 2,500 casualties; the U.S. II Corps had lost more than 4,200 men, and the British corps another 4,000. All the Allies had to show for their losses was the British bridgehead over the Garigliano, the French capture of Monte Belvedere, and the small mountain bridgehead of the Americans on the Rapido. The Allied ploy had failed. The Anzio

German medics struggle to evacuate a wounded comrade from the steep, treacherous flanks of Monte Cassino. In such terrain, it took as long as eight hours for the wounded on both sides to reach field hospitals; many were killed by artillery fire or mines while en route.

landing had not forced a withdrawal from the Gustav Line. On the contrary, the German defenses were more impenetrable than ever.

In early February, both sides brought in fresh units from the Adriatic front. Vietinghoff added the 1st Paratroop and the 90th Panzergrenadier divisions to his Gustav Line positions and shifted the 29th Panzergrenadier back to Anzio. Alexander augmented the British X Corps on the Garigliano with the British 5th Division from the Eighth Army. He also transferred two elite divisions, the New Zealand 2d and Indian 4th, which joined with the British 78th and a combat group of the U.S. 1st Armored Division to form the New Zealand II Corps under Lieut. General Sir Bernard Freyberg.

Freyberg promptly triggered one of the most fiercely debated controversies of the war—the bombing of Monte Cassino abbey. Both combatants were ostensibly committed to protecting Italy's cultural and historical monuments. The Allies permitted exceptions only for "military necessity." In the eyes of many Allied troops, the abbey was a threat that had to be destroyed. As one officer explained: "Wherever you went, there was the monastery, looking at you." Major General F. S. Tuker, whose Indian 4th Division had replaced the battle-weary 34th Division, put it more bluntly. He told Freyberg: "I must have the monastery reduced by heavy bombers."

Freyberg's request for an aerial bombardment sparked a high-level dispute. Clark opposed it. He argued that bombing the monastery would not only hand the Germans a propaganda victory but also create stronger fortifications by reducing the buildings to rubble. Alexander, however, felt he could not deny the request if Freyberg insisted it was a military necessity. And Freyberg did.

The matter went all the way to General Sir Henry Maitland Wilson, the supreme allied commander of the Mediterranean theater. Wilson sent his deputy, Lieut. General Jacob Devers, and his air commander, Lieut. General Ira Eaker, to investigate. The two American generals made a low-altitude pass over the abbey in a Piper Cub and thought they saw evidence that supported Freyberg's contention that the Germans were making use of the buildings. In fact, General Senger had forbidden his troops to enter the monastery, and no Germans were within its walls.

To avoid being hit by stray bombs, the Indian 4th Division pulled out of the hard-won positions they had inherited from the 34th Division on a boomerang-shape ridge that the Americans called Snakeshead, close to the slopes of Monte Cassino. The next morning, February 15, two waves of Allied bombers dropped nearly 600 tons of explosives on the abbey.

When the bombing stopped and the surviving monks and refugees stumbled out of the ruins and made their way to safety, German paratroopers took position in the rubble. "Now," Senger said later, "we would occupy the abbey without scruple. The Germans had a mighty, commanding strongpoint, which paid for itself in all the subsequent fighting." The Germans also reoccupied the abandoned ground and were fully prepared to receive the attacking Allies. Over the next few days, the Royal Sussex, a British battalion in the Indian 4th Division, lost half its men trying to take Hill 593, the high ground on Snakeshead ridge. The 4th/6th Rajputana Rifles and two battalions of Gurkhas were also repulsed with heavy losses.

Meanwhile, 2,000 feet below, a battalion of Maoris from the New Zealand 2d Division seized the Cassino railroad station, located just a quarter-mile from where Highway 6 curves around Monastery Hill into the Liri Valley. But on February 18, tanks and infantry of the 211th Panzergrenadier Regiment counterattacked. Taking advantage of a smoke screen that the New Zealanders had laid down to conceal their movements, the Germans broke through on two sides and drove the Maoris from the station.

Snow and freezing rain soon made offensive operations impossible. Nearly a month would pass before they resumed, and by then, one of the toughest units in the Wehrmacht, the 1st Paratroop Division, would be defending the blood-soaked bottleneck that blocked the road to Rome.

While the fighting raged on the Cassino front, Hitler's longed-for counterattack at Anzio began. On February 10, Mackensen's forces recaptured Aprilia on the Anzio-Albano road north of the beachhead. The Germans now had a springboard for the final attack to the sea. The front was quiet

The Cassino Front

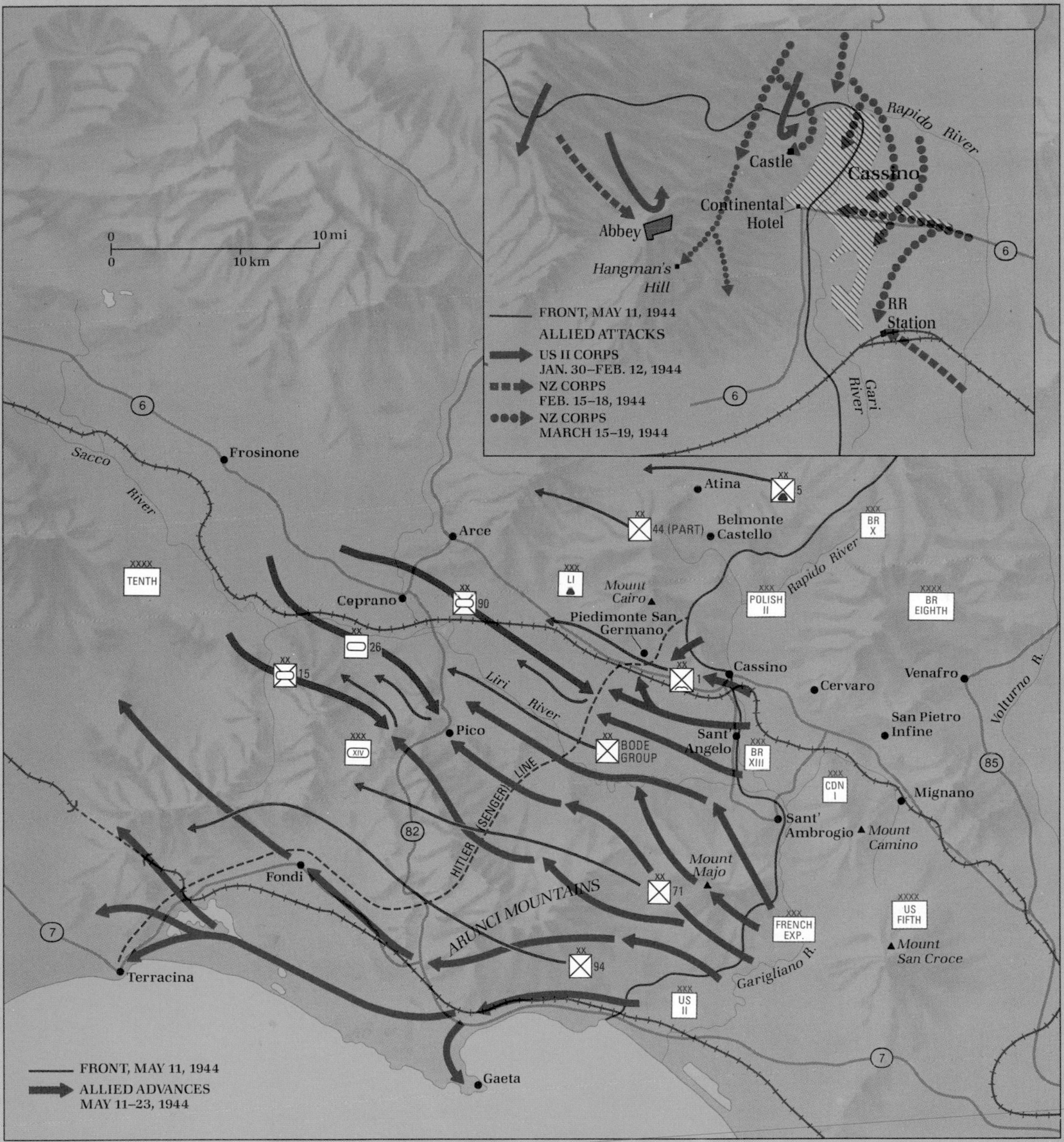

The key point of the Gustav Line was the town of Cassino *(inset)*, located behind the swift-flowing Rapido River and at the base of the Monte Cassino massif, which was dominated by the famous medieval abbey of Saint Benedict. Together, the town and the abbey controlled access to the Liri Valley and the road to Rome. Between January and March of 1944, the Allies made three futile efforts to smash through the mountain barrier into the valley below. Both the abbey and the town were reduced to rubble, but the German defenders clung to the ruins. In May, the Allies finally shifted heavy reinforcements to the south and broke through the German lines along the coast opposite the Aurunci Mountains. With their right flank shattered, the Germans were forced to fall back along their entire front. Despite reinforcements, attempts to make a stand at the Hitler Line were brushed aside, and the Allies rolled on toward Rome.

for a few days while the last reinforcements rolled in, bringing the total strength of Mackensen's army to more than 125,000, about 25 percent more than Lucas had. Notable among the arrivals was an elite infantry training unit from Berlin that was known as the Lehr Regiment. They were favorites of Hitler, who valued their Aryan looks, political reliability, and textbook performances in field exercises.

As so often happened in crucial battles, Hitler now intervened directly in every detail of the planning. He ordered the assault mounted on a narrow front, so that the artillery could deliver a creeping barrage "reminiscent of those used in World War I." He also insisted that the Lehr Regiment be assigned to the vanguard, even though the men had no combat experience. Hitler expected Mackensen's troops to overrun the Allies in three days.

Kesselring and Mackensen preferred a broader front to reduce the effectiveness of Allied artillery and planes and to tie down more enemy troops. But the generals felt compelled to follow all the Führer's orders—except for the creeping barrage; there was simply not enough ammunition for it. A half-hour-long bombardment would have to suffice.

The attack began at 6:30 a.m. February 16, the day after the Allies bombed Monte Cassino. The I Paratroop Corps, with the 4th Paratroop and 65th divisions, drove west of the Anzio-Albano road against the British. East of the road, the Hermann Göring Panzer Division mounted a diversionary feint near Cisterna. In the center, the LXXVI Panzer Corps delivered the main blow. The plan called for the Lehr Regiment, the 3d Panzergrenadier, and the 114th and 715th divisions to break through the U.S. 45th Division. The 29th Panzergrenadier and the 26th Panzer divisions would then exploit the opening and drive to the sea.

The chief of the German Fourteenth Army, General Eberhard von Mackensen, walks through an Italian meadow in May 1944, shortly before he was relieved of his command.

German troops strain to free a truck bogged down in the mud near Anzio. Heavy February rains turned much of the already marshy terrain into a quagmire, forcing Mackensen's attacking panzers to stay on roads, where they were savaged by Allied artillery and naval gunfire.

The Allies, however, were prepared to meet the onslaught. Initially, the only significant German success was the attack by the 4th Paratroop, which penetrated almost two miles through the British 56th Division. In two days of heavy fighting, the Germans managed to push the British and the Americans back to their final defense line, just seven miles from the sea. But they could go no farther. The Allies, aided by powerful naval and air support, refused to break. The big guns that Lucas had so painstakingly amassed had done their job.

The spectacular results Hitler expected had not been achieved. Adding insult to injury, the Lehr Regiment had broken, and the men had fled; Kesselring wrote later that they acted "disgracefully." On February 20, the Germans broke off the attack. In five days, they had lost more than 5,000 men. The fact that Allied losses were comparable was small consolation.

Another casualty of the battle was General Lucas. On February 22, at Alexander's insistence, Clark relieved Lucas of command, making the American corps commander the scapegoat for the Allied failure to force Kesselring out of the Gustav Line. But Kesselring himself was not among the second-guessers. "It would have been the Anglo-American doom to overextend themselves," he said after the war. "The landing force was initially weak, only a division or so of infantry, and without armor. It was a halfway measure as an offensive, and that was your basic error."

Clark replaced Lucas with Major General Lucian K. Truscott, Jr., the commander of the U.S. 3d Division. Truscott had only one week to settle in before the Germans struck again near Cisterna, against positions held by his former division. After the Hermann Göring Panzer, 26th Panzer, and 362d divisions made slight gains, the Americans pushed them back. When a second attack failed, Kesselring called a halt. He and Mackensen concluded that they lacked the strength to eradicate the Anzio beachhead. The German air and artillery inferiority was simply too great to overcome.

But would the Führer accept their bleak assessment? In early March, Kesselring dispatched Westphal to Berchtesgaden to explain. Hitler at first accused Westphal of "slandering his troops" and ordered twenty officers of all arms and ranks brought from the front so that he could interview them personally. For three hours, Westphal argued that losses had been heavy and that the troops were "exhausted to a frightening degree." Hitler became uncharacteristically subdued. "He said, with obvious emotion, that he knew well how great was the war-weariness that afflicted the people and also the Wehrmacht," Westphal recalled. "A victory on a large scale, for instance on the eastern front, was impossible, for we had not the strength. That was why he had hoped that success would attend the assault." As Westphal was leaving, Field Marshal Wilhelm Keitel, chief of the armed forces high command, remarked: "You were lucky. If we old fools had said even half as much, the Führer would have had us hanged."

Shortly after Westphal returned to Kesselring's headquarters, the Cassino front exploded again. The silence that had ensued when foul weather set in on February 19 persisted through the first half of March as Freyberg regrouped the New Zealand Corps for one more crack at the Gustav Line. Believing that mountain attacks had been proved futile, he now focused on Cassino, reasoning that the town offered easier access to Monte Cassino and hence to the Liri Valley. The New Zealand Division would attack the town from the east while the Indian 4th Division attacked from the north. The two units would then seize Monte Cassino while the 78th Division and elements of the 1st Armored entered the Liri Valley.

When the weather finally cleared on March 15, the Allied command unleashed its air power in what was, at the time, the most massive aerial bombardment ever mounted. In a raid lasting more than three hours, a total of about 500 bombers obliterated Cassino. The bombers struck at fifteen-minute intervals, dropping more than 1,000 tons of explosives on the smoking, quaking town. In the pauses between sorties and for forty minutes afterward, the Allied artillery took over, booming another 2,500 tons of shells at the target. The ground shook in a five-mile radius around the town, as if an earthquake had struck.

The display awed Allied observers. "I remember no spectacle in war so gigantically one-sided," a British war correspondent said. "Above, the beautiful, arrogant, silver-gray monsters performing their mission with what

Cassino lies shattered after the massive Allied air raid of March 15. Although not a single building remained intact, the defending German paratroopers survived in bunkers and tunnels, then turned the wreckage of the town into an intricate maze of hidden strongpoints.

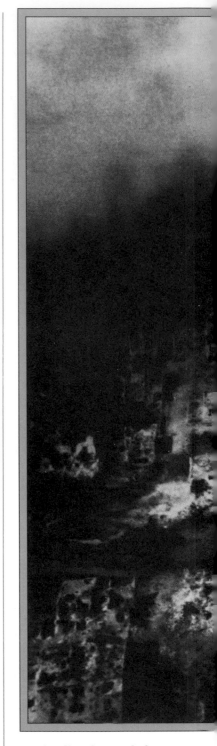

looked from below like a spirit of utter detachment; below, a silent town, suffering all this in complete passivity."

The 1st Paratroop Division in Cassino waited it out in cellars and dug-outs. Breathing amid the smoke and dust was a "desperate and urgent business," one officer recalled. Another felt sudden empathy with U-boat crews dodging depth charges beneath the sea. A few soldiers were buried so deeply that it took hours to dig out.

When the shelling finally stopped, the lead New Zealand troops moved into Cassino, picking their way through the rubble, block by block. Suddenly, to their astonishment, paratroopers amid the debris opened up with rifles, machine guns, and mortars. The heaviest fire came from the ruined

Outfitting the Wehrmacht's Paratroopers

The German paratroopers who fought as infantry in Sicily and then in the hell that was Cassino—seen in the background photograph—continued to wear a distinctive battle dress that was originally designed for paratroop operations. Most notable was a long, loose-fitting gabardine smock or coverall that reached to the knees *(opposite)*. Also unique was the paratroop helmet. Lacking a front brim and the swept-down portion at the back protecting the neck, it was lighter than the regular issue helmet. The trousers, looser than those of other German uniforms, tucked into lace-up jump boots with heavy rubber soles. The paratroopers carried light, rapid-fire weapons *(below)* that handled easily but provided them impressive firepower.

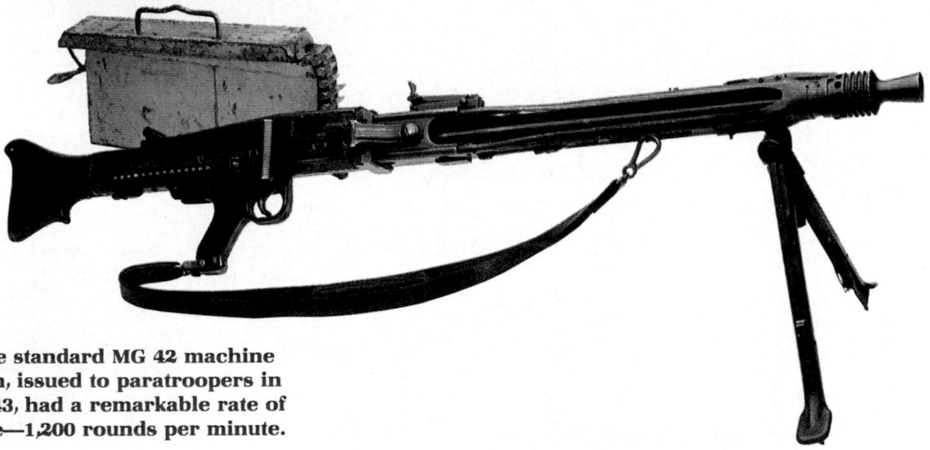

The standard MG 42 machine gun, issued to paratroopers in 1943, had a remarkable rate of fire—1,200 rounds per minute.

The FG 42 rifle, designed specially for paratroopers, was a versatile weapon. It could fire either single shots or machine-gun bursts.

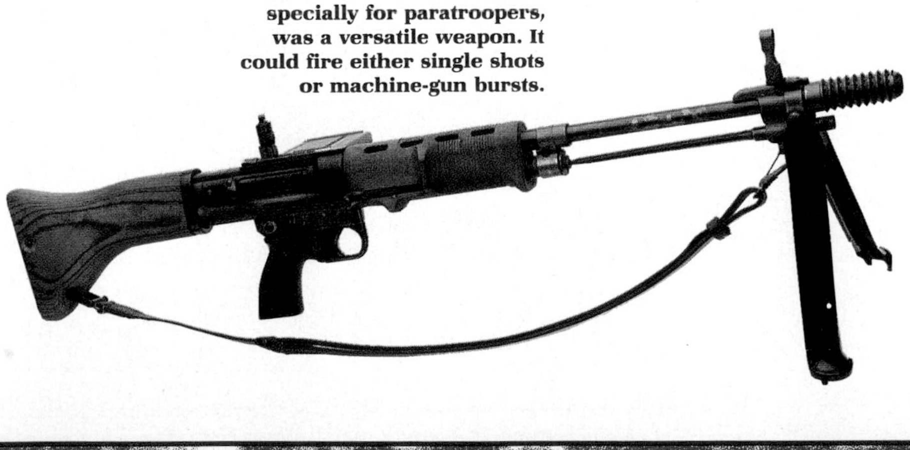

The coverall had four large pockets for equipment and canned rations. Other items hung from a shoulder strap and belt: a light haversack, gas mask, mess kit, pistol, bayonet, and tucked into the belt, hand grenades. Paratroopers sometimes looped a bandoleer of ammunition around their necks. The bowl-like helmet was usually camouflaged with a cloth cover.

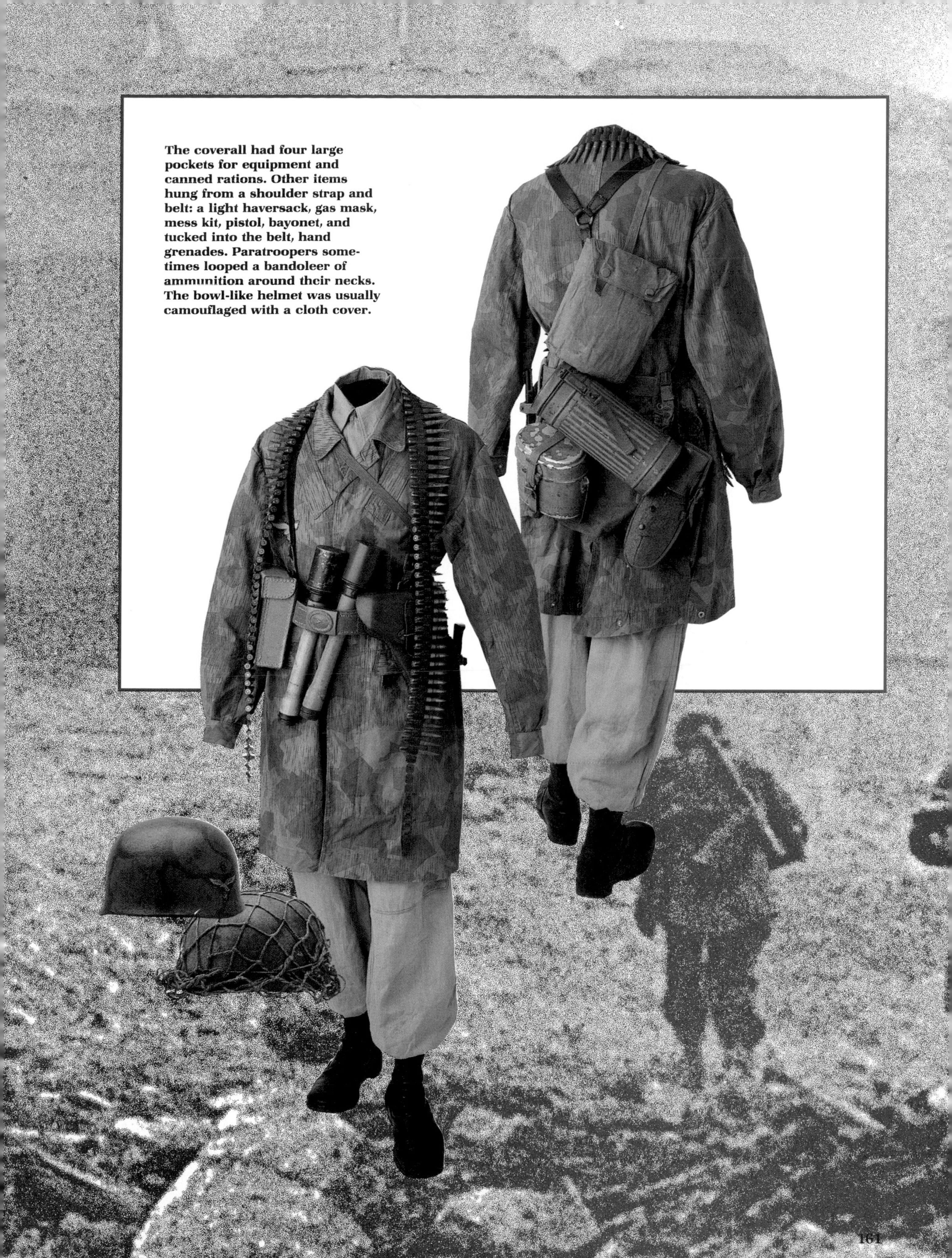

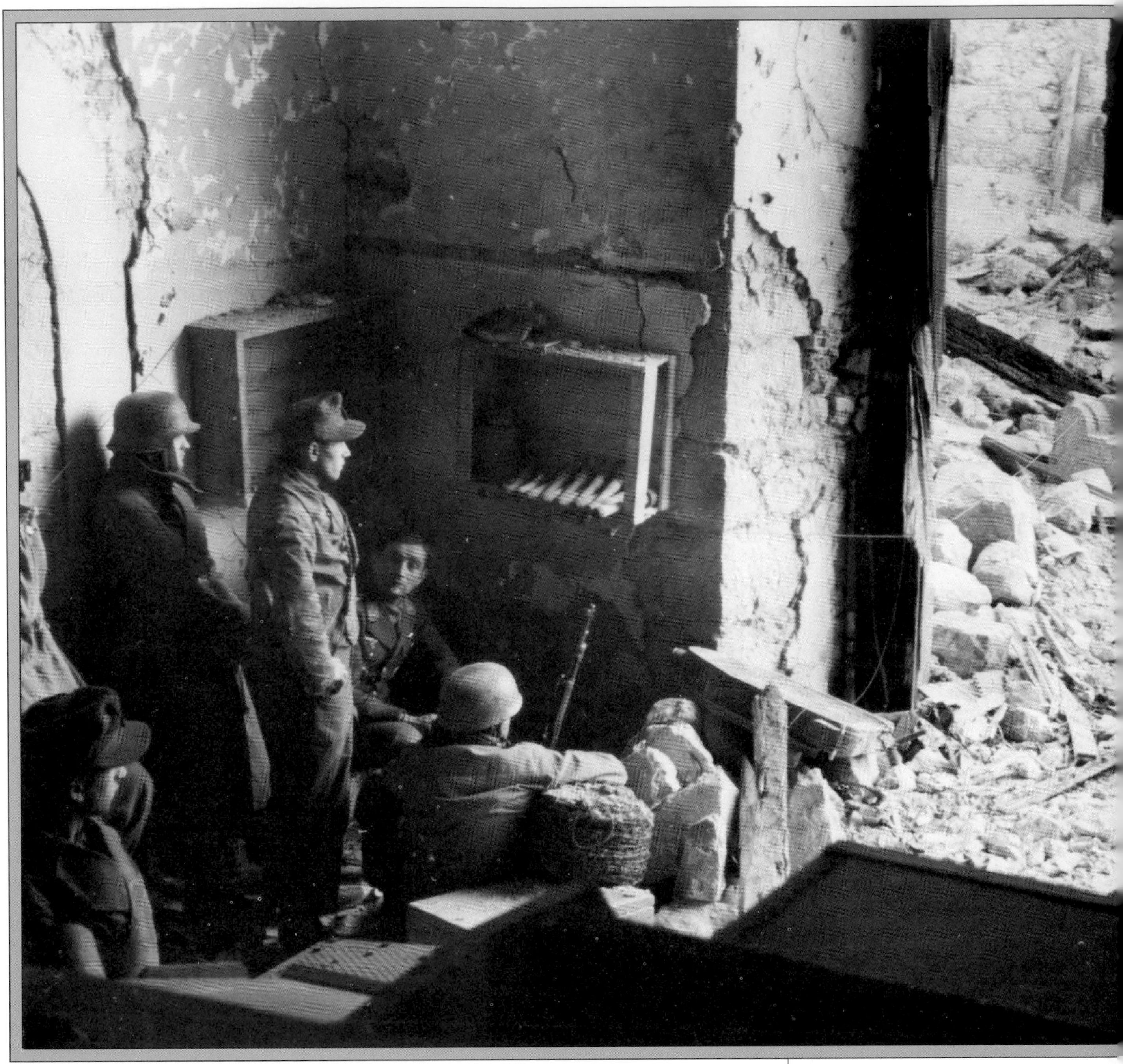

Continental Hotel on slightly elevated ground. (The Excelsior was its real name, but it was mistakenly called the Continental, and is so known in history.) Far from eliminating German resistance, the bombing had produced even more impenetrable bulwarks. That night, a torrential rain turned the bomb craters into ponds and the ground into a soupy morass, denying Freyberg the use of his tanks.

The paratroopers remained immovable. "What we are going through here is beyond description," a veteran machine gunner wrote in his diary. "I never experienced anything like this in Russia, not even a second's peace, only the dreadful thunder of guns and mortars and planes over and above. Everything is in the hands of fate, and many of the boys have met theirs already." During the next nine days, the paratroopers wore down six battalions of New Zealand infantry in the gutted town. Behind Cassino, they isolated a battalion of Gurkhas on Hangman's Hill, a knoll just 250 feet

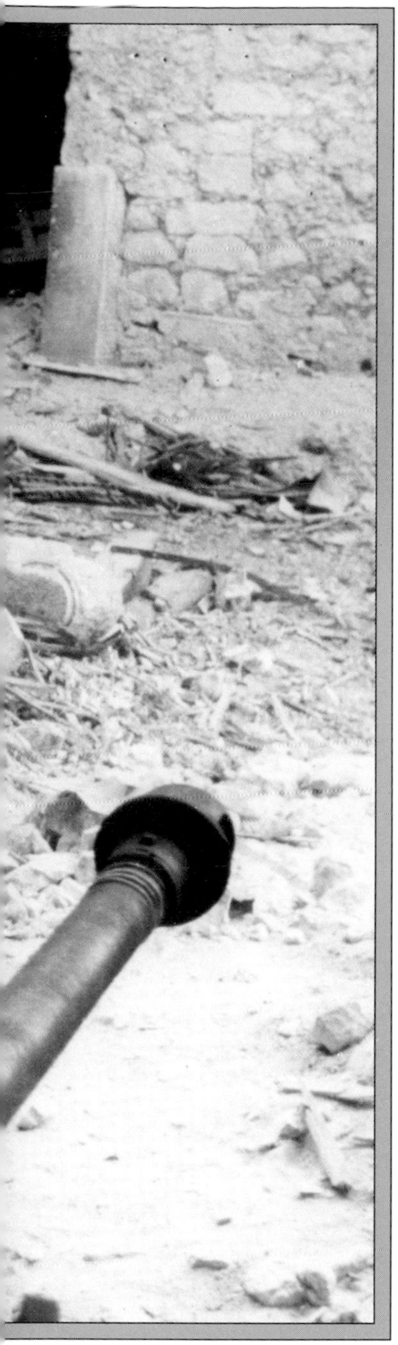

Grenades lined up on a shelf in readiness, German troops await an Allied attack in the ruins of one of Cassino's thick-walled buildings, adjacent to a dug-in assault gun. The German defenders also concealed tanks in the rubble.

below the abbey, and other Indian division troops on nearby Castle Hill, named for its ruined medieval fort.

When Alexander called a halt on March 23, the battered combatants stood roughly where they had been before the fighting began. The Gurkhas, with difficulty, evacuated their perch on Hangman's Hill, their wounded passing directly through the German lines under a Red Cross flag. All Freyberg had gained from the unprecedented bombing, the expenditure of more than 600,000 artillery shells, and the loss of 2,000 troops were Castle Hill, part of Cassino, and the train station.

Alexander tipped his cap to his foe. "The tenacity of these German paratroopers is quite remarkable," he said. "They were subjected to the whole of the Mediterranean Air Force under the greatest concentration of firepower that has ever been put down. I doubt if there are any other troops in the world who could have stood up to it and then gone on fighting with the ferocity they have."

A lull descended on the Cassino and Anzio fronts in late March. Luftwaffe pilots dropped strings of antipersonnel bombs on the troops at Anzio—GIs called the fliers Popcorn Pete—while German railroad guns, dubbed Anzio Annie by the Allies, kept up harassing fire. The Allies, in turn, took full advantage of their air superiority to pummel the German supply lines.

Kesselring ordered the construction of two fallback positions: the Hitler Line, which crossed the mountains and the Liri Valley five to ten miles behind the Gustav Line, and another closer to Rome called the C-Position, which the Allies named the Caesar Line. He found himself in a familiar situation—unsure where the Allies would strike next. General Richard Heidrich, commander of the 1st Paratroop Division, expected one more attempt to break the Gustav Line. But Kesselring thought that another amphibious invasion was a stronger possibility. To counter the threat, he stationed strong reserve divisions near the key ports of Civitavecchia and Leghorn, north of Rome. It was exactly what the Allies wanted him to do.

Heidrich's instincts proved correct. Far from abandoning his hope of breaking into the Liri Valley, Alexander was planning an even more powerful blow. It would begin with a ruse. To exploit Kesselring's fear of an amphibious assault, the British commander sent the U.S. 36th Division to the Naples-Salerno area to conduct landing exercises, while Allied planes reconnoitered the beach at Civitavecchia. The Canadian I Corps, an Eighth Army reserve unit, simulated radio traffic with the Americans to make the Germans think that a joint American-Canadian operation was planned.

Meanwhile, Alexander regrouped his forces. In early March, he secretly began transferring almost the entire British Eighth Army, under Lieut.

General Sir Oliver Leese, from the Adriatic front to the Cassino front. In addition to English and Commonwealth troops, this polyglot force of more than 265,000 included the Polish Corps of Lieut. General Wladyslaw Anders, as well as units from Belgium, Yugoslavia, Lebanon, the West Indies, and even Italy. Alexander assigned them to positions previously occupied by the American Fifth Army, opposite Cassino, on either side of Highway 6.

At the same time, he shifted the Fifth Army, now 350,000 strong, to the area running from south of Sant'Angelo to the Tyrrhenian coast. The U.S. II Corps, augmented by the 85th and 87th Infantry divisions, was placed between Minturno and the sea, where the British X Corps had been. It, in turn, was moved to Leese's right flank, under his command. The French remained on the Americans' right, but now occupied the Garigliano bridgehead, captured by the British in January. Juin's force had also been strengthened with the addition of the 1st Motorized Infantry and the Moroccan 4th divisions, as well as 12,000 fierce Berber tribesmen from the Atlas Mountains of North Africa. These tribesmen, called *goumiers* because they were organized in *goums*, or companies, were renowned as scouts and infamous for bringing back the severed ears of their dead enemies.

By May 11, Alexander had thirteen divisions crammed into the Cassino front and was ready to unveil his plan, dubbed Operation Diadem. The Germans, who had only four divisions, still thought they faced no more than six. Diadem called for the Fifth and the Eighth armies to attack simultaneously. Four days into the offensive, Truscott's VI Corps at Anzio, reinforced to 90,000 men, would break out, cut Highway 7, and link up with the Eighth Army at Valmontone, twenty miles southeast of Rome on Highway 6, trapping the German armies retreating from the south. Alexander used a boxing analogy to describe the plan: The Fifth and Eighth armies would deliver the first punch, a powerful right cross at the Gustav Line, followed by a left hook from VI Corps at Anzio.

May 11th passed uneventfully on the German side. Even though everyone knew an Allied attack could begin at any moment, several senior commanders were away. Senger was on home leave, Westphal on sick leave. That afternoon, Vietinghoff left for Germany to receive a decoration for valor from Hitler. At 11:00 p.m., the massed artillery of the two Allied armies opened up—all 1,660 guns in an ear-shattering cannonade. Just before midnight, the Allies moved out—the Americans and the French on the left, the British in the center, and the Poles on the right.

Although the attack achieved complete surprise, the deeply dug-in Germans fought back fiercely. At the end of the first day, the Allied results were disappointing. Assaulting the flanks of Monte Cassino, the Poles briefly held a point about 1,800 yards northwest of the abbey, called Phantom

Pleased with the success of his defensive strategy in and around Cassino, Field Marshal Albert Kesselring cheerfully waves his riding crop from the rear of a tracked motorcycle during a March visit to Belmonte Castello, a hill town near the front.

Ridge, as well as Hill 593. But counterattacks by the 1st Paratroop Division drove them back with heavy losses. The British XIII Corps managed to throw two vehicular bridges over the Rapido but could not break out of their shallow bridgehead. American gains along the coast were small, although their artillery hurt the German 94th Infantry Division severely.

Only the French made significant progress. They attacked in the rugged Aurunci Mountains where Kesselring, relying on the terrain to repel the enemy, had left only a thin screen of troops. The Moroccan 2d Division, spearheaded by the tireless goumiers, captured two key heights in the Monte Majo area. The next afternoon, they took Monte Majo, splitting the German 71st Division and exposing the left wing of the XIV Panzer Corps. The French attack put the entire Gustav Line in jeopardy.

Allied aircraft, pounding German lines of communications and supply depots without letup, knocked out the Tenth Army field headquarters and severely damaged Kesselring's own command post. The field marshal could not get a clear picture of the battle. Late on May 13, he ordered the 90th Panzergrenadier Division to rush to the 71st Division's aid. By that time, it was too late to dislodge the French. The British had added a third bridge across the Rapido, and the Americans were advancing along the coast. The German front was crumbling.

By May 16, the French and the Americans had broken through the Gustav Line between the Liri Valley and the coast. The next day, the British and Canadians reached the mouth of the valley, while the Poles attacked Monte Cassino and the town. The 1st Paratroop Division was about to be cut off.

Polish infantrymen wearing British uniforms scramble up one of the knife-edge ridges leading toward Monte Cassino during the last—and finally successful—Allied attack on the heights in May 1944. The exiled Poles fought furiously, suffering almost 4,000 casualties.

A battalion commander recorded his desperation: "Impossible to get wounded away. Great number of dead on the slopes—stench—no water—no sleep for three nights—amputations being carried out at battle headquarters." Gazing down from the bloodstained heights, the paratroopers watched an endless ribbon of Allied vehicles rolling into the valley.

On May 17, Kesselring ordered the Cassino area evacuated. Late that night, the surviving paratroopers escaped into the hills. The battalion at the monastery blew up its ammunition and slipped away. The next morning, the British occupied the town and Polish infantrymen moved uncontested onto the crest of Monte Cassino. All they found were several seriously wounded paratroopers and two medics. The agonizing fight for Saint Benedict's mountaintop was finally over.

Kesselring's withdrawal to the Hitler Line, hastily renamed the Senger

Line to disassociate the Führer from defeat, brought his reeling troops no respite. The Allies were pushing forward everywhere. On May 20, the Algerian 3d Infantry Division, backed by tanks, penetrated the Senger Line southeast of Pico and gained a foothold in the town. The Algerian attack paved the way for fresh Allied gains on both flanks. Vietinghoff sent two panzergrenadier divisions from the Liri Valley to reinforce the 26th Panzer Division fighting the Algerians. On May 24, the U.S. II Corps seized Terracina, where the Senger Line met the sea. The fall of the ancient Roman fortress town opened Highway 7 all the way to Cisterna, above Anzio.

The day before, Truscott's VI Corps at Anzio had begun a drive to break through Mackensen's Fourteenth Army. By May 25, the U.S. 1st Armored and 3d Infantry divisions, aided by close air support, had worked their way

A triumphant Pole pulls a German soldier from a wood-reinforced dugout near Piedimonte San Germano on May 27. Once past Monte Cassino, the Poles moved fast to capture Piedimonte, which was supposed to anchor the next German defensive line astride Highway 6.

through extensive minefields into Cisterna. That day, an American engineer patrol moving south from Cisterna on Highway 7 met a U.S. II Corps patrol heading north from Terracina. Four months after the landing, the long-planned linkup was at last a fact.

Kesselring, with Hitler's grudging consent, ordered a pullback to the Caesar Line, the last fortified barrier short of Rome. He informed Vietinghoff and Mackensen that the battle had reached its "decisive phase."

Kesselring was right—but for a reason he knew nothing about. A difference of opinion between Clark and Alexander was about to create a situation that would allow the bulk of his forces to escape. According to Alexander's plan, Truscott's VI Corps was supposed to drive northeastward to Valmontone to block Highway 6 and trap Vietinghoff's Tenth Army. But Clark disagreed. Not only did he think that few Germans would be caught there, he was also determined that his Fifth Army should gain the ultimate prize—Rome. "We not only wanted the honor of capturing Rome," he said, "but we felt we more than deserved it." Furthermore, he knew that the cross-channel invasion of France was about to unfold. On May 25, Clark ordered Truscott to shift the bulk of his forces northwest, toward the Alban Hills. Instead of VI Corps being a trapdoor snapping shut at Valmontone, it would be the Fifth Army's spearhead for a drive on Rome.

Truscott's units moving toward Valmontone faced only light resistance. But those moving northeast in accordance with Clark's orders ran directly into the formidable Caesar Line, held by three full-strength units, the 4th Paratroop, the 65th, and the 3d Panzergrenadier divisions. After several costly frontal assaults failed, the Americans finally penetrated the line by a surprise nighttime infiltration. A patrol from the U.S. 36th Division discovered a small gap in the defenses near Velletri. On May 30, two regiments broke through to Highway 7. By the following day, the entire division was behind the Caesar Line.

Mackensen was slow to tell Kesselring of the breakthrough. For the field marshal, this was the last straw in what had been an uneasy relationship. Mackensen, who had anticipated Clark's decision to attack toward Rome through the Alban Hills, was still angry with his superior for refusing to authorize a withdrawal from Cisterna earlier in the fighting. And he had bitterly resented being ordered to send his Fourteenth Army's reserves to support Vietinghoff's Tenth Army near Terracina. He had dragged his feet, and the reserves arrived too late to help. Kesselring, in turn, blamed him for the disaster, which he claimed "gave the Americans the victory." This time when the disgruntled army commander asked to step down, Kesselring accepted, replacing him with General Joachim Lemelsen.

Clark ordered an all-out offensive against the remnants of the Caesar

To elude the increasingly powerful Allied air raids and artillery bombardments on the Anzio front, this headquarters section of a panzer division has set up a combined command post and barracks in a railroad tunnel near the town of Aprilia in May 1944.

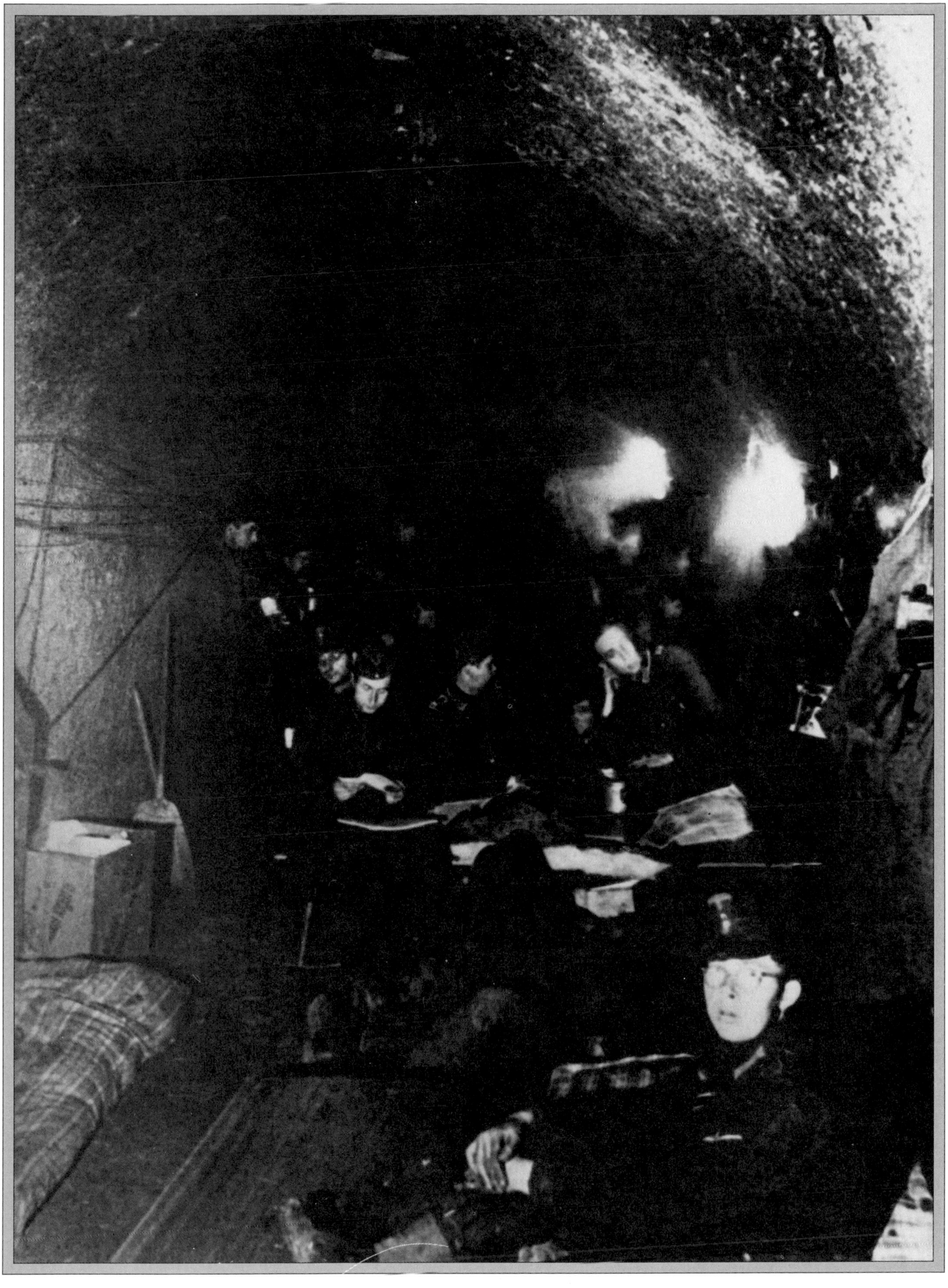

Line. The Germans were in no condition to resist. Senger's XIV Panzer Corps, which had held the Cassino heights for four months, had been whittled down to just fourteen tanks. The improvised character of the German units was illustrated by the prisoners taken at Velletri. They belonged to more than fifty different companies. Vietinghoff, who had been intermittently ill for months, was evacuated to a hospital; Westphal collapsed from nervous exhaustion.

When Valmontone fell on June 2, Kesselring ordered a general retreat. Rearguard units checked the Americans long enough for the battered troops of the Tenth and Fourteenth armies to stream into Rome. Kesselring briefed Hitler by phone on June 3. The Führer agreed to treat Rome as an open city to preclude serious fighting in the city.

Fearing a popular uprising if word of the retreat spread, Kesselring ordered his top officers to attend the opera that evening. The next day, the retreating Germans clattered through the streets. The Italians were fascinated by the endless procession of artillery pieces and trucks. A German officer noticed several Italians were waving little American flags and smiling. Suddenly he realized that he was wearing a captured Allied jacket. "We're still Germans," he told them. "The Americans will be coming soon."

The vanguard of the U.S. II Corps moving up Highway 6 reached the southern outskirts of the city late on the afternoon of June 4. General Clark, following close behind, stopped to pose for a photograph beside a sign reading *Roma*, but a sniper spoiled the moment by peppering the signpost with bullets. Only a few isolated skirmishes broke out as the lead units reached the Piazza Venezia in the heart of the city shortly after 7:00 p.m. Clark's moment on the world's center stage lasted just two days, however. On June 6, Overlord, the long-awaited Normandy invasion knocked his triumph out of the headlines.

In the coming months, Alexander would lose seven veteran divisions, including his best mountain troops, the redoubtable French Expeditionary Corps, to the Allied force assembling for the invasion of southern France. To replace them, he would get only the U.S. 92d Infantry Division, the U.S. 10th Mountain Division, and a division from Brazil. His air support would also be reduced, as one bomber group and twenty-three fighter squadrons were diverted to southern France. Kesselring would fare better. Hitler allowed him to keep the seasoned Hermann Göring Panzer Division, previously scheduled to go to France, and sent him eight more divisions, although some were of dubious quality.

In the concentrated fighting in May, Kesselring's armies suffered more than 38,000 casualties. The German commander's task now was to delay the Allies through the summer until a new defensive line could be com-

Sprinting past the burning hulk of a German Tiger tank, troops of the U.S. 88th Division rush down a wide boulevard into the center of Rome. The day before the Americans arrived, Kesselring received Hitler's permission to abandon the city without a fight.

pleted in northern Italy. Named the Gothic Line for the Germanic tribes that overran Rome in A.D. 410, this 180-mile barrier, from south of Spezia on the west coast along a spur of the Apennines to Pesaro on the Adriatic, would eventually be even more formidable than the Gustav Line.

In the fortnight following the fall of Rome, the Germans moved nearly 100 miles across the uneven terrain north of the capital to the Lake Trasimeno area. The steady retreat discouraged Senger—"what a change since the days of Cassino," he lamented. At Lake Trasimeno, Kesselring held off the Allies for eight days before falling back again.

When Hitler issued a no-withdrawal order at the end of June, Kesselring flew to Germany to confront him. The field marshal had a "knack" with the Führer, Westphal wrote, "which often enabled him to get his own way." Kesselring argued heatedly that only by maneuver and withdrawal could he save his two armies, armies that the Reich could ill afford to lose. If given a free hand, he guaranteed he could halt the Allies in the northern Apennines. Hitler grudgingly relented.

The Allies captured Leghorn on July 19 and entered Pisa four days later. Kesselring dropped back again, this time to the Arno River, where his troops held out for another ten days. The dispensation that had saved

Smoke billows from Florence's ancient Santa Trinità Bridge, blown into the Arno River by German engineers to impede the Allied advance. German forces held the Arno Line for nearly three weeks before retreating northward to the Gothic Line.

Rome was denied the lovely old city of Florence. The Germans had destroyed all the bridges, except the famous Ponte Vecchio, which was suitable only for foot traffic.

The two months of fire-and-fall-back combat had cost Germany another 63,000 casualties. But a decisive victory still eluded the Allies. In late August, Alexander tried again, this time with an all-out assault on the Adriatic side of the front. He called it Operation Olive.

As in the Diadem campaign, Alexander built a charade into the plan—a feint along the Arno near Florence midway between Italy's two coasts. It caught the Germans off guard. Vietinghoff was on leave on August 25 when Eighth Army forces crossed the Metauro River twelve miles south of the Gothic Line near the Adriatic coast. Six days later, British and Canadian infantry breached the line near the village of Monte Gridolfo. By September 1, the gap was fifteen miles wide, but the weather came to Kesselring's aid. Heavy rains stalled the Allies in the hills northwest of Pesaro.

When the Eighth Army bogged down, Fifth Army attacked, farther west. On September 10, the Americans hit the seam of the Tenth and Fourteenth armies, amid the steep slopes of Il Giogo Pass. Heavy fighting persisted for six more days before German resistance collapsed, opening a thirty-mile-wide gap in the Gothic Line.

When the Allies had marched out of Rome in early June, they had confidently expected to be at Rimini by the end of July. But they had not taken into account how much their pursuit would be impeded by the transfer of troops to southern France and by Kesselring's maneuvering.

By the end of September, Allied soldiers in the Apennines could see the Po Valley through the haze. The Gothic Line was at their backs. But in sporadic fighting during the next several weeks, they gained only a few more miles. Senger, who had assumed command of the Fourteenth Army because of General Lemelsen's poor health, compared his front to a thick cloth being jabbed with a spear—eventually, it would rip. But not yet.

When the bad weather arrived, the Germans manned an improvised line running from Spezia on the west coast to a point ten miles south of Bologna and on to the Adriatic, below Ravenna. The Alpine peaks beyond the Po Valley were already mantled with snow. Alexander's forces were exhausted and suddenly short of ammunition.

On October 23, Kesselring suffered a severe concussion when his staff car, traveling in thick fog over roads clogged with military traffic, ran into a towed artillery piece. Command of his army group fell to Vietinghoff.

The two-month-long stalemate ended in early December when the British Eighth Army, aided by a massive partisan uprising, seized Ravenna. But winter storms in the mountains kept the American Fifth Army pinned in place. Vietinghoff withdrew the Tenth Army to a line northwest of Ravenna to prevent its right wing from being cut off.

A few weeks later, it was his turn to surprise the Allies. On December 26, the LI Mountain Corps launched Operation Winter Thunderstorm, a limited counterattack down the Serchio Valley on the western end of the front. It was designed to relieve pressure on the *Monte Rosa* Alpine division, one of five Italian divisions still fighting with Vietinghoff's army group. The Germans caught the Americans completely unprepared. They drove the inexperienced 92d Division five miles backward, unbalancing the entire Fifth Army. Their objective achieved, the Germans withdrew with a small, but satisfying victory.

Both sides now settled down for another excruciating winter. As the Allies probed for incremental gains, the Germans attempted to strengthen their fallback positions. Although Vietinghoff's front still stretched from sea to sea, his military situation was deteriorating rapidly. Behind his lines, bands of Italian guerrillas harassed what remained of his bomb-shattered transportation system, setting roadblocks and blowing up railroad tracks. Beginning in January, the 50,000 tons of supplies that normally arrived each month from Germany ceased altogether, and his troops were forced to live off the land. To keep provisions moving forward, the Germans commandeered whatever they could lay their hands on—private automobiles, city buses, trucks, even oxen—and stretched their dwindling fuel supplies by mixing alcohol and benzene with gasoline and diesel oil.

In early April, the Allies launched yet another offensive. By now, they enjoyed a two-to-one superiority in artillery and manpower, and a three-to-one advantage in armor. On the eve of the attack, Hitler refused Vietinghoff's request to withdraw his forces to prepared positions behind the Ticino and Po rivers. One angry staff officer called the Führer's decision the equivalent of a death sentence for the Tenth and Fourteenth armies.

Exhausted and dejected, a wounded German soldier rests by the roadside in a northern Italian town during the long, 150-mile retreat from central Italy in the summer of 1944.

The end came with startling suddenness. On April 9, the British Eighth Army struck near Lake Comacchio, north of Ravenna. Five days later, the American Fifth Army hit Bologna. On April 20, Hitler's fifty-sixth and final birthday, the Americans broke out into the open country, and Vietinghoff, on his own authority, ordered the retreat he had requested several weeks earlier. But it was too late. The following day, the two Allied armies linked up behind Bologna and raced for the Po River to get behind the fleeing Germans. Lacking bridging equipment, many units were trapped, and by April 29, the Allies were across the Po and had sealed off all escape routes.

With his troops finally cornered, Vietinghoff agreed to a cease-fire, effective May 2, 1945—exactly 570 days after the tortuous, grinding, yard-by-yard struggle for Italy had begun on Sicily's southernmost tip. ✠

Bitter Fruits of Alliance with Hitler

The news of Italy's surrender to the Allies was still crackling on the shortwave radios on the evening of September 8, 1943, when the Wehrmacht flashed out the code: *Ernte einbringen!* (Bring in the harvest!). German troops all along the Italian boot swept into position to disarm their former Axis comrades.

Even though Marshal Pietro Badoglio, who replaced Mussolini as head of the government, had pledged to continue fighting, Hitler smelled the odor of deceit. Thus, when the Germans heard the broadcast of the armistice, they responded like angry hornets, seizing the weapons of tens of thousands of Italian soldiers and shooting anyone who refused to cooperate. King Victor Emmanuel III and Badoglio fled to the Adriatic coast, narrowly escaping the Germans' grasp, but the ordinary citizens, especially the Jews, were left to face the fury of the frustrated Reich.

Despite the fact that Italy's army was in disarray and virtually leaderless, some officers were moved by the impulse to resist. General Don Ferrante Gonzaga, an old soldier who had been highly decorated in World War I, refused to hand over his pistol when a German major demanded it. "A Gonzaga never lays down his arms!" he shouted, then fell in a hail of gunfire.

Exhausted by war, most Italians merely wanted to get on with their lives. But others took to the hills. By early spring, partisan bands, armed with weapons captured from the Germans or dropped by Allied aircraft, began to strike back. And after the fall of Rome in June 1944, they became even more aggressive. Groups such as the Stella Rossa (Red Star) stepped up their activities from railroad sabotage to almost daily attacks on German troops and their loyal Italian collaborators.

Retribution was swift and merciless. Not content to kill active guerrillas, the Germans moved into Stella Rossa's home district, a cluster of villages known as Marzabotto, located near Bologna, and burned every house to the ground. As the inhabitants ran outside to escape the flames, the Germans slaughtered them with machine guns. More than 1,800 men, women, and children died in the massacre.

On the day of Italy's surrender, a German soldier keeps a wary

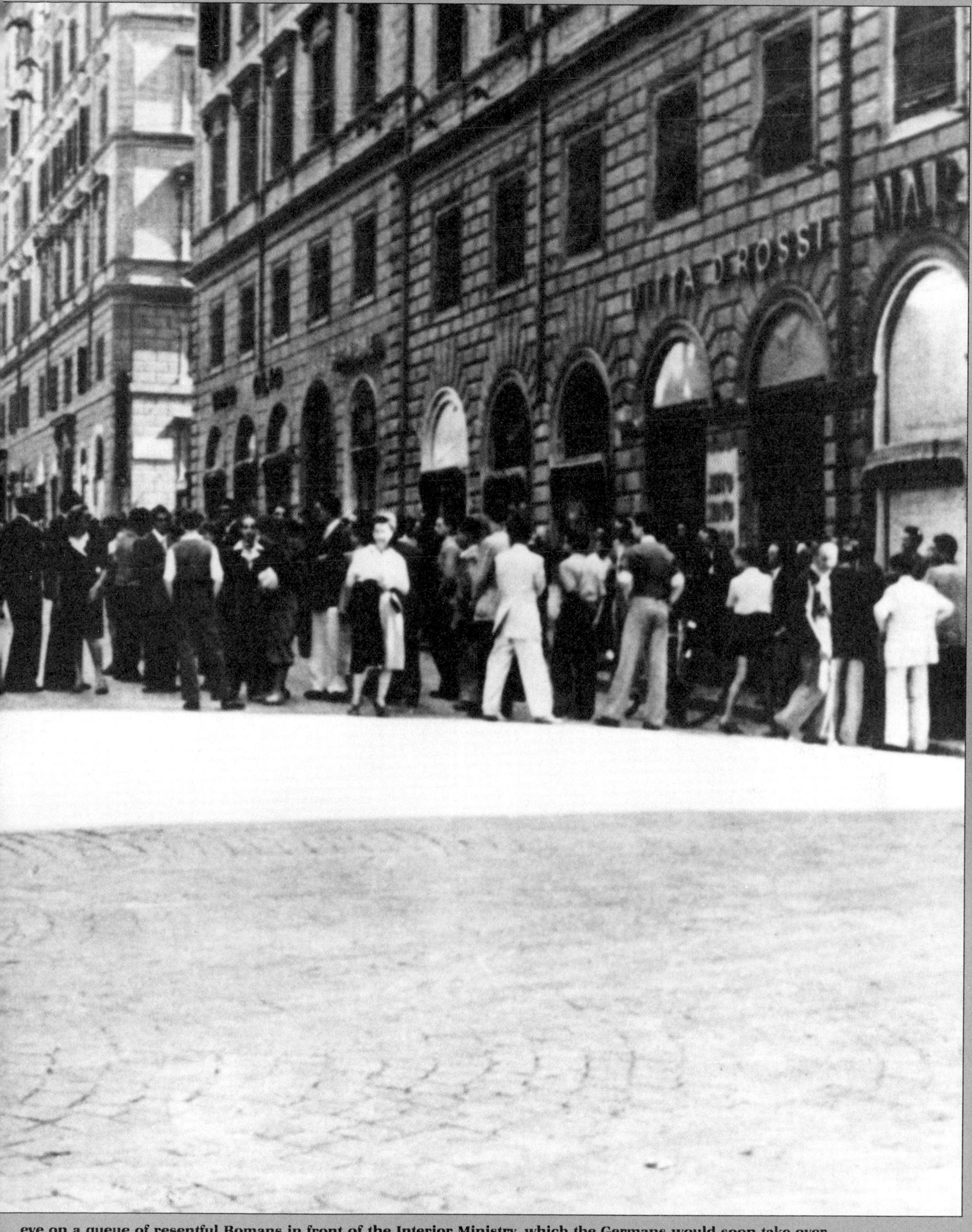

eye on a queue of resentful Romans in front of the Interior Ministry, which the Germans would soon take over.

A German Fist on Rome

As a token resistance to the German seizure of Rome, Italian soldiers defend the Porta San Paolo—a gate in the old city wall.

An Italian officer leads a German soldier into a captivity that probably lasted only a few hours. The Germans moved quickly to crush Italian resistance and reestablish control in Rome.

An SS assault gun leads a German convoy into Rome as stunned Italians stand aside.

Italian soldiers surrender as they abandon a burning building in Rome.

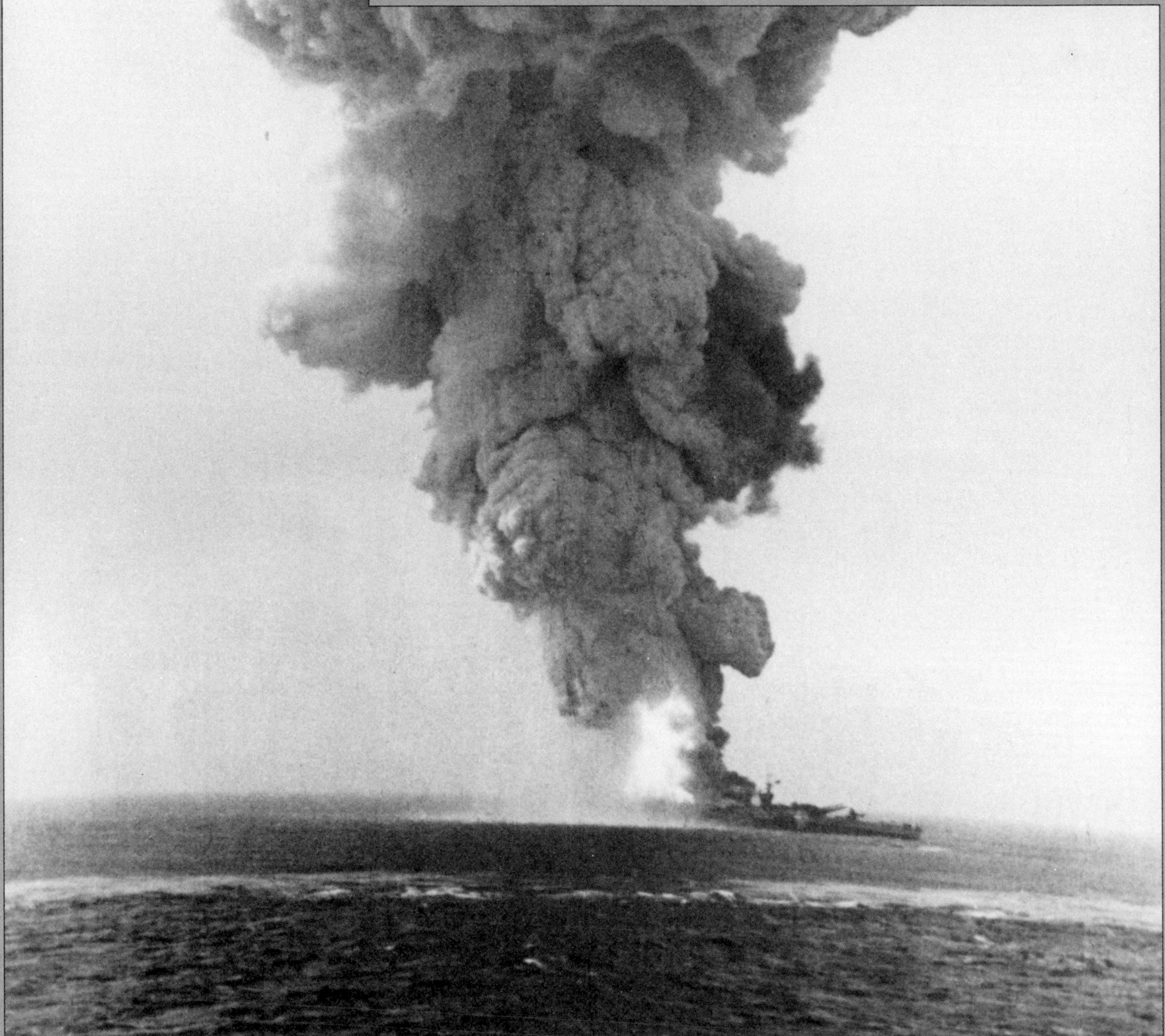

Suppressing the Italian Military

When Italy capitulated, the nation's 1.7 million soldiers, deployed across a broad swath of Europe from the Soviet Union to the Balkans, suddenly found themselves at the mercy of their former German comrades in arms. Their fate depended largely on their political leanings—and luck.

Because the Germans lacked the means to control such a large number of prisoners, Field Marshal Albert Kesselring encouraged the Italians to discard their uniforms and melt into the civilian world. The majority succeeded in doing so. But 40,000 less fortunate ones found themselves interned as slave laborers and shipped to work camps inside Germany to meet the Reich's worsening manpower shortage.

A few soldiers who still believed in the Axis cause were accepted into the Wehrmacht. Others opted for the army of the new Italian Social Republic, the fascist state led by Benito Mussolini, reduced now to a German puppet. Antifascists joined guerrilla bands or handed over their weapons to the partisans.

Italy's sailors had fewer choices. Defying furious attacks by the Luftwaffe, the fleet steamed at full speed for Allied ports in Malta and North Africa. Although the battleship *Roma* was sunk, four other battleships, seven cruisers, and eight destroyers made it to safe harbor.

A group of anxious Italian officers *(inset)* gathers around a German officer to hear news about the German takeover.

Smoke from the *Roma* billows skyward after a bombing strike by the Luftwaffe. The Italian flagship went to the bottom with more than 1,300 men aboard.

Their weapons already piled on the ground, Italian soldiers submit to their SS captors in a courtyard near Milan.

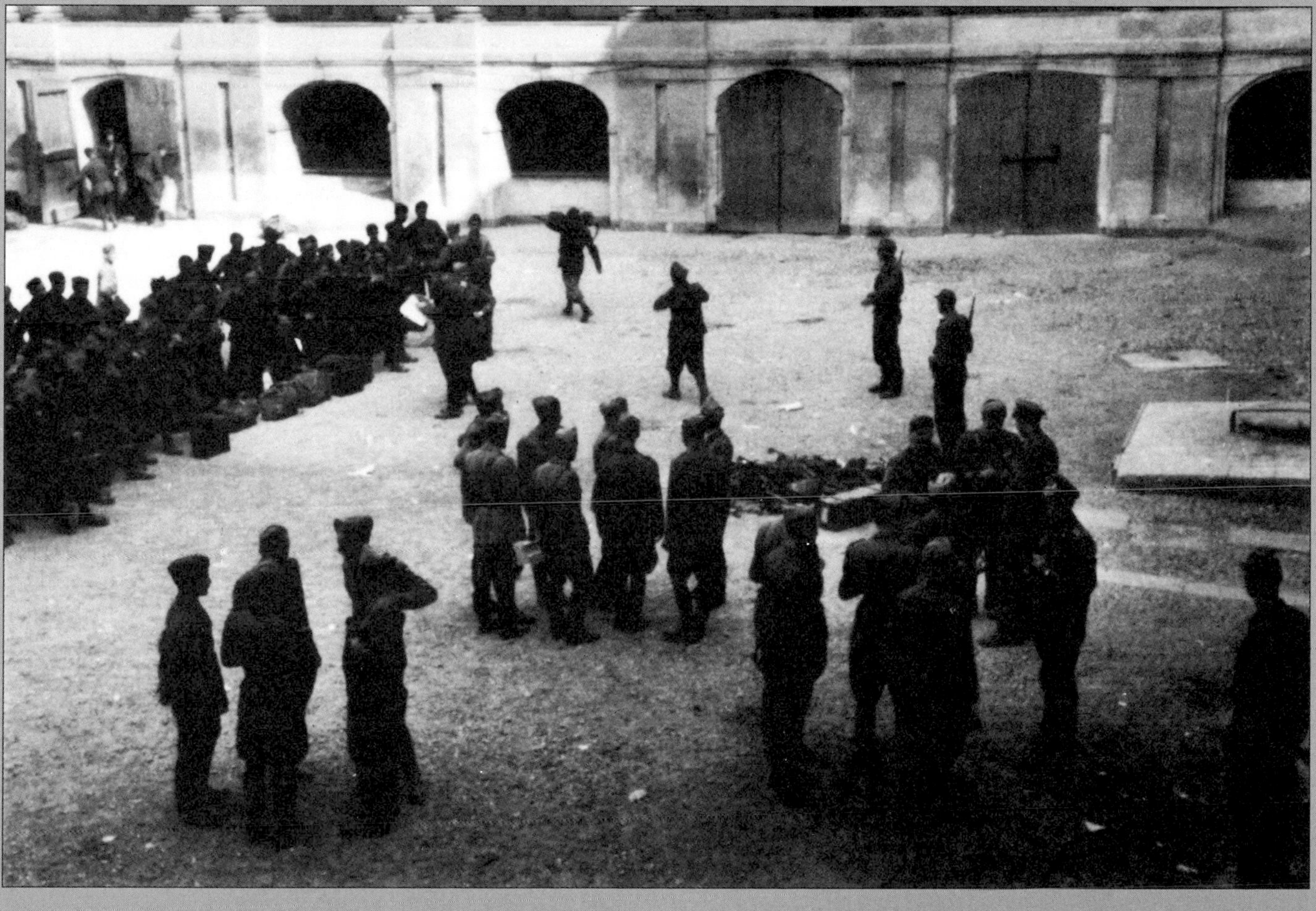

Striking Fear in the Populace

"The Germans are all over the town, and they have begun looting in earnest," reported an American diarist who remained in Rome during the occupation and wrote under the pseudonym Jane Scrivener. "They stop people in the street and take their jewels, rings, chains, watches, and money from them at the muzzle of a revolver. They are also stealing bicycles and motorcars. They simply stop the cyclist or motorist, take the machine, and leave the owner afoot. There is no redress. Their attitude is: 'Well, and what are you going to do about it?' "

There was worse treatment in store for many Italians. Thousands

A German officer stops motorists at a roadblock near Rome to check their papers. The Germans tried to intimidate the Italian people by imposing random identification checks.

SS men guard handcuffed Jews in the northern Italian province of Varese near the Swiss border.

of them would be slaughtered indiscriminately in retaliation for their acts of resistance against the oppressors. The German military commander in the city of Naples clearly set the tone of vengeance when he proclaimed that anyone who "acts openly or surreptitiously against the German armed forces will be executed. Each German soldier wounded or killed will be avenged 100 times."

In the meantime, the SS cracked down on the Jews of Italy, who had remained relatively sheltered under the regime of Mussolini. The Germans dispatched about 8,000 of them to Nazi death camps.

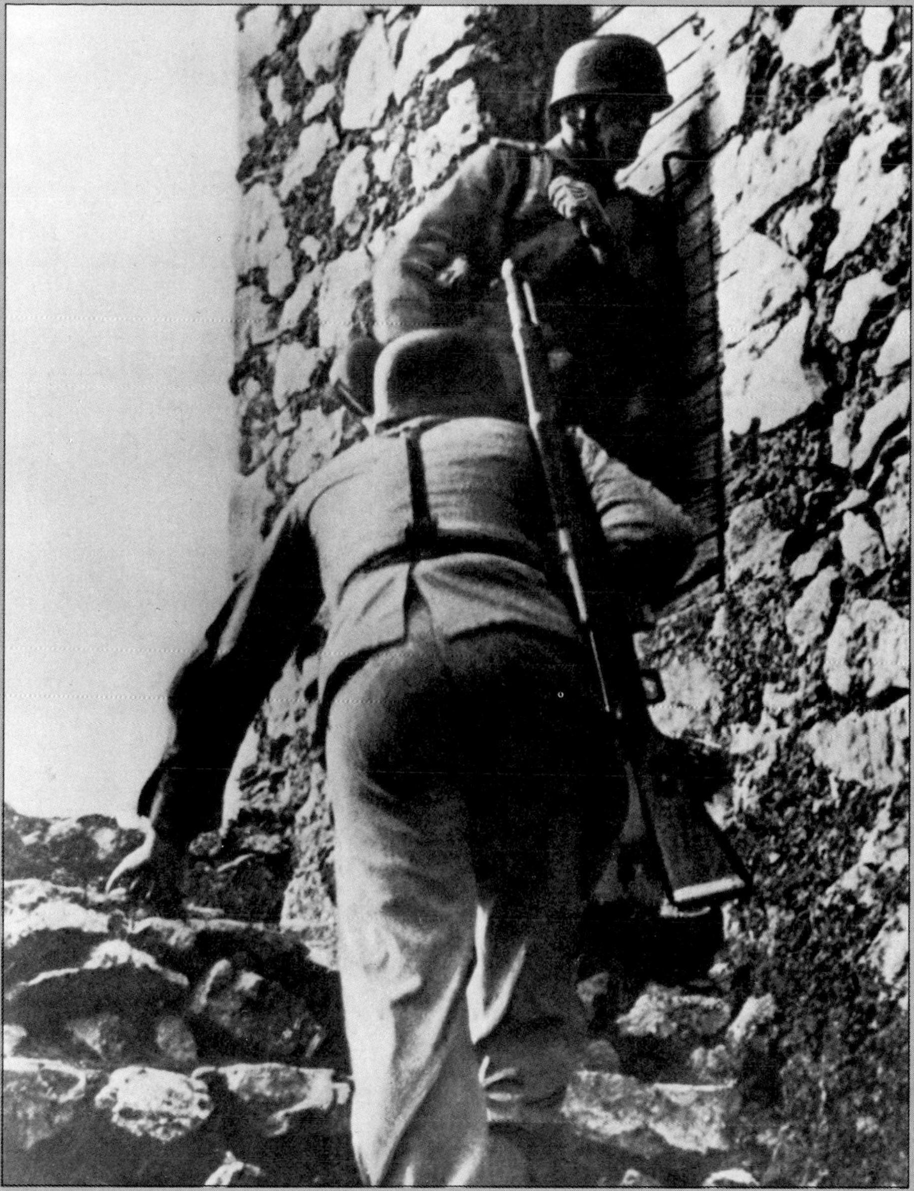

German soldiers conduct a house-to-house search in an Italian village. Such intrusions became a frightening, everyday occurrence in the spring of 1944.

Civilians who have been rounded up in Milan are herded into a truck for transport to Germany as forced laborers.

A locomotive pulling a train loaded with German ammunition lies upside down, tipped over by charges laid by Italian partisans.

The bodies of thirty-two SS men who were killed by a partisan bomb lie on Rome's Via Rasella. The Germans massacred 330 Italians in retaliation.

The corpses of fifty-two Italian civilians who were executed by the Germans for partisan activities dangle gruesomely from the balconies of the Rittmeyer Palace in Trieste.

Resistance and Reprisals

Some Allied leaders had hoped that the Italian soldiers would turn their weapons against the Germans. But the timing of the armistice caught the Italian army by surprise, and acts of resistance by the troops proved sporadic and ineffectual.

A resistance movement slowly emerged, then gained steam as more and more former soldiers brought their combat skills to the cause. Using hit-and-run tactics, they killed or kidnapped approximately 7,500 German soldiers during the summer of 1944. Sabotage of military installations and communications added to the havoc. By the last days of the war, the partisans numbered more than 200,000.

The raids infuriated the Germans, who made good on their vow to execute an "appropriate number of hostages" each time a soldier became a target of violence. Entire villages were assembled and forced to witness hangings. Bodies were left dangling for hours, then cut down and buried, as a German edict put it, "without ceremony and without the assistance of any priest."

Acknowledgments

The editors thank the following individuals and institutions for their help: Germany: Berlin—Heidi Klein, Bildarchiv Preussischer Kulturbesitz; Wolfgang Streubel, Ullstein Bilderdienst. Freiburg—Florian Berberich, Militärgeschichtliches Forschungsamt. Koblenz—Meinrad Nilges, Bundesarchiv. Munich—Elisabeth Heidt, Süddeutscher Verlag Bilderdienst. Rösrath-Hoffnungstahl—Helga Müller, Archiv Piekalkiewicz. Italy: Milan—Bruna Carnevali, Mondadori Editore; Alberto Crivelli, Mario Sannella, Farabola; Mariko Derpa, Publifoto; Ando and Luciana Gilardi, Fototeca Storica Nazionale. Rome—Aldo Fuga Casanova, Ufficio Storico Marina Militare; Gabriella Cerulli, Associazione Nazionale Partigiani d'Italia; Ettore Tanzanella, Biblioteca Storia Contemporanea. United States: North Carolina—Wolfgang O. Horn. Virginia—George A. Petersen, National Capital Historical Sales.

Picture Credits

Credits from left to right are separated by semicolons, from top to bottom by dashes. Cover: Robert Hunt Library, London. 4: AP/Wide World Photos, New York. 6, 7: Map by R. R. Donnelley and Sons Company, Cartographic Services. 9: Süddeutscher Verlag Bilderdienst, Munich. 10, 11: British Official, except inset, bottom left, AP/Wide World Photos, New York. 14, 15: Ullstein Bilderdienst, Berlin. 17: Robert Hunt Library, London. 19: U.S. Army Signal Corps, CA148. 21: Roger-Viollet, Paris. 22, 23: Artwork by John Batchelor, photographed by Larry Sherer. 24, 25: Ullstein Bilderdienst, Berlin. 27: The Hulton Picture Company, London. 29: Map by R. R. Donnelley and Sons Company, Cartographic Services. 31: Ullstein Bilderdienst, Berlin. 33: Map by R. R. Donnelley and Sons Company, Cartographic Services. 34, 35: Imperial War Museum, London. 36, 37: Eliot Elisofon for LIFE. 39-49: Courtesy Dr. Wolfgang O. Horn. 50: Library of Congress, D731552. 53: Mondadori, Milan. 54, 55: Map by R. R. Donnelley and Sons Company, Cartographic Services. 56: Camera Press, London. 57: The Hulton Picture Company, London. 58, 59: Mondadori, Milan. 62, 63: Bob Landry for LIFE. 64: Süddeutscher Verlag Bilderdienst, Munich. 65-67: Larry Sherer, courtesy George A. Petersen. 68, 69: Bildarchiv Preussischer Kulturbesitz, Berlin. 70: Courtesy George A. Petersen. 71: Mondadori, Milan. 72: Imperial War Museum, London. 75: Süddeutscher Verlag Bilderdienst, Munich. 76, 77: Mondadori, Milan. 79: Map by R. R. Donnelley and Sons Company, Cartographic Services. 80: The Hulton Picture Company, London. 81: Farabola, Milan. 83: Bettmann Newsphotos, New York. 84, 85: Ullstein Bilderdienst, Berlin. 86, 87: Roger-Viollet, Paris. 88, 89: Bundesarchiv, Koblenz (2); Bildarchiv Preussischer Kulturbesitz, Berlin. 90, 91: Bundesarchiv, Koblenz; Fototeca Storica Nazionale, Milan. 92, 93: Bundesarchiv, Koblenz. 94, 95: Süddeutscher Verlag Bilderdienst, Munich; Bundesarchiv, Koblenz. 96, 97: Fototeca Storica Nazionale, Milan; National Archives, 208-PU-142Y-1. 98: Mondadori, Milan. 101: Map by R. R. Donnelley and Sons Company, Cartographic Services. 103: Bundesarchiv, Koblenz. 105-107: Archiv Gerstenberg, Wietze. 109: Map by R. R. Donnelley and Sons Company, Cartographic Services. 110, 111: National Archives, 242-JRP-9-168. 113: Fototeca Storica Nazionale, Milan. 114, 115: Camera Press, London; Ullstein Bilderdienst, Berlin. 119: Bibliothek für Zeitgeschichte, Stuttgart. 120: Bundesarchiv, Koblenz. 121: Imperial War Museum, London. 123: Map by R. R. Donnelley and Sons Company, Cartographic Services. 124, 125: Bundesarchiv, Koblenz; Armées, Paris. 127: Mondadori, Milan. 128, 129: Imperial War Museum, London. 130, 131: The Bettmann Archive, New York, inset Alinari, Florence (2). 132, 133: Bundesarchiv, Koblenz. 134, 135: Robert Hunt Library, London, inset Archiv J. K. Piekalkiewicz, Rösrath-Hoffnungstahl. 136, 137: Süddeutscher Verlag Bilderdienst, Munich; Imperial War Museum, London. 138: Bundesarchiv, Koblenz—Imperial War Museum, London. 139: Süddeutscher Verlag Bilderdienst, Munich. 140, 141: UPI/Bettmann, New York. 142: Bundesarchiv, Koblenz. 145: Mondadori, Milan. 147: Map by R. R. Donnelley and Sons Company, Cartographic Services. 148, 149: Imperial War Museum, London—Camera Press, London. 150, 151: Bundesarchiv, Koblenz. 152: Archiv J. K. Piekalkiewicz, Rösrath-Hoffnungstahl. 153: Bundesarchiv, Koblenz. 155: Map by R. R. Donnelley and Sons Company, Cartographic Services (2). 156: Ullstein Bilderdienst, Berlin. 157: Roger-Viollet, Paris. 158, 159: Camera Press, London. 160, 161: Larry Sherer courtesy George A. Petersen, background Mondadori, Milan. 162, 163, 165: Bundesarchiv, Koblenz. 166: Imperial War Museum, London. 167: Archives Tallandier/Photothèque USIS, Paris. 169: Ullstein Bilderdienst, Berlin. 171: Robert Hunt Library, London. 172, 173: Publifoto, Milan. 175: Robert Hunt Library, London. 176, 177: Ullstein Bilderdienst, Berlin. 178, 179: Bettmann Newsphotos, New York; Publifoto, Milan—Süddeutscher Verlag Bilderdienst, Munich (2). 180: Library of Congress, LC7489C—Ufficio Storico della Marina Militare, Rome. 181: National Archives, 242JRP-67-23. 182: Mondadori, Milan—Fototeca Storica Nazionale, Milan. 183: Publifoto, Milan—Fototeca Storica Nazionale, Milan. 184, 185: Moro, Rome—Fototeca Storica Nazionale, Milan; Publifoto, Milan.

Bibliography

Books

Angolia, John R., and Adolf Schlicht, *Uniforms & Traditions of the German Army, 1933-1945* (Vol. 3). San Jose, Calif.: R. James Bender, 1987.

Avagliano, Faustino, ed., *Il Bombardamento di Montecassino*. Montecassino: N.p., 1980.

Bender, Roger James, *Air Organizations of the Third Reich: The Luftwaffe*. Mountain View, Calif.: R. James Bender, 1972.

Bender, Roger James, and Richard D. Law, *Uniforms, Organization and History of the Afrikakorps*. San Jose, Calif.: R. James Bender, 1973.

Bender, Roger James, and George A. Petersen, *"Hermann Göring."* San Jose, Calif.: R. James Bender, 1975.

Bergot, Erwan, *The Afrika Korps*. New York: Charter Books, 1975.

Blumenson, Martin:
Anzio. Philadelphia: J. B. Lippincott, 1963.
Bloody River. Boston: Houghton Mifflin, 1970.
Kasserine Pass. Boston: Houghton Mifflin, 1967.
Salerno to Cassino. Washington, D.C.: Government Printing Office, 1969.

Böhmler, Rudolf, *Monte Cassino*. Transl. by R. H. Stevens. London: Cassell, 1964.

Carell, Paul, *The Foxes of the Desert*. Transl. by Mervyn Savill. New York: E. P. Dutton, 1961.

Connell, Charles, *Monte Cassino*. London: Elek Books, 1963.

Davis, Melton S., *Who Defends Rome?* New York: Dial Press, 1972.

D'Este, Carlo, *Bitter Victory*. New York: E. P. Dutton, 1988.

Edwards, Roger, *German Airborne Troops, 1936-1945*. London: Macdonald and Jane's, 1974.

Esposito, Vincent J., ed., *The West Point Atlas of American Wars, Volume II, 1900-1953*. New York: Praeger, 1959.

Farrar-Hockley, Anthony, *Student*. New York: Ballantine Books, 1973.

Fisher, Ernest F., Jr., *Cassino to the Alps*. Washington, D.C.: Government Printing Office, 1977.

Foley, Charles, *Commando Extraordinary*. London: Longmans, Green, 1954.

Forty, George, *The Long Road Back*. Vol. 2 of *Afrika Korps at War*. London: Ian Allan, 1978.

Gallo, Max, *Mussolini's Italy*. Transl. by Charles Lam Markmann. New York: Macmillan, 1973.

Garland, Albert N., and Howard McGaw Smyth, *Sicily and the Surrender of Italy*. Washington, D.C.: Government Printing Office, 1965.

Garrett, Richard, *The Raiders*. Devon, England: David & Charles, 1980.

Graham, Dominick, *Cassino*. New York: Ballantine Books, 1970.

Graham, Dominick, and Shelford Bidwell, *Tug of War*. New York: St. Martin's Press, 1986.

Hapgood, David, and David Richardson, *Monte Cassino*. New York: Congdon & Weed, 1984.

Hibbert, Christopher, *Anzio*. New York: Ballantine Books, 1970.

Hogg, Ian, *The Weapons That Changed the World*. New York: Arbor House, 1986.

Howe, George F., *Northwest Africa*. Washington, D.C.: Government Printing Office, 1957.

Jackson, W. G. F.:
The Battle for Italy. London: B. T. Batsford, 1967.
The Battle for Rome. New York: Charles Scribner's Sons, 1969.

Kesselring, Albert, *Kesselring: A Soldier's Record*. Transl. by Lynton Hudson. New York: William Morrow, 1954.

Kirkpatrick, Ivone, *Mussolini*. New York: Hawthorn Books, 1964.

Kühn, Volkmar, *Mit Rommel in der Wüste*. Stuttgart: Motorbuch Verlag, 1987.

Kurzman, Dan, *The Race for Rome*. Garden City, N.Y.: Doubleday, 1975.

Lewin, Ronald:
The Life and Death of the Afrika Korps. London: B. T. Batsford, 1977.
Rommel as Military Commander. London: B. T. Batsford, 1968.

Linklater, Eric, *The Campaign in Italy*. London: His Majesty's Stationery Office, 1951.

Lucas, James, *Panzer Army Africa*. London: Macdonald and Jane's, 1977.

Macksey, Kenneth:
Afrika Korps. New York: Ballantine Books, 1968.
Rommel. New York: Mayflower Books, 1979.

Majdalany, Fred, *The Battle of Cassino*. Boston: Houghton Mifflin, 1957.

Mason, David, *Salerno*. New York: Ballantine Books, 1972.

Miksche, F. O., *Paratroops*. New York: Random House, 1943.

Moorehead, Alan, *Eclipse*. New York: Harper & Row, 1945.

Morris, Eric, *Salerno*. New York: Stein and Day, 1983.

Piekalkiewicz, Janusz, *The Battle for Cassino*. Indianapolis: Bobbs-Merrill, 1980.

Pond, Hugh:
Salerno. Boston: Little, Brown, 1961.
Sicily. London: William Kimber, 1962.

Rommel, Erwin, *The Rommel Papers*. Ed. by B. H. Liddell Hart, transl. by Paul Findlay. New York: Da Capo Press, 1982.

Schmidt, Heinz Werner, *With Rommel in the Desert*. London: George G. Harrap, 1951.

Scrivener, Jane, *Inside Rome with the Germans*. New York: Macmillan, 1945.

Senger und Etterlin, F. M. von:
German Tanks of World War II. Ed. by Peter Chamberlain and Chris Ellis, transl. by J. Lucas. Munich: J. F. Lehmanns Verlag, 1968.
Neither Fear nor Hope. Transl. by George Malcolm. Novato, Calif.: Presidio Press, 1989.

Shepperd, G. A., *The Italian Campaign, 1943-1945*. New York: Praeger, 1968.

Simpson, Keith, *History of the German Army*. Greenwich, Conn.: Bison Books, 1985.

Skorzeny, Otto:
La Guerre Inconnue. Paris: Albin Michel, 1975.
Secret Missions. New York: E. P. Dutton, 1950.

Smith, Denis Mack, *Mussolini*. New York: Alfred A. Knopf, 1982.

Vaughan-Thomas, Wynford, *Anzio*. London: Longmans, Green, 1961.

Warlimont, Walter, *Inside Hitler's Headquarters, 1939-1945*. Transl. by R. H. Barry. New York: Praeger, 1964.

Weeks, John S., *Airborne Equipment*. Newton Abbot, England: David & Charles, 1976.

Westphal, Siegfried, *The German Army in the West*. London: Cassell, 1951.

Whiting, Charles, *Kasserine*. New York: Stein and Day, 1984.

Wilhelm, Maria de Blasio, *The Other Italy*. New York: W. W. Norton, 1988.

Young, Desmond, *Rommel*. New York: Quill, 1978.

Other Publications

Flamm, Paul F., ed., *Combat History of the 84th Chemical Mortar Battalion*. Washington, D.C.: Department of the Army, n.d.

Gericke, Walter, "Feind bei Anzio-Nettuno gelandet!" *Der deutsche Fallschirmjäger*, September 1954.

Hermann, Ernst, "Alarm bei Anzio-Nettuno." *Der deutsche Fallschirmjäger*, May-June 1959.

Nofi, A. A., "Sicily: The Race for Messina, 10 July-17 August 1943." *Strategy & Tactics*, November-December 1981.

Otte, Alfred, "Im Feuer der Schiffsartillerie." *Der deutsche Fallschirmjäger*, March 1979.

R. B., "Die 5. Kompanie/Rgt. 3 in Cassino." *Der deutsche Fallschirmjäger*, May 1964.

Index

Numerals in italics indicate an illustration of the subject mentioned.

A
Abwehr: and Allied invasion planning, 51, 144
Acate River: 61
Acerno, Italy: 118, 119
Acquafondata, Italy: *124-125*
Adolff, Paul: 75
Adrano, Sicily: 79, 82
Afrikakorps: 5, 6, 20; Kasserine Pass offensive, 28-32; retreat from El Alamein, 7-8, *9, 10-11,* 25; strength of, 8, 9, 21; surrender of, 38
Agropoli, Italy: 107
Aircraft: A-36 fighter-bomber (American), 82; B-17 bomber (American), 104, 116; B-25 bomber (American), 77, 116; B-26 bomber (American), 116; C-47 transport (Allied), 71; DFS 230 gliders, *88, 90-91;* Fieseler Storch spotter plane, 86, *94, 95;* Folke Wulfe 190 fighter, 72; glider and rocket bombs, 112; Heinkel 111 (bomber), *14-15,* 96; Junkers, 18; Junkers 52 transport, 16, 35, 43, *76-77;* Junkers 87 dive bomber (Stuka), 16; Messerschmitt fighter, 18; Piper Cub (American), 154; Spitfire fighter, *48*
Alban Hills: 145, 148, 168
Albania: 99
Alexander, Sir Harold: 26, 38, 51, 77; and Anzio landing, 145, 157; and bombing of Monte Cassino, 135, 153, 154, 163; commander of 15th Army Group, 143; drive on Gustav Line, 143, 144, 153; German Tenth Army, attempt to trap, 168; and Operation Diadem, 163-164; and Operation Olive, 173; and transfer of troops for Allied invasion of southern France, 170
Alexandria, Egypt: 5
Algiers: Allied landings at, 5, 7, 9, 13, 15, 17
Allies: air superiority of, 7, 82, 84, 144, 163; amphibious capability of, 99, 144, 145, 148; British counterintelligence activities, 51; command problems in Italian campaign, 168; command problems in Tunisian campaign, 26-28; diversity of national units on Italian front, 164, 170; ground troop reliance on air support, 100, 103; historical and cultural property, policy on, 153; Italy, plans for invasion of, 103; Polish Corps, 138, 164-165, *166, 167;* Stalin, promise of western front support, 144
Altavilla, Italy: 113
Anders, Wladyslaw: 164
Anderson, Kenneth: 26
Anzio: Allied breakout from, 164, 167-168; Allied landing at, 145, 146, *148-149,* 150-158; Allied naval and air support at, 157; German counterattack at, 154-156, *157,* 158; German propaganda leaflets at, *148;* lull in fighting at, 163; panzer division headquarters at, *169*
Anzio Annie: 163
Aprilia, Italy: 150, 154, 169
Arabs: relations with Allies and Germans, 18, *47*
Armed forces high command (OKW): 12, 16, 21, 51, 99, 100, 102, 105, 106, 122
Armored vehicles: armored personnel carriers, *31;* Bren gun carrier (British), *72;* M-3 light tanks (American), 18; Panzer IV tanks, *19;* Panzer VI Tiger I tanks, 20, *22-23,* 60, 63, 107, *171;* Sherman tanks (American), 61, 74; SS assault gun, *179*
Army: attrition in units, 170; battle group in action at Salerno beachhead, *110-111;* Battle Group Schmalz, 64, 69, 70, 73, 76, 82; captured German troops in North Africa, *36-37;* casualties, 38, 85, 170, 173, *175;* casualties, recording of on battlefield, *127;* command structure in Sicily, 54; engineers, 143; Fourteenth Army, 168, 170, 173; German scorn for Italian units, 8, 68; historic and cultural property, policy toward, 130, 153; medics evacuating wounded, *153;* minelaying by, 9-12, 78, 126; mule transport on Italian front, *119;* observation posts, *25,* 126; panzer division headquarters, *169;* panzer engineers, 9; planning for Italian capitulation, 100; rearguard units, tactics of, 119, 126; reprisals for Italian partisan activity, 176, 183, *184-185;* sappers, *98;* Sixth Army, 12, 107; supply problems in Italian theater, *119,* 174; Tenth Army, 102, *103,* 116, 117, 118, 122, 126, 146, 165, 168, 170, 173, 174; training and camp life in Tunisian campaign, *44-49;* transfer of relics from Monte Cassino, *132-133*
Army (armored units): 8th Panzer Regiment, 30; 15th Panzergrenadier Division, 54, 55, 56, 58, 64, 69, 78, 79, 112, 118, 125, 127, 128, 143, 147, 150; Fifth Panzer Army, 7, 20, 26, 33, 39; XIV Panzer Corps, 55, 109, 112, 118, 123, 128, 130, 146, 165, 170; German-Italian Panzer Army, 7; 90th Panzergrenadier Division, 128, 144, 153, 165; Panzergrenadier Regiment Africa (Special Unit 288), 28; 79th Panzergrenadier Regiment, 108; LXXVI Panzer Corps, 112, 118, 123, 126, 156; 16th Panzer Division, 104, 107, 108, 109-112, 113, 118, 122-123, 128; 10th Panzer Division, 7, 20, 21, 26, 28, 30, 39; 3d Panzergrenadier Division, 106, 118, 124-125, 150, 156, 168; 21st Panzer Division, 7, 25, 26, 28, 30; 29th Panzergrenadier Division, 55, 77, 78, 79, 82, 112, 113, 118, 128, 144, 150, 153, 156; 26th Panzer Division, 112, 118, 128, 156, 158, 167; 211th Panzergrenadier Regiment, 154
Army (infantry units): LI Mountain Corps, 174; 44th Division, 143; Lehr Regiment, 156, 157; 90th Light Infantry Division, 26, 34; 94th Division, 146, 165; 114th Division, 148, 156; 164th Division, 26; 715th Division, 148, 150, 156; 71st Division, 165; 65th Division, 126, 128, 148, 156, 168; 362d Division, 148, 158
Army Group Africa: 32
Arnim, Jürgen von: 20, 32, 38; in command post at Pont-du-Fahs, *24;* Kasserine Pass offensive, 26, 28, 29
Arno River: 171, 173
Artillery: antiaircraft gun (four-barreled), *128-129;* assault gun, *162-163;* coastal defense guns (Italian), *57;* 88-mm antiaircraft gun, 72, 73, 108; 88-mm antiaircraft gun used as antitank weapon, *19,* 20, 74; *Nebelwerfer* (rocket launcher), *113;* 105-mm howitzer (German), *45, 48-49;* self-propelled guns, *120;* 75-mm self-propelled gun *(Stürmgeschutz), 114-115;* 280-mm railroad gun, *150-151,* 163
Augusta, Sicily: British troops in, *68-69*
Avellino, Italy: 115
Awards: Iron Cross, 34; Knight's Cross of the Iron Cross, 86; Luftwaffe ground combat badge, *65*

B
Badoglio, Pietro: and armistice with Allies, 100, 104, 105; escape from German occupying troops, 106; as Italian premier, 78, 176
Balck, Hermann: 109, 112
Balkans: Italian army disarmed in, 106; potential Allied invasion site, 51, 99, 100, 102, 122
Barbara Line: 117, 126
Bardo (museum): 42
Barenthin, Walther: 18
Bastico, Ettore: 12
Battipaglia, Italy: 113, 116, 118
Bayerlein, Fritz: 7
Belgium: units with British Eighth Army, 164
Belmonte Castello, Italy: Kesselring at, *165*
Benedict of Nursia, Saint: 130
Benghazi, Libya: British supply problems at, 24-25; German aircraft over harbor, *14-15;* German withdrawal from, 5
Berchtesgaden: 158
Bergengrün, Helmut: 61
Bernhardt Line: 117, 126, 127; Italian POWs working at, *124*
Biferno River: 122
Bizerte, Tunisia: 7, 16, 17, 18, 20, 36, 38; German counterattack at, *27*
Böhmler, Rudolf: 73
Bologna, Italy: 173, 174
Brazil: units with Allies on Italian front, 170
British army: Canadian I Corps, 163; commandos, 70, 108, 122, 148; Durham Light Infantry Regiment, 74, 75; Eighth Army, 5, 6-7, 9, 13, 15, 25, 33, 34, 38, 55, 57, 58, 70, 77, 103, 104, 115, 118, 122, 123, 126, 128, 153, 163-164, 173, 174; 11th Brigade, 20; 5th Division, 68, 153; 50th Division, 70,

73; 51st (Highland) Division, *58-59;* 56th Division, 108, 121, 127, 157; First Army, 7, 17, 38; 1st Division, 148, 150; 1st Paratroop Brigade, 71-73; 46th Division, 108, 121; 4th/6th Rajputana Rifles, 154; glider operations by, 57, 58; Gurkhas, 154, 162-163; Indian 4th Division, 153, 154, 158, 163; King's Dragoon Guards, 121; Maoris, 154; New Zealand Corps, 25, 34; New Zealand II Corps, 153, 158; New Zealand 2d Division, 153, 154, 158, 159-162; paratroopers, 20; Royal Sussex, 154; 7th Armored Division, 121; 78th Division, 17, 122, 153, 158; signalman under fire, *114;* X Corps, 108, 113, 121, 125, 143, 145, 146, 152, 153, 164; XIII Corps, 165; 36th Brigade of Guards, 18
British counterintelligence activities: 51
Broich, Fritz von: 32
Buelowius, Karl: 30
Buerat, Libya: 21, 24

C

Caesar Line: 163, 168-170
Cairo, Egypt: Shepheard's Hotel, 21
Calabria, Italy: Allied invasion, 99, 104, 112; German withdrawal to from Sicily, 79, 83, 84
Calore River: 107, 113
Caltagirone, Sicily: 60, 64
Campoleone, Italy: 150
Canada: German prisoners shipped to, 37
Canaris, Wilhelm: 144
Cape Serrat: 20, 38
Carthage: German troops touring at, *39, 43*
Casablanca: Allied landings at, 5, 7, 13, 15; conference at, 52
Cassino, Italy: 135, 146; bombing of, *158-159;* fighting at, *145,* 150, 152, 154, 158-159, *160-163,* 164; German paratroopers in, *142*
Castellano, Giuseppe: *105*
Castle Hill: 163
Catania, Sicily: 68, 69, 70, 73, 74, 75, 76, 77, 82
Cerami, Sicily: 79
Chiunzi Pass: 108
Chott Djerid: 13, 34
Churchill, Winston: 15, 52, 100, 144, 145
Cisterna, Italy: 150, 156, 157, 167, 168
Civitavecchia, Italy: 163
Clark, Mark: and Anzio landing, 145, 150, 157; attacks on Gustav Line, 151-152; and bombing of Monte Cassino, 153; halts Fifth Army offensive operations at Bernhardt Line, 127-128; invasion of French North Africa, 15; invasion of Italy, 103, 112, 114, 115, 146; and liberation of Rome, 168, 169
Comando Supremo: 5, 8, 12, 21, 25, 26, 30, 51
Conrath, Paul: 60, 61, *64,* 68
Continental Hotel (Cassino): fighting at, 159-162
Corsica: 99, 103
C-Position: 163. *See also* Caesar Line
Cramer, Johann: 7
Crete: 106

D

Darlan, Jean François: 15-16
Devers, Jacob: 154
Diamare, Gregorio: and attack on abbey, 135; leaves Monte Cassino for Rome, *137;* transfer of relics from Monte Cassino, 132, *133*
Djebel Abiod, Tunisia: 17
Djebel Ahmera, Tunisia: 20
Düppenbecker, Herbert: 108

E

Eaker, Ira: 154
Eastern Task Force (Allies): 17
Eboli, Italy: 113, 116
Egypt: coastal road, German retreat on, *10-11*
Eisenhower, Dwight D.: 38; as commander in chief, 26; invasion of Italy, 103; and Italian armistice, 104, *105;* Rome as objective of, 122
El Alamein: battle of, 5, 6, 7, 9
Enfidaville, Tunisia: 38
Enna, Sicily: 77; Italian headquarters at, 54, 56, 64
Etna Line: 55, 77, 78, 79, 82
Excelsior Hotel: *See* Continental Hotel

F

Faïd, Tunisia: 26
Faïd Pass: 28
Fassl, Erich: 75
Feltre, Italy: 77
Fériana, Tunisia: 28
Fischer, Wolfgang: 20
Florence, Italy: demolition of bridges in, *172-173*
Foggia, Italy: airfields at, 99, 102, 103, 117, 122
Fosso Bottaceto: 75, 76
France: threat of Allied landings in, 13, 99. *See also* Vichy France
Frascati, Italy: Kesselring's headquarters at, 104, 144
Fredendall, Lloyd: 26-28
French Expeditionary Corps: in Italian theater of operations, 143, 145, 146, 152, 164, 165, 170; in North Africa, 38
French Expeditionary Corps units: Algerian 3d Division, 143, 167; 1st Motorized Infantry, 164; *goumiers* (Berbers), 164, 165; Moroccan 4th Division, 164; Moroccan 2d Division, 143, 165
French Morocco: Allied landings in, 5, 9, 15
French North Africa: French reactions to Allied invasion, 13-16
Freyberg, Sir Bernard: 158, 162, 163; and bombing of abbey at Monte Cassino, 153, 154
Fuka, Egypt: 12

G

Gabès, Tunisia: German defensive position at, 7, 13, 17-18, 33, 34
Gaeta, Italy: 109
Gafsa, Tunisia: 26, 28
Garigliano River: 117, 127, 143, 145, 146, 148, 153
Gavin, James: 61
Gela, Italy: American beachhead at, 58, 60-61, *62-63,* 64
Gerlach, Heinrich: 94, 95, 96
Gibraltar: 13
Gonzaga, Don Ferrante: 176
Göring, Hermann: 100, 106; and German command structure in Sicily, 54; meeting with Rommel and Hitler at Wolf's Lair, 12-13; organizes namesake unit, 65
Gothic Line: 102, 171, 173
Gran Sasso d'Italia: 86; lodge at, *92*
Greece: potential Allied invasion site, 51, 99
Gustav Line: 117, 122, *124-125,* 126, 128, 129, 143, 145, 146, 151, 153, 158, 163, 164, 165, 171
Guzzoni, Alfredo: 54-56, 57, 58, 60, 61, 64, 68, 78

H

Hangman's Hill: 162-163
Heidrich, Richard: 122, 163
Heilmann, Ludwig: 70, 71, 73, 74, 76
Henschel Company: 22
Hill 593: 154, 165
Hill 445: 152
Hitler, Adolf: approves withdrawal to Caesar Line, 168; and counterattack at Anzio, 151, 154-157, 158; and defense of Sicily, 77, 78, 83; and defensive plans for Italy, 102, 103; doubts over Italian allies, 52, 53, 78, 86, 100, 106, 176; and German defeat in North Africa, 38; greets rescued Mussolini, *97;* hold at all costs defensive orders, 128; insistence on personal approval of every major military decision in Italy, 128; and Kesselring, 100, 102, 129, 168, 171; meeting with Mussolini at Feltre, 77-78; meeting with Rommel at Wolf's Lair, 12-13, 21; monitors situation in Cassino sector, 143; orders rescue mission for Mussolini, 86, 103; Rome, agrees to treat as open city, 170; Rome, defensive plans for, 122; and Rommel, 5, 6, 8, 34; and secret weapons, 112, 151; sends Arnim to Tunisian second front, 20; strategic plans of, 6, 13, 38, 51, 99; and Vatican, distrust of, 100; and Vietinghoff, 117, 164, 174
Hitler Line: 163, 166
Horn, Wolfgang: photographs of North African war by, *39-49*
Hube, Hans: 77, 78, 79, 82, 83, 84

I

Il Giogo Pass: 173
Infantry weapons: bazookas (American), 58-60; FG 42 rifle, *160;* MG 42 machine gun (Spandaus), 119, *160; panzerfaust* antitank weapon, *145; Shu* mine, 126; "S" mine (Bouncing Betty), 12, 126
Italian army: and Afrikakorps, 8, 12; Aosta Division, 79, 82; Centauro Division, 25, 30; Comando Supremo, 5, 8, 12, 21, 25, 26, 30, 51; command structure on Sicily, 54; evacuation from Sicily, 84; fate of following armistice, 106, *180-181,* 185; 5th Bersaglieri, 25; Livorno Division, 55, 58, 60, 61; Mobile Group E, 58; *Monte Rosa* Alpine Division, 174; Napoli Division, 64, 69; Sixth Army, 54; Spezia Division, 34; strength of, 52, 54, 100, 181; Superga Division, 18; in Tunis, *17*
Italian navy: abandons base on Sicily, 68; fails to challenge Allied fleet in Mediterranean, 52; flees for Allied ports after armistice, 106, 181
Italian Social Republic: 181
Italy: Allied objectives in, 38, 51-52, 103; armistice with Allies, 100, 103, 104-105, 176; depletion of military strength, 52; effect of terrain on Allied campaign, 117-118; Fascist Grand Council, 78; German initial defensive strategy in, 102, 117-118; German intimidation of civilian population, *182-183;* Jews, and German occupation, 176, *182,* 183; losses in North Africa, effects of, 32, 38; Mussolini's resignation, 78, 100; partisan activity in, 173, 174, 176, 181, *184,* 185; political crisis in, 77-78; royal family, flight of, 106; units with British Eighth Army, 164

J

Jews: fate of in German-occupied Italy, 176, *182,* 183
Juin, Alphonse-Pierre: in Italian theater of operations, 143, 145, 152, 164; in North Africa, 15

K

Kasserine Pass, battle of: 25, 28-32, 39
Keitel, Wilhelm: on Hitler's relations with general staff, 158
Kesselring, Albert: and Anzio landings, 148-150, 151, 156, 157, 158; appointed commander of all forces in Italy, 129; and Caesar Line, 168, 170; at Cassino front, *165;* Cassino front, orders evacuation of, 166; defensive strategy for Italy, 100, 102, 103, 117, 118, 122, 126, 163, 171; and Gustav Line, 117, 128, 129, 143-144, 145, 146, 157, 163, 165; and Italian capitulation, 106, 109, 181; Naples, orders for demolition in, 121; relinquishes command due to injury from auto accident, 173; and retreat from Rome, 170, 171; and Rommel, 8, 32-33; with Rommel in Egypt, *4;* and Salerno landings, 107, 109, 113, 116; and Sicilian theater of operations, 54-56, 58, 60, 64-68, 77, 79, 82-83; survives Allied bombing raids, 104, 165; and Termoli landings, 122; and Tunisian offensive, 20, 26, 30, 32; and Vietinghoff, 126
Keyes, Geoffrey: 143, 146, 152

L

La Goulette, Tunisia: *40*
Lake Comacchio: 174
Lake Garda: Rommel's headquarters at, 102
Lake Trasimeno: fighting at, 171
La Molina Pass: 108
Lampedusa: Italian surrender of, 53
Lebanon: units with British Eighth Army, 164
Leese, Sir Oliver: 164
Leghorn, Italy: 99, 163, 171
Le Kef, Tunisia: 30
Lemelsen, Joachim: 126, 168, 173
Lentini, Sicily: 70, 73
Leonardi, Priamo: 68
Leonforte, Sicily: 77
Lessouda, Tunisia: 28
Libya: German retreat from, 9
Liri Valley: 127, 128, 130, 146, 152, 154, 158, 163, 165, 167
Longstop Hill: *See* Djebel Ahmera
Lowry, Frank: 148
Lucas, John: 145, 146, 148, 150, 156; relieved of command at Anzio, 157
Luftwaffe: antiaircraft crews, 150; at Anzio beachhead, 150, 163; attack on Italian fleet, 106, *180,* 181; cuff titles of Hermann Göring Panzer Division, *65, 66;* declining strength of in western Mediterranean sector, 52; ground crew for Stuka, *106-107;* and invasion of Sicily, 56, 58, 64, 82; in North Africa, 7, 16, 18, 35; paratrooper battle dress and weapons, *160-161;* recruiting posters, *65;* and rescue of Mussolini, *86-97;* at Salerno beachhead, 106, 108, 112; at Termoli beachhead, 123; in Tunisia, 16, 18; uniforms of Hermann Göring Panzer Division, *66-67*
Luftwaffe (ground units): 5th Paratroop Regiment, 18; I Paratroop Corps, 156; 1st Paratroop Division, *50, 55, 71,* 102, 106, 118, 122, 128, 138, *142,* 153, 154, 159-162, 163, 165-166; 1st Paratroop Engineer Battalion, 74; 1st Paratroop Machine-Gun Battalion, 70, 71, 73, 74; 4th Paratroop Division, 150, 156, 157, 168; 4th Paratroop Regiment, 76; Hermann Göring Panzer Division, 54, 55, 56, 58, 60, 61, 64, 65, 69, 70, 78, 82, 109, 112, 118, 121, 124, 128, 132, 150, 156, 158, 170; paratroop-engineer battalion, 17; paratroopers, *120, 138;* paratroopers as regular infantry preparing for assault, *27;* paratroopers in Sicily, *75,* 82; Ramcke's Paratroop Brigade, 8, 12; 2d Paratroop Division, 100, 106; 3d Paratroop Regiment, 69-70, 73, 76

M

Mackensen, Eberhard von: *156;* at Anzio beachhead, 150, 154-158, 167-168
Maiori, Italy: 107, 108
Malati Bridge: 70, 73
Malta: 13, 112, 181; British bases on, 6
Mareth Line: 7, 25, 26, 30, 33, *34,* 35
Marseilles, France: 144
Martin, William: 51
Martuba: 5
Marzabotto: massacre in, 176
Mateur, Tunisia: 17, 18
Matronola, Martino: 132, 137
Médenine: battle at, 33-34
Mediterranean Sea: Axis supply routes across, 6, 35; and Italian fleet, 52; Royal Navy control in, 35
Medjerda Valley: 39
Medjez-el-Bab, Tunisia: 18, 20, 44, 45, 48
Menton, Colonel: 28
Mersa Brega Line: 5, 12, 15, 21, 24
Messagero, Il (newspaper): *80*
Messe, Giovanni: 25, 32, 38
Messina, Sicily: 55, 68, 77, 79, 82, 83, 84
Metauro River: 173
Mignano Gap: 127, 128
Milan, Italy: reaction to Mussolini's resignation, *81;* SS guarding Italian prisoners in, *181*
Minturno, Italy: 146, 164
Monte Belvedere: 152
Monte Cassino: 117, 146; abbey at, *130-131,* 144; Allied bombing of abbey, *134-135,* 137, 153; Allied casualties at, 152; Allied leaflets used at, *134;* German medics and wounded at, *153;* and German propaganda, *152;* German troops occupy bombed abbey, *138-139,* 142, 154; German withdrawal to defensive position at, 128; Polish units, successful assault of, 165, *166;* postwar condition and reconstruction, *140-141;* refugees leaving abbey after Allied bombing, *136-137;* safeguarding of abbey relics, *132-133*
Montecorvino, Italy: airfield at, 113
Monte Gridolfo, Italy: 173
Monterotondo, Italy: 106
Monte Trocchio, Italy: 124
Montgomery, Bernard Law: 38; assault on Mareth Line, 34, *35;* assumes command of Eighth Army, 6; defeats Rommel at Médenine, 33; at El Alamein, 7; invasion of Sicily, 57, 70, 76, 77; Italy theater of operations, 103, 112, 115, 122, 128; in pursuit of Afrikakorps, 9, 12, 13, 25, 30
Mors, Otto-Harald, 91
Mount Camino: 128
Mount Etna: 68
Mount La Difensa: 127, 128
Mount Majo: 165

Mount Sammucro: 117, 128
Murphy, Robert: 15
Mussolini, Benito: 20, 85, 176, 183; forced resignation and arrest of, 78, 80, 100; and German offers to boost defense of Italy, 52-54; head of puppet regime in northern Italy, 97, 181; meets with Hitler at Feltre, 77-78; and Rommel, 5, 6, 8; and Skorzeny rescue operation, *86-97*, 103

N

Naples, Italy: Allied base for amphibious operations, 144, 163; as Allied objective, 99, 102, 103, 108, 116, 117, 118; Allied occupation of, 121-122; damage to harbor, 118, *121*, 122; German withdrawal from, *120*, 121
National Socialist German Workers' party: *See* Nazi party
Navy: torpedo boats evacuated from Sicily, 68; U-boats blocked from Mediterranean, 52
Nazi party: police units as nucleus of Hermann Göring Panzer Division, 65; propaganda offensive over Monte Cassino attack, 140
Nehring, Walther: 16, 17, 18, 20
Nettuno, Italy: 148
North Africa: German commitment for defense, 13; German defeat and surrender in, 35, *36-37*, 38

O

OKW: *See* Armed forces high command
Oliveto Citra, Italy: 118
Operation *Achse* (Axis): 100, 105-106
Operation *Alarich: 52-53*, 100
Operation Anvil: 144
Operation Diadem: 164-165
Operation *Frühlingswind* (Spring Wind): 26
Operation Husky: 57, *58-59;* Allied ship convoys for, *56*
Operation Lehrgang (Training Tour): 82-84
Operation *Morgenluft* (Morning Air): 26
Operation Olive: 173
Operation Overlord: 144, 145, 170
Operation *Richard:* 148
Operation Torch: 5, 9, 13-16
Operation Winter Thunderstorm: 174
Oran, Algeria: Allied landings at, 5, 7, 13, 15

P

Pachino Peninsula: 57, 58
Paestum, Italy: 118
Palermo, Sicily: Allied occupation of, 77
Pantelleria: Allied attack on, *53*
Patton, George S.: in command of II Corps, 38; invasion of French North Africa, 15; invasion of Sicily, 58, 77
Penta, Italy: 116
Pesaro, Italy: 171
Pescara, Italy: 106, 128
Phantom Ridge: 164-165
Piano Lupo, Sicily: 60, 61
Piedimonte San Germano: captured German troops at, *167*
Pisa, Italy: 102, 171
Pohl, Ritter von: 150
Poland: units with British Eighth Army, 164
Pont-du-Fahs, Tunisia: 24
Ponte Grande: 58
Ponte Primosole: *See* Primosole Bridge
Popcorn Pete: 163
Po River: 174
Po Valley: 117, 173
Pratica di Mare air base: 96
Primosole Bridge: *72;* fighting at, 70-75, 77

R

Radio Rome: 105
Rapido River: 117, 124, 143, 145, 146, 148, 151-152, 165
Rastenburg, East Prussia: 97
Ravenna, Italy: 173, 174
Reich: Italians transported as slave laborers, 106, 181, *183*
Rhodes: 106
Richthofen, Wolfram von: 104
Riemenschneider, Tilman: 46
Rimini, Italy: 102, 173
Roatta, Mario: 104, 106
Rodt, Eberhard: 79, 82
Rome, Italy: Allied bombing of, 78, 80; Allied liberation of, 170, *171;* as Allied objective, 99, 117, 122, 127, 128, 144, 145, 146, 148, 168, 170; Allied POWs paraded in by Germans, *cover;* declared an open city, 100, 170; German defense and occupation of, 102, 105-106, *176-179;* German withdrawal from, 170, 171; reaction to Mussolini's resignation, *80;* safeguarding of relics in, 132, *133*
Rommel, Erwin: and Arnim, 20, 25, 29; and command structure, 20; defensive strategy for Italy, 102, 103, 122; at El Alamein, 7; Kasserine Pass offensive, 26, 28-32; and Kesselring, *4*, 129; leaves North Africa, 34; medical problems of, 6; meeting with Hitler and Göring at Wolf's Lair, 12-13, 21; promotion to field marshal, 6; retreat from Egypt, 5, 8, 9, 12, 15, 24, 25; strategic plans of, 12-13, 33, 34; supply problems in North Africa, 6, 8, 21, 32
Roosevelt, Franklin D.: 100, 145
Royal Air Force (RAF): aerial reconnaissance photographs by, *10-11;* air superiority of in North Africa, 7; attacks on Axis supply convoys to North Africa, 6; and German retreat in North Africa, 5, 8, 9
Rumania: oil fields in, 99

S

St. Anselm's monastery: 132, 137
St. Paul's monastery: 132
Salerno, Italy: Allied invasion at, 104, 106-117; Allied naval losses at, 112; as Allied target, 102, 103, 113; German containment of Allied beachhead, 109, *110-111*, 112, 113, *114-115*
San Fratello, Sicily: 79, 82
Sangro River: 126, 128
San Pietro Infine, Italy: 128
Sant'Angelo, Italy: 146, 164
Santo Stefano, Sicily: 77, 78, 79
Sardinia: 13, 51, 53, 99, 103
Sbeitla, Tunisia: 7, 30
Sbiba, Tunisia: 7
Schlegel, Julius: *133*
Schmalz, Wilhelm: 69, *70*
Scrivener, Jane: 182
Sele River: 107, 113
Senger Line: 166-167
Senger und Etterlin, Frido von: 128, 130, 135, 146, 147, 148, 164, 170, 171; and abbey at Monte Cassino, 154; assumes command of Fourteenth Army, 173; with Diamare at Monte Cassino, *137*
Serchio Valley: 174
Ships: *Jean Bart* (French), 15; LST (Allied), *148-149; Newfoundland* (British cruiser), 72; *Roma* (Italian battleship), 106, *180*, 181; *Savannah* (U.S. cruiser), 61; Siebel ferries, *84*
Sicily: Allied and Axis casualties, 85; Allied invasion target, 51-52, 53, 54; Allied landings on, 55-58; Axis defenses, strengthening of, 54; German counterattack on Allied beachheads, 60-61, *62-63*, 64; German evacuation of, 78-83, *84-85;* German withdrawal to from North Africa, 38; Italian coastal defense guns, *57;* strategic importance of, 52
Sickenius, Rudolf: 109
Sidi Barrani: 5
Sidi-Bou-Zid, Tunisia: 26, 28, 30
Siebel, Fritz: 84
Simeto River: 70, 71, 74
Sirte, Libya: 24
Skorzeny, Otto: and rescue of Mussolini, *86-87, 92-94*
Smith, Walter B.: *105*
Snakeshead Ridge: 154
Sollum-Halfaya Line: 5
Sorrento Peninsula: 118
Spezia, Italy: 171, 173; Italian fleet at, 52, 106
SS *(Schutzstaffel):* guarding Italian soldiers in Milan, *181;* and Italian Jews, *182*, 183; partisan attack on in Rome, *184*. *See also* Waffen-SS
Stalin, Joseph: Allied assurances to of second front, 144
Stalingrad: encirclement of Sixth Army at, 12
Stangenberg, Franz: 73, 74
Stella Rossa (Red Star): 176
Strait of Gilbraltar: 52
Strait of Messina: 52, 83, 99, 103; Axis lifeline across, 68, 77
Student, Kurt: 86, 88, 89, 96
Suez Canal: 38

Syracuse: Italian surrender of, *58*, 68

T

Taranto, Italy: Allied invasion target, 103; Italian fleet at, *52*, 106
Tarhuna-Homs Line: 25
Tebessa, Algeria: Allied supply base at, 29, 30
Tébourba, Tunisia: fighting at, 18, *19*, 20, *21*
Tehran Conference: 144
Termoli, Italy: 122, 123
Terracina, Italy: 167
Thala, Tunisia: 30, 32
Thélepte, Tunisia: 30
Ticino River: 174
Times of London: 72, 76
Tobruk: German withdrawal from, 5, 12
Trieste: German reprisals for partisan activity in, *184-185*
Trigno River: 123, 125
Tripoli, Libya: 25
Troina, Sicily: fighting at, 79-82
Truscott, Lucian K., Jr.: 77, 157, 164, 167, 168
Tuker, F. S.: 153
Tunis, Tunisia: Allied objective, 16-17, 38; Allied race for, 17-20; antiquities in, *42*; bazaars and city life in, *41, 42;* German occupation and defense of, 16, 20, *40;* Italian troops in, *17;* Jewish cemetery in, *42*
Tunisia: Afrikakorps withdraws to Mareth Line in, 7, 25; Axis casualties in, 38; German convoys in, *31;* German defense of, 9, 12, 13, 16, 18, 20-21, 33; German surrender in, 38

U

Ultra: and Italian theater of operations, 122; and North African theater of operations, 6, 21, 33
United States: German prisoners shipped to, 37; postwar congressional inquiry, 148
United States army: attack on abbey at Monte Cassino, 140; Combat Force B, 20; 18th Infantry, 20; 88th Division, *171;* 85th Infantry Division, 164; 82d Airborne Division, 61, 115; 87th Infantry Division, 164; Fifth Army, 103, 118, 123, 126, 127-128, 145, 150, 164, 168, 173, 174; 1st Armored Division, 17, 18, 28, 34, 61, 150, 153, 158, 167; 509th Parachute Infantry Battalion, 148; 45th Division, 113, 114, 118, 156; military police and prisoners, *83;* 92d Infantry Division, 170, 174; 9th Infantry Division, 32; paratrooper attack on Sicily, 56-57, 64; Rangers, 58, 61, 108, 109, 121, 148, 150; II Corps, 7, 15, 26, 28, 30, 32, 38, 143, 146, 152, 164, 167, 168, 170; Seventh Army, 55, 57-58, 77, *83;* Signal Corps, combat newsreels taken by, *19;* VI Corps, 108, 113, 145, 150, 164, 167-168; 10th Mountain Division, 170; 3d Division, 77, 118, 119, 124, 127, 148, 150, 157, 167; 34th Division, 125, 152, 153, 154; 36th Division (Texas National Guard), 108, 128, 146-148, 151, 163, 168
United States navy: 60; friendly fire by, 64

V

Valmontone, Italy: 164, 168, 170
Vatican: 137; Hitler's distrust of, 100
Velletri, Italy: 168, 170
Vichy France: and French colonies, 15; German military occupation of, 16
Victor Emmanuel III: and armistice, 100, 104; flees German occupation troops, 176; and resignation of Mussolini, 78
Vienna, Austria: 86, 96
Vietinghoff, Heinrich von: 102, *103;* and Bernhardt Line, 127; and Caesar Line, 168; and Gustav Line, 144, 145, 146, 150, 153, 164; in hospital, 170; and Operation Winter Thunderstorm, 174; replaces injured Kesselring as commander, 173; and Salerno beachhead, 107, 109, 112, 113, 115, 116-117; Salerno beachhead, withdrawal from, 118; and Senger Line, 167; and surrender of Tenth and Fourteenth armies, 174; at Volturno front, 122-124, 126
Vietri sul Mare, Italy: 104, 108
Vizzini, Sicily: 70
Volturno River: 118, 121, 122, 123, 126; casualties at, *127;* fighting at, *98*, 124-125

W

Waffen-SS: and rescue of Mussolini, 86
Ward, Orlando: 28
Waters, John K.: 18
Weber, Friedrich: *24*
Wehrmacht: *See* Army, Luftwaffe, Navy
Welvert, Joseph: 18
West Indies: units with British Eighth Army, 164
Westphal, Siegfried: 8, 144, 146, 164, 170, 171; briefs Hitler on failed counterattack at Anzio, 158; as Kesselring's chief of staff, 143
Wilson, Sir Henry Maitland: 154
Witzig, Rudolf: 17
Wolf's Lair: Rommel's meeting with Hitler at, 12-13

Y

Yugoslavia: 99; units with British Eighth Army, 164

Z

Zanuck, Darryl F.: 18
Ziegler, Heinz: 28, 30